The World's First Love

FULTON J. SHEEN

The World's First Love

IGNATIUS PRESS   SAN FRANCISCO

Cover art by Sister Mary Grace, O.P.
Cover design by Roxanne Mei Lum

Reprinted 1996 Ignatius Press, San Francisco
ISBN 0–89870–597–5
Library of Congress catalogue number 96–83643
Printed in the United States of America ∞

Contents

PART I

The Woman the World Loves

I

Love Begins with a Dream

Every person carries within his heart a blueprint of the one he loves. What seems to be "love at first sight" is actually the fulfillment of desire, the realization of a dream. Plato, sensing this, said that all knowledge is a recollection from a previous existence. This is not true as he states it, but it is true if one understands it to mean that we already have an ideal in us, one that is made by our thinking, our habits, our experiences, and our desires. Otherwise, how would we know immediately, on seeing persons or things, that we loved them? Before meeting certain people we already have a pattern and mold of what we like and what we do not like; certain persons fit into that pattern, others do not.

When we hear music for the first time, we either like or dislike it. We judge it by the music we already have heard in our own hearts. Jittery minds, which cannot long repose in one object of thought or in continuity of an ideal, love music that is distracting, excited, and jittery. Calm minds like calm music: the heart has its own secret melody, and one day, when the score is played, the heart answers: "This is it." So it is with love. A tiny architect works inside the human heart drawing sketches of the ideal love from the people it sees, from the books it reads, from its hopes and daydreams, in the fond hope that the eye may one day see the ideal and the hand touch it. Life becomes satisfying the moment the dream is seen walking, and the person appears as the incarnation of all that one loved. The liking is instantaneous—because, actually, it was there waiting for a long time. Some go through life without ever meeting *what they call* their ideal. This could be very disappointing, if the ideal never really existed. But the absolute ideal of every heart does exist, and it is God. All human love is an initiation into the Eternal. Some find the Ideal in substance without passing through the shadow.

God, too, has within Himself blueprints of everything in the universe. As the architect has in his mind a plan of the house before the house is built, so God has in His Mind an archetypal idea of every flower, bird, tree, springtime, and melody. There never was a brush touched to canvas or a chisel to marble without some great pre-existing idea. So, too, every atom and every rose is a realization and concretion of an idea existing in the Mind of God from all eternity. All creatures below man correspond to the pattern God has in His Mind. A tree is truly a tree because it corresponds to God's idea of a tree. A rose is a rose because it is God's idea of a rose wrapped up in chemicals and tints and life. *But it is not so with persons.* God has to have two pictures of us: one is what we *are*, and the other is *what we ought to be*. He has the model, and He has the reality: the blueprint and the edifice, the score of the music and the way we play it. God has to have these two pictures because in each and every one of us there is some disproportion and want of conformity between the original plan and the way we have worked it out. The image is blurred; the print is faded. For one thing, our personality is not complete in time; we need a renewed body. Then, too, our sins diminish our personality; our evil acts daub the canvas the Master Hand designed. Like unhatched eggs, some of us refuse to be warmed by the Divine Love, which is so necessary for incubation to a higher level. We are in constant need of repairs; our free acts do not coincide with the law of our being; we fall short of all God wants us to be. St. Paul tells us that we were predestined, before the foundations of the world were laid, to become the sons of God. But some of us will not fulfill that hope.

There is, actually, only one person in all humanity of whom God has one picture and in whom there is a perfect conformity between what He wanted her to be and what she is, and that is His Own Mother. Most of us are a minus sign, in the sense that we do not fulfill the high hopes the Heavenly Father has for us. But Mary is the equal sign. The Ideal that God had of her, that she *is*, and in the flesh. The model and the copy are perfect; she is all that was foreseen, planned, and dreamed. The melody of her life is played just as it was written. Mary was thought, conceived, and planned as the equal sign between ideal and history, thought and reality, hope and realization.

That is why, through the centuries, Christian liturgy has applied to her the words of the Book of Proverbs. Because she is what God wanted us all to be, she speaks of herself as the Eternal blueprint in the Mind of God, the one whom God loved before she was a creature. She is even pictured as being with Him not only at creation but also before creation. She existed in the Divine Mind as an Eternal Thought before there were any mothers. She is the Mother of mothers—*she is the world's first love*.

> The Lord possessed me in the beginning of His ways, before He made anything, from the beginning. I was set up from eternity, and of old, before the earth was made. The depths were not as yet, and I was already conceived; neither had the fountains of waters as yet sprung out; the mountains with

their huge bulk had not as yet been established: before the hills I was brought forth. He had not yet made the earth, or the rivers, or the poles of the world. When He prepared the heavens, I was present; when with a certain law and compass He enclosed the depths; when He established the sky above and poised the fountains of waters; when He compassed the sea with its bounds and set a law to the waters that they should not pass their limits; when He balanced the foundations of the earth; I was with Him, forming all things, and was delighted every day, playing before Him at all times, playing in the world: and my delights were to be with the children of men. Now, therefore, ye children, hear me: Blessed are they that keep my ways. Hear instruction, and be wise, and refuse it not. Blessed is the man that heareth me and that watcheth daily at my gates and waiteth at the posts of my doors. He that shall find me shall find life and shall have salvation from the Lord (Prov 8:22–35).

But God not only thought of her in eternity; He also had her in mind at the beginning of time. In the beginning of history, when the human race fell through the solicitation of a woman, God spoke to the Devil and said, "I will establish a feud between thee and the woman, between thy offspring and hers; she is to crush thy head, while thou dost lie in wait at her heels" (Gen 3:15). God was saying that, if it was by a woman that man fell, it would be through a woman that God would be revenged. Whoever His Mother would be, she would certainly be blessed among women, and because God Himself chose her, He would see to it that all generations would call her blessed.

When God willed to become Man, He had to decide on the time of His coming, the country in which He would be born, the city in which He would be raised, the people, the race, the political and economic systems that would surround Him, the language He would speak, and the psychological attitudes with which He would come in contact as the Lord of History and the Savior of the World.

All these details would depend entirely on one factor: the woman who would be His Mother. To choose a mother is to choose a social position, a language, a city, an environment, a crisis, and a destiny.

His Mother was not like ours, whom we accepted as something historically fixed, which we could not change; He was born of a Mother whom He chose before He was born. It is the only instance in history where both the Son willed the Mother and the Mother willed the Son. And this is what the Creed means when it says "born of the Virgin Mary". She was called by God as Aaron was, and Our Lord was born not just of her flesh but also by her consent.

Before taking unto Himself a human nature, He consulted with *the Woman*, to ask her if she would give Him *a man*. The Manhood of Jesus was not stolen from humanity, as Prometheus stole fire from heaven; it was given as a gift.

The first man, Adam, was made from the slime of the earth. The first woman was made from a man in an ecstasy. The new Adam, Christ, comes from the new Eve, Mary, in an ecstasy of prayer and love of God and the fullness of freedom.

We should not be surprised that she is spoken of as a thought by God before the world was made. When Whistler painted the picture of his mother, did he not have the image of her in his mind before he ever gathered his colors on his palette? If you could have preexisted your mother (not *artistically*, but *really*), would you not have made her the most perfect woman that ever lived—one so beautiful she would have been the sweet envy of all women, and one so gentle and so merciful that all other mothers would have sought to imitate her virtues? Why, then, should we think that God would do otherwise? When Whistler was complimented on the portrait of his mother, he said, "You know how it is; one tries to make one's Mummy just as nice as he can." When God became Man, He too, I believe, would make His Mother as nice as He could—and that would make her a perfect Mother.

God never does anything without exceeding preparation. The two great masterpieces of God are Creation of man and Re-creation or Redemption of man. Creation was made for unfallen men; His Mystical Body, for fallen men. Before making man, God made a garden of delights—as God alone knows how to make a garden beautiful. In that Paradise of Creation there were celebrated the first nuptials of man and woman. But man willed not to have blessings, except according to his lower nature. Not only did he lose his happiness; he even wounded his own mind and will. Then God planned the remaking or redeeming of man. But before doing so, he would make another Garden. This new one would be not of earth but of flesh; it would be a Garden over whose portals the name of sin would never be written—a Garden in which there would grow no weeds of rebellion to choke the growth of the flowers of grace—a Garden from which there would flow four rivers of redemption to the four corners of the earth—a Garden so pure that the Heavenly Father would not blush at sending His Own Son into it—and this "flesh-girt Paradise to be gardened by the Adam new" was Our Blessed Mother. As Eden was the Paradise of Creation, Mary is the Paradise of the Incarnation, and in her as a Garden were celebrated the first nuptials of God and man. The closer one gets to fire, the greater the heat; the closer one is to God, the greater the purity. But since no one was ever closer to God than the woman whose human portals He threw open to walk this earth, then no one could have been more pure than she. In the words of Lawrence Housman:

A garden bower in flower
Grew waiting for God's hand:
Where no man ever trod,
This was the Gate of God.
The first bower was red—
Her lips which "welcome" said.
The second bower was blue—
Her eyes that let God through.
The third bower was white—
Her soul in God's sight.
Three bowers of love
Now Christ from heaven above.

This special purity of hers we call the Immaculate Conception. It is not the Virgin Birth. The word "immaculate" is taken from two Latin words meaning "not stained". "Conception" means that, at the first moment of her conception, the Blessed Mother in the womb of her mother, St. Anne, and in virtue of the anticipated merits of the Redemption of her Son, was preserved free from the stains of Original Sin.

I never could see why anyone in this day and age should object to the Immaculate Conception; all modern pagans believe that they are immaculately conceived. If there is no Original Sin, then *everyone* is immaculately conceived. Why do they shrink from allowing to Mary what they attribute to themselves? The doctrine of Original Sin and the Immaculate Conception are mutually exclusive. If Mary alone is *the* Immaculate Conception, then the rest of us must have Original Sin.

The Immaculate Conception does not imply that Mary needed no Redemption. She needed it as much as you and I do. She was redeemed in advance, by way of prevention, in both body and soul, in the first instant of conception. *We* receive the fruits of redemption in our soul at Baptism. The whole human race needs redemption. But Mary was de-solidarized and separated from that sin-laden humanity as a result of the merits of Our Lord's Cross being offered to her at the moment of her conception. If we exempted her from the need of redemption, we would also have to exempt her from membership in humanity. The Immaculate Conception, therefore, in no way implies that she needed no redemption. She did! Mary is the first effect of redemption, in the sense that it was applied to her at the moment of her conception and to us in another and diminished fashion only after our birth.

She had this privilege, not for her sake, but for *His* sake. That is why those who do not believe in the Divinity of Christ can see no reason for the special privilege accorded to Mary. If I did not believe in the Divinity of Our Lord— which God avert—I should see nothing but nonsense in any special reverence given to Mary above the other women on earth! But if she is the Mother of God, Who became Man, then she is unique, and then she stands out as the new Eve of Humanity—as He is the new Adam.

There *had* to be some such creature as Mary—otherwise God would have found no one in whom He could fittingly have taken His human origin. An honest politician seeking civic reforms looks about for honest assistants. The Son of God beginning a new creation searched for some of that Goodness which existed before sin took over. There would have been, in some minds, a doubt about the Power of God if He had not shown a special favor to the woman who was to be His Mother. Certainly what God gave to Eve, He would not refuse to His Own Mother.

Suppose that God in making over man did not also make over woman into a new Eve! What a howl of protest would have gone up! Christianity would have been denounced as are all male religions. Women would then have searched for a female religion! It would have been argued that woman was always the slave of man and even God intended her to be such, since He refused to make the new Eve as He made the new Adam.

Had there been no Immaculate Conception, then Christ would have been said to be less beautiful, for He would have taken His Body from one who was not humanly perfect! There ought to be an infinite separation between God and sin, but there would not have been if there was not one Woman who could crush the cobra's head.

If you were an artist, would you allow someone to prepare your canvas with daubs? Then why should God be expected to act differently when He prepares to unite to Himself a human nature like ours, in all things, save sin? But having lifted up one woman by preserving her from sin, and then having her freely ratify that gift at the Annunciation, God gave hope to our disturbed, neurotic, gauche, and weak humanity. Oh, yes! He is our Model, but He is also the Person of God! There ought to be, on the human level, Someone who would give humans hope, Someone who could lead us to Christ, *Someone who would mediate between us and Christ as He mediates between us and the Father.* One look at her, and we know that a human who is not good can become better; one prayer to her, and we know that, because she is without sin, we can become less sinful.

And that brings us back to the beginning. We have said that everyone carries within his heart a blueprint of his ideal love. The best of human loves, no matter how devoted they be, must end—and there is nothing perfect that ends. If there be anyone of whom it is possible to say, "This is the last embrace", then there is no perfect love. Hence some, ignoring the Divine, may try to have a multiplicity of loves make up for the ideal love; but this is like saying that to render a musical masterpiece one must play a dozen different violins.

Every man who pursues a maid, every maid who yearns to be courted, every bond of friendship in the universe, seeks a love that is not just *her* love or *his* love but something that overflows both her and him that is called "our love". Everyone is in love with an ideal love, a love that is so far beyond sex that sex is forgotten. We all love something more than we love. When that overflow ceases, love stops. As the poet puts it: "I could not love thee, dear, so much, loved I not honour more." That ideal love we see beyond all creature-love, to which we instinctively turn when flesh-love fails, is the same ideal that God had in His Heart from all eternity—the Lady whom He calls "Mother". She is the one whom every man loves when he loves a woman—whether he knows it or not. She is what every woman wants to be when she looks at herself. She is the woman whom every man marries in ideal when he takes a spouse; she is hidden as an ideal in the discontent of every woman with the carnal aggressiveness of man; she is the secret desire every woman has to be honored and fostered; she is the way every woman wants to command respect and love because of the beauty of her goodness of body and soul. And this blueprint love, whom God loved before the world was made, this Dream Woman before women were, is the one of whom every heart can say in its depth of depths: "She is the woman I love!"

2

When Freedom and Love Were One: The Annunciation

The modern age, which gives primacy to sex, justifies promiscuity and divorce on the grounds that love is by its nature free—which, indeed, it is. All love is free love, in a certain sense. To be devoid of love is of the essence of hell. Scripture tells us: "Where the spirit of the Lord is, there is liberty" (2 Cor 3:17). The ideal life is fulfilled—not in subjection to an absolute law but in the discriminating response of an educated affection.

The formula that love is free is right. The interpretation of this can often be wrong. Those husbands who leave one wife for another may justify their infidelity on the grounds that "one must be free to live his own life". *No one* is ever selfish or voluptuous without covering up his demands with a similar parade of ideals. Behind many contemporary affirmations of the freedom of love is a false rationalization, for although love involves freedom, not all freedom involves love. I cannot love unless I am free, but, because I am free, still I may not love as I please. A man can have freedom without love—for example, he who violates another is free in his action when there is no one around to restrain him—yet he certainly has no love. A robber is free to ransack a house when the owners are away, but it is absurd to say that he loves the owners because he is free to steal. The purest liberty is that which is given, not that which is taken.

What many moderns mean by freedom in love is freedom *from* something without being free *for* anything. True love wants to be free *from* something *for* something. A young man wants to be free from the parental yoke—that he may love someone besides his parents and thus prolong his life. Freedom of love is, therefore, inseparable from service, from altruism and goodness. The press wants freedom from restraint in order to be free to express truth; a man wants to be free from political tyranny in order to work out his own prosperity for him here below and for his destiny in the life hereafter. Love demands freedom from one thing in order to place itself freely at the service of another. When a man falls in love, he seeks the sweet servitude of affection and devotion to another. When a man falls in love with God, he immediately goes out in search of a neighbor. But to be utterly free from all restraint, a man would have to be alone; but then he would have no one to love. This is precisely the ideal of Sartre, who says: "Others are hell." The basis of his philosophy is that anything restraining the ego is nothing. But every other man, and every other thing, restrains the ego—therefore, they are nothing. Truly, indeed, if a man sets out to be free in the sense of living life only on his own terms, he finds himself in the nihilism of hell. Sartre forgets that to fall in love means to fall into something, and that something is responsibility. Thus, the same love that demands freedom to exercise itself also seeks the curbs to limit it. The liberty of love, therefore, is not license. Freedom implies not just a mere choice but also responsibility for choice.

There are three definitions of freedom: two of them are

false, and one is true. The first false definition is "Freedom is the right to do whatever I *please*." This is the liberal doctrine of freedom, which reduces freedom to a physical, rather than to a moral, power. Of course we are free to do whatever we please: for example, we can turn a machine gun on our neighbor's chickens, or drive an automobile on the sidewalk, or stuff a neighbor's mattress with used razor blades—but *ought* we to do these things? This kind of freedom, in which everyone is allowed to seek his own benefit, produces confusion. There is no liberalism of this particular kind without a world of conflicting egotisms, where no one is willing to submerge himself for the common good. In order to overcome this confusion of everyone's doing whatever he pleases, there arose the second false definition of freedom, namely, "Freedom is the right to do whatever you *must*." This is totalitarian freedom, which was developed in order to destroy individual freedom for the sake of society. Engels, who with Marx wrote the *Philosophy of Communism*, said: "A stone is free to fall because it *must* obey the law of gravitation." So man is free in Communist society because he must obey the law of the dictator.

The true concept of freedom is "Freedom is the right to do whatever we *ought*", and *ought* implies goal, purpose, morality, and the law of God. True freedom is within the law, not outside it. I am free to draw a triangle, if I give it three sides, but not, in a stroke of broad-mindedness, fifty-seven sides. I am free to fly on condition that I obey the law of aeronautics. In the spiritual realm, I am also most free when I obey the law of God.

In order to escape the implications of freedom (namely, its involvement in responsibility), there are those who would deny individual freedom either communally (as do the Communists) or biologically (as do some Freudians). Any civilization that denies free will is, generally, a civilization that is already disgusted with the choices of its freedom, because it has brought unhappiness upon itself. Those who make the theoretical denial of free will are those who, in practice, confuse freedom by identifying it with license. One will never find a professor who denies freedom of the will who does not also have something in his life for which he wishes to shake off responsibility. He disowns the evil by disowning that which made evil possible, namely, free will. On the golf course, such deniers of freedom blame the golf clubs but never themselves. The excuse is like the perennial one of the little boy who broke the vase: "Someone pushed me." That is, he was forced. When he grows up, he becomes a professor, but instead of saying: "I was pushed", he says: "The concatenation of social, economic, and environmental factors, so weighted down with the collective psychic heritage of our animal and evolutionary origin, produced in me what psychologists called a compulsive Id." These same professors who deny freedom of the will are the ones who sign their names to petitions to free Communists in the name of freedom, after they have already abused the privilege of American freedom.

The beauty of this universe is that practically all gifts are conditioned by freedom. There is no law that a young man should give the gift of a ring to the young lady to whom he is engaged. The one word in the English language that proves the close connection between gifts and freedom is "thanks". As Chesterton said: "If man were not free, he could never say, 'Thank you for the mustard'."

Freedom is ours really to give away because of something we love. Everyone in the world who is free wants freedom first of all as a means: he wants freedom in order to give it away. Almost everyone actually gives freedom away. Some give their freedom of thinking away to public opinion, to moods, to fashions, and to the anonymity of "they say" and thus become the willing slaves of the passing hour. Others give their freedom to alcohol and to sex and thus experience in their lives the words of Scripture: "He who commits sin is the slave of sin." Others give up their freedom in love to another person. This is a higher form of surrender and is the sweet slavery of love of which Our Savior spoke: "My yoke is sweet and my burden light." The young man who courts a young woman is practically saying to her: "I want to be your slave all the days of my life, and that will be my highest and greatest freedom." The young woman courted might say to the young man: "You say you love me, but how do I know? Have you courted the other 458,623 young eligible ladies in this city?" If the young man knew his metaphysics and philosophy well, he would answer: "In a certain sense, yes, for by the mere fact that I love you, I reject them. The very love that makes me choose you also makes me spurn them—and that will be for life."

Love therefore is not only an affirmation; it is also a rejection. The mere fact that John loves Mary with his whole heart means that he does not love Ruth with any part of it. Every protestation of love is a limitation of a wrong kind of free love. Love, here, is the curbing of the freedom understood as license, and yet it is the enjoyment of perfect freedom—for all that one wants in life is to love that person. True love always imposes restrictions on itself—for the sake of others— whether it be the saint who detaches himself from the world in order more readily to adhere to Christ or the husband who detaches himself from former acquaintances to belong more readily to the spouse of his choice. True love, by its nature, is uncompromising; it is the freeing of self from selfishness and egotism. Real love uses freedom to attach itself unchangeably to another. St. Augustine has said: "Love God, and then do whatever you please." By this he meant that if you love God, you will never do anything to wound Him. In married love, likewise, there is perfect freedom, and yet *one* limitation that preserves that love, and that is the refusal to hurt the beloved. There is no moment more sacred in freedom than that when the ability to love others is suspended and checked by the interest one has in the pledged one of his heart; there then arises a moment when one abandons the seizure and the capture for the pleasure of contemplating it and when the need to possess and devour disappears in the joy of seeing another live.

And an interesting insight into love is this—that, to just the extent that we reject love, we lose our gifts. No refugee from Russia sends a gift back to a dictator; God's gifts, too, are dependent on our love. Adam and Eve could have passed on to posterity extraordinary gifts of body and soul had they but loved. They were not *forced* to love; they were not asked to say, "I love", because words can be empty; they were merely asked to make an act of choice between what is God's and what is not God's, between the choices symbolized in the alternatives of the garden and the tree. If they had had no freedom, they would have turned to God as the sunflower does to the sun; but, being free, they could reject the whole for the part, the garden for the tree, the future joy for the immediate pleasure. The result was that mankind lost those gifts that God would have passed on to it, had it only been true in love.

What concerns us now is the restoration of these gifts through another act of freedom. God could have restored man to himself by simply forgiving man's sin, but then there would have been mercy without justice. The problem confronting man was something like that which confronts an orchestra leader. The score is written and given to an excellent director. The musicians, well skilled in their art, are free to follow the director or to rebel against him. Suppose that one of the musicians decides to hit a wrong note. The director might do either of two things: either he might ignore the mistake, or he might strike his baton and order the measure to be replayed. It would make little difference, for that note has already gone winging into space, and since time cannot be reversed, the discord goes on and on through the universe, even to the end of time. Is there any possible way by which this voluntary disharmony can be stopped? Certainly not by anyone in time. It could be corrected on condition that someone would reach out from eternity, would seize that note in time and arrest it in its mad flight. But would it still not be a discord? No, it could be made the first note in a new symphony and thus be made harmonious!

When our first parents were created, God gave them a conscience, a moral law, and an original justice. They were not compelled to follow Him as the director of the symphony of creation. Yet they chose to rebel, and that sour note of original revolution was passed on to humanity, through human generation. How could that original disorder be stopped? It could be arrested in the same way as the sour note, by having eternity come into time and lay hold of a man by force, compelling him to enter into a new order where the original gifts would be restored and harmony would be the law. But this would not be God's way, for it would mean the destruction of human freedom. God could lay hold of a note, but He could not lay hold of a man by force without abusing the greatest gift that He gave to man—namely, freedom, which alone makes love possible.

Now we come to the greatest act of freedom the world has ever known—the reversal of that free act which the Head of humanity performed in Paradise when he chose non-God against God. It was the moment in which that unfortunate choice was reversed, when God in His Mercy willed to re-make man and to give him a fresh start in a *new* birth of free-dom under God. God *could* have made a perfect man to start humanity out of dust as He had done in the beginning. He could have made the new man start the new humanity from nothing as He had done in making the world. And He could have done it without consulting humanity, but this would have been the invasion of human privilege. God would not take a man out of the world of freedom without the free act of a free being. God's way with man is not dictatorship, but cooperation. If He would redeem humanity, it would be *with* human consent and not *against it*. God could destroy evil, but only at the cost of human freedom, and that would be too high a price to pay for the destruction of dictatorship on earth—to have a dictator in Heaven. Before remaking hu-manity, God willed to consult with humanity, so that there would be no destruction of human dignity; the particular person whom He consulted was a woman. In the beginning, it was man who was asked to ratify the gift; this time it is a woman. The mystery of the Incarnation is very simply that of God's asking a woman freely to give Him a human nature. In so many words, through the angel, He was saying: "Will you make Me a man?" As from the first Adam came the first Eve, so now, in the rebirth of man's dignity, the new Adam will come from the new Eve. And in Mary's free consent we have the only human nature that was ever born in perfect liberty.

The story of this rebirth of freedom is told in the Gospel of St. Luke (1:26–35):

> When the sixth month came, God sent the angel Gabriel to a city of Galilee called Nazareth, where a virgin dwelt betrothed to a man of David's lineage;

His name was Joseph, and the virgin's name was Mary.

Into her presence the angel came, and said,

"Hail, thou who art full of grace; the Lord is with thee; Blessed art thou among women."

She was much perplexed at hearing him speak so,

And cast about in her mind, what she was to make of such a greeting.

Then the angel said to her, "Mary, do not be afraid;

"Thou hast found favour in the sight of God.

"And behold, thou shalt conceive in thy womb, and shalt bear a son and shalt call him Jesus. He shall be great, and men will know him for the Son of the most High;

"The Lord will give him the throne of his father, David,

"And He shall reign over the house of Jacob eternally;

"His Kingdom shall never have an end."

But Mary said to the angel, "How can that be, since I have no knowledge of man?"

And the angel answered her, "The Holy Spirit will come upon thee and the Power of the most High will overshadow thee.

"Thus the holy thing which is to be born of thee shall be known for the Son of God."

The angel Gabriel, as God's spokesman, here asks Mary if she will freely give the Son of God a human nature, that He may also be the Son of man. A creature was asked by the Creator if she would freely cooperate with God's plan to take humanity out of the mire and to let him be ravished totally by God. Mary at first is troubled as to how she can give God a manhood, since she is still a virgin. The angel settles the problem by telling her that God Himself, through His Spirit, will work that miracle within her.

But from our point of view there seems to be another difficulty. Mary was chosen by God to be His Mother and was even prepared for that honor by being preserved free from the

primal sin that had infected all humanity. If she were so prepared, would she be free to accept or to reject, and would her
answer be the full fruit of her free will? The answer is that her
redemption was already completed but that she had not yet
accepted or ratified it. It was, in a way, something like our
dilemma. We are baptized as infants, and our bodies become
temples of God, as our souls have been filled with infused
virtues. We become not just creatures made by God but partakers in Divine nature. All this is done in Baptism before our
freedom blossoms, the Church standing responsible for our
spiritual birth as our parents did for our physical birth. Later
on, however, we ratify that original endowment by the free
acts of our moral lives—by receiving the sacraments, by
prayers, and by sacrifices. So, too, Mary's redemption was
completed—as our Baptism was completed—but she had not
yet accepted, ratified, or confirmed it before she gave her
consent to the angel. She was planned for a role in the drama
of redemption by God, as a child is planned for a musical
career by his physical parents, but it was not fulfilled until this
moment. The Holy Trinity never possesses a creature without
the consent of his will. When, therefore, Mary had heard
how this was to take place, she uttered words that are the
greatest pledge of liberty and the greatest charter of freedom
the world has ever heard: "Be it done unto me according to
thy word." As in Eden there took place the first espousals of
man and woman, so, in her, there took place the first espousals of God and man, eternity and time, omnipotence and
bonds. In answer to the question "Will you give me a man?"
the marriage ceremony of love becomes bathed with new
depths of freedom: "I will." And the Word was conceived in
her.

Here, then, is *freedom of religion*; God respects human freedom by refusing to invade humanity and to establish a beach-

head in time without the free consent of one of His creatures. *Freedom of conscience* is also involved: before Mary could claim as her own the great gifts of God, she had to ratify those gifts by an act of will in the Annunciation. And there is *the freedom of a total abandonment to God*: our free will is the only thing that is really our own. Our health, our wealth, our power—all these God can take from us. But our freedom he leaves to us, even in hell. Because freedom is our own, it is the only perfect gift that we can make to God. And yet here a creature totally, yet freely, surrendered her will, so that one might say that it was not a matter of Mary's will doing the will of her Son but of Mary's will being lost in that of her Son. Later on in His life he would say: "If the Son of Man makes you free, you will be free indeed." If this be so, then no one has ever been more free than this belle of Liberty, the lady who sang the *Magnificat*.

But there is another freedom revealed through Mary. In human marriage there is something personal and also something impersonal or racial. What is personal and free is love, because love is always for a unique person; thus, jealousy is the guardian of monogamy. What is impersonal and automatic is sex, since its operation is to some extent outside human control. Love belongs to man; sex belongs to God, for the effects of it are beyond our determination. Whenever a mother gives birth to a babe, she freely wills the act of love that made her and her husband two in one flesh. But there is also the unknown, the free element in their love, namely, the decision whether a child will be born of the union—whether it will be a boy or a girl and the exact time of birth and even the moment of its conception are lost in some unknown night of love. We are thus accepted by our parents rather than willed by them—except indirectly.

But with Mary there was perfect freedom. Her Divine Son

was not accepted in any unforeseen or unpredictable way. He was *willed*. There was no element of chance; nothing was impersonal, for He was fully willed in mind and in body. How is this true? He was willed in *mind*, because, when the angel explained the miracle, Mary said: "Be it done unto me according to thy word." Then he was willed in Body for *now*, not in some past obscure night; conception took place as in the full effulgence of the brightness of the morn does the Divine Spirit of Love begin weaving the garment of flesh for the Eternal Word. The time was deliberately chosen; the consent was voluntary; the physical cooperation was free. It was the only birth in all the world that was truly willed and, therefore, truly free.

Every birth partakes of the nature of the plant kingdom, in that the flower has its roots on the earth, although its blossoms open to the heavens. In generation, the body comes from parents who are of the earth; the soul comes from God, Who is in Heaven. In Mary, there was hardly any earth at all except herself; all was Heaven. The other love that conceived within her was the Holy Spirit; the Person born of her was the Eternal Word—the union of the Godhead and manhood was through the mysterious alchemy of the Trinity. She alone was of earth, and yet she, too, seemed more of Heaven.

Other mothers know that a new life beats within them, through the pulsations within the body. Mary knew that Divine Life beat within her, through her soul in communion with an angel. Other mothers become conscious of motherhood through physical changes; Mary knew through the message of an angel and the overshadowing of the Holy Spirit. Nothing that comes from the body is as free as that which comes from the mind: there are mothers who yearn for children, but they have to wait upon processes subject to nature. In Mary alone a Child waited *not* on nature but on her acceptance of the Divine will. All she had to say was *Fiat*, and she conceived. This is what all birth would have been without sin—a matter of human wills uniting themselves with the Divine will and, through the union of bodies, sharing in the creation of new life through the usual processes of human generation. The Virgin Birth is, therefore, synonymous with Birth in Freedom.

Mary!—we poor creatures of earth are stumbling over our freedoms, fumbling over our choices. Millions of us are seeking to give up their freedom—some by repudiating it, because of the burden of their guilt—some, by surrendering it to the moods and fashions of the time—others, by absorption into Communism, where there is only one will, which is the dictator's, and where the only love is hate and revolution!

We speak much of freedom today, Mary, because we are losing it—just as we speak most of health when we are sick. Thou art the Mistress of Freedom because thou didst undo the false freedom that makes men slaves to their passions by pronouncing the word God Himself said when He made light and again when thy Son redeemed the world—*Fiat*! Or, be it done unto me according to God's will. As the "no" of Eve proves that the creature was made by love and is therefore free, so thy *Fiat* proves that the Creature was made *for* love as well. Teach us, then, that there is no freedom except in doing, out of love, what thou didst do in the Annunciation, namely, saying *Yes* to what Jesus asks.

3

The Song of the Woman:
The Visitation

One of the most beautiful moments in history was that when pregnancy met pregnancy—when childbearers became the first heralds of the King of Kings. All pagan religions begin with the teachings of adults, but Christianity begins with the birth of a Child. From that day to this, Christians have ever been the defenders of the family and the love of generation. If we ever sat down to write out what we would expect the Infinite God to do, certainly the last thing we would expect would be to see Him imprisoned in a carnal ciborium for nine months; and the next to last thing we would expect is that the "greatest man ever born of woman", while yet in his mother's womb, would salute the yet imprisoned God-Man. But this is precisely what took place in the Visitation.

At the Annunciation the archangel told Mary that her cousin Elizabeth was about to become the mother of John the Baptist. Mary was then a young girl, but her cousin was "advanced in years", that is, quite beyond the normal age of conceiving. "See, moreover, how it fares with thy cousin Elizabeth; she is old, yet she too has conceived a son; she who was reproached with barrenness is now in her sixth month, to prove that nothing is impossible with God. And Mary said, 'Behold the handmaid of the Lord, let it be done unto me according to thy word.' And with that the angel left her" (Lk 1:36–38).

The birth of Christ is without regard to man; the birth of John the Baptist is without regard to age! "Nothing is impossible with God." The Scripture continues the story:

> In the days that followed, Mary rose up and went with all haste to a city of Juda, in the hill country where Zachary dwelt; and entering in she gave Elizabeth greeting. No sooner had Elizabeth heard Mary's greeting, than the child leaped in her womb; and Elizabeth herself was filled with the Holy Ghost; so that she cried out with a loud voice, "Blessed art thou among women and blessed is the fruit of thy womb. How have I deserved to be thus visited by the mother of my Lord? Why, as soon as ever the voice of thy greeting sounded in my ears, the child in my womb leaped for joy. Blessed art thou for thy believing; the message that was brought to thee from the Lord shall have fulfillment" (Lk 1:39–45).

Mary "went with all haste"; she is always in a hurry to do good. With deliberate speed she becomes the first nurse of Christian civilization. The woman hastens to meet a woman. They serve best their neighbor who bear the Christ within their hearts and souls. Bearing in herself the Secret of Salvation, Mary journeys five days from Nazareth to the city of Hebron, where, according to tradition, rested the ashes of the founders of the people of God: Abraham, Isaac, and Jacob.

> *The terraced fields of Juda*
> *pregnant with seed*
> *called out to her*
> *as she passed,*

>*praising the Child*
>*she was yet to bear;*
>*invoking His Blessing*
>*on their expectancy.*[1]

"She gave Elizabeth greeting"; springtime served the autumn. She, who is to bear Him Who will say: "I came not to be ministered unto but to minister", now ministers unto her cousin, who bears only His trumpet and His voice in the wilderness. Nothing so provokes the service of the needy as the consciousness of one's own unworthiness when visited by the grace of God. The handmaid of the Lord becomes the handmaid of Elizabeth.

On hearing the woman's greeting, the child whom Elizabeth bore within her "leaped in her womb". The Old Testament is here meeting the New Testament; the shadows dissolve with joy before the substance. All the longings and expectations of thousands of years as to Him Who would be the Savior are now fulfilled in this one ecstatic moment when John the Baptist greets Christ, the Son of the Living God.

Mary is present at three births: at the birth of John the Baptist, at the birth of her own Divine Son, and at the "birth" of John the Evangelist, at the foot of the Cross, as the Master saluted him: "Behold thy mother!" Mary, the Woman, presided at the three great moments of life: at a birth on the occasion of the Visitation, at a marriage at the Marriage Feast of Cana, and at a Death, or surrender of Life, at the Crucifixion of her Divine Son.

"The child leaped in her womb, and Elizabeth herself was filled with the Holy Ghost." A Pentecost came before Pente-

[1] Calvin Le Compte, *I Sing of a Maiden* (Macmillan, 1949).

cost. The physical body of Christ within Mary now fills John the Baptist with the Spirit of Christ; thirty-three years later the Mystical Body of Christ, His Church, will be filled with the Holy Spirit, as Mary, too, will be, in the midst of the Apostles abiding in prayer. John is sanctified by Jesus. So Jesus is not as John—not man alone, but God as well.

The second part of the second most beautiful prayer in the world, the Hail Mary, is now about to be written; the first part was spoken by an angel: "Hail (Mary) full of grace; the Lord is with thee; blessed art thou among women" (Lk 1:28).

Now Elizabeth adds the second part in a "loud voice"; "Blessed art thou among women, and blessed is the fruit of thy womb (Jesus)." Old age is here not jealous of youth or privilege, for Elizabeth makes the first public proclamation— that Mary is the Mother of God: "How have I deserved to be thus visited by the mother of my Lord?" She learned it less from Mary's lips than from the Spirit of God nestling over her womb. Mary received the Spirit of God through an angel; Elizabeth was the first to receive it through Mary.

Cousin-nurse at birth, Mother-nurse at death. There is nothing Mary has that is for herself alone—not even her Son. Before He is born, her Son belongs to others. No sooner does she have the Divine Host within herself than she rises from the Communion rail of Nazareth to visit the aged and to make her young. Elizabeth would never live to see her son lose his head to the dancing stepdaughter of Herod, but Mary would live and die at once in seeing her Son taste death, that death might be no more.

Thomas Merton has compared John the Baptist in his mother's womb to the contemplative, such as the Trappist, for John the Baptist as the first "Anchorite" lives for God in secret.

Why do you fly from the drowned shores of Galilee,
From the sands and the lavender water?
Why do you leave the ordinary world, Virgin of Nazareth,
The yellow fishing boats, the farms,
The wine smelling yards and low cellars
Or the oil press, and the women by the well?
Why do you fly those markets,
Those suburban gardens,
The trumpets of the jealous lilies,
Leaving them all, lovely among the lemon trees?

You have trusted no town
With the news behind your eyes.
You have drowned Gabriel's word in thoughts like seas
And turned toward the stone mountain
To the treeless places.
Virgin of God, why are your clothes like sails?

The day Our Lady, full of Christ,
Entered the dooryard of her relative
Did not her steps, light steps, lay on the paving leaves like
    gold?
Did not her eyes grey as doves
Alight like the peace of a new world upon that house, upon
    miraculous Elizabeth?

Her salutation
Sings in the stone valley like a Charterhouse bell:
And the unborn saint John
Wakes in his mother's body,
Bounds with the echoes of discovery.
Sing in your cell, small anchorite!
How did you see her in the eyeless dark?

What secret syllable
Woke your young faith to the mad truth
That an unborn baby could be washed in the Spirit of God?
Oh burning joy!
What seas of life were planted by that voice!
With what new sense
Did your wise heart receive her Sacrament,
And know her cloister Christ?

You need no eloquence, wild bairn,
Exulting in your heritage,
Your ecstasy is your apostolate,
For whom to kick is contemplata tradere.
Your joy is the vocation
Of Mother Church's hidden children—
Those who by vow lie buried in the cloister or the hermitage
The speechless Trappist, or the grey, granite Carthusian,
The quiet Carmelite, the barefoot Clare
Planted in the night of contemplation,
Sealed in the dark and waiting to be born.

Night is our diocese and silence is our ministry
Poverty our charity and helplessness our tongue-tied sermon.
Beyond the scope of sight or sound we dwell upon the air
Seeking the world's gain in an unthinkable experience.
Waiting upon the first far drums of Christ the Conqueror,
Planted like sentinels upon the world's frontier.[2]

Elizabeth, describing how the God–Man hidden within
Mary worked on her soul and the new life within her old
body, exclaimed: "Why, as soon as ever the voice of thy greet-

[2] Thomas Merton, "The Quickening of St. John the Baptist", from *The Tears of the Blind Lions*.

ing sounded in my ears, the child in my womb leaped for joy. Blessed art thou for thy believing; the message that was brought to thee from the Lord shall have fulfillment" (Lk 1:44, 45). Eve had believed the serpent; Elizabeth now praises Mary for blotting out the ruin of Eve by believing in God.

But no sooner did an unborn child leap with joy in a prison house of flesh than a song leaped with joy to Mary's lips. To sing a song is to possess one's soul. Maria, the sister of Moses, sang after the miraculous crossing of the Red Sea. Deborah sang after the defeat of the Canaanites. Wherever liberty is, there the free sing. Elizabeth's husband sang the *Benedictus* to usher in the New Order, for Our Lord came "not to destroy the law but to fulfill it". Yet only as a Mirror, in whom Elizabeth sees reflected the unborn Emmanuel, does Mary glow with the song of those future days when He alone shall be the Light of the World. Mary smiles through tears of joy, and she makes rainbow of a song. At least until the Birth, the Woman shall have mirth. After those nine months He, Who is sheathed within her flesh, would say: "I come not to bring peace, but the sword" (Mt 10:34).

The *Magnificat* is the hymn of a mother with a Child Who is at once the "Ancient of Days". Like a great artist, who has finished a painting in a few months, Mary could say: "In how short a time, and yet it is my life", so the song sprang from Mary's lips like a jet in a few seconds—and yet she was a lifetime in composing it.

She gathered up the soul melodies of her people—a song of David, a song above all which Hannah sang centuries before at the door of the tabernacle of Shiloh, when she brought her infant son Samuel, "to lend him to the Lord as long as He liveth" (1 Sam 1:28). But Mary makes their words and her own refer not to the past but to the future, when the Law of Fear will give way to the Law of Love, and when another life, another kingdom, will arise in a towering flight of sanctity and praise.

"My soul magnifies the Lord: My spirit has found joy in God, Who is my Saviour." The faces of women had been veiled for centuries, and the faces of men were veiled, too, in the sense that men hid themselves from God. But now that the veil of sin is lifted, the Woman stands upright and looks at the face of God to praise Him. When the Divine enters into the human, then the soul thinks less of asking than of loving Him. The lover seeks no favors from the beloved; Mary has no petitions but only praise. As the soul becomes detached from things and is conscious of itself and of its destiny, it knows itself only in God. The egotist magnifies himself, but Mary magnifies the Lord. The carnal think first of body, and the mediocre think of God as an afterthought. In Mary nothing takes precedence over Him Who is God the Creator, the Lord of history, and the Savior of mankind.

When our friends praise us for our deeds, we thank them for their kindness. When Elizabeth extols Mary, Mary glorifies her God. Mary receives praise as a mirror receives light: she stores it not, nor even acknowledges it, but makes it pass from her to God to Whom is due all praise, all honor and thanksgiving. The shortened form of this song is: "Thank God." Her whole personality is to be at the service of her God. Too often do men praise God with our tongues, while our hearts are far from Him. "Words go up, but thoughts remain below." But it was the soul and spirit of Mary, and not her lips, that overflowed in words, because the secret of Love within had already burst its bonds.

Why magnify God, Who cannot become less by subtraction through our atheism or greater by the addition of our praise? It is true—not in Himself does God change stature through our recognition, any more than, because a simpleton mocks the beauty of a Raphael, the painting loses its beauty. But, in us, God is capable of increase and decrease as we are lovers or sinners. As our ego inflates, the need of God seems to be less; as our ego deflates, the need of God appears in its true hunger.

The love of God is reflected in the soul of the just, as the light of the sun is magnified by a mirror. So Mary's Son is the Sun, for she is the moon. She is the nest—He the Fledgling Who will fly to a higher Tree and will then call her home. She calls Him her Lord or Savior, even though she is preserved free from the stain of Original Sin, for it is due entirely to the merits of the Passion and Death of her Divine Son. In herself she is nothing, and she has nothing. He is everything! Because He has looked graciously upon the lowliness of His handmaid—because He Who is Mighty, He whose name is Holy, has wrought these wonders for me.

The proud end in despair, and the last act of despair is suicide or the taking of one's life, which is no longer bearable. The humble are necessarily the joyful, for where there is no pride, there can be no self-centeredness, which makes joy impossible.

Mary's song has this double note; her spirit rejoices because God has looked down on her lowliness. A box that is filled with sand cannot be filled with gold; a soul that is bursting with its own ego can never be filled with God. There is no limit on God's part to His possession of a soul; it is the soul alone that can limit His welcome, as a window curtain limits the light. The more empty the soul is of self, the greater the room in it for God. The larger the emptiness of a nest, the bigger the bird that can be housed therein. There is an intrinsic relation between the humility of Mary and the Incarnation of the Son of God within. She whom the heavens could not contain now tabernacles the King of the Heavens Himself. The Most High looks on the lowliness of His handmaid.

Mary's self-emptying, alone, would not have been enough, had not He Who is her God, her Lord and Savior, "humbled Himself". Though the cup be empty, it cannot hold the ocean. People are like sponges. As each sponge can hold only so much water and then reaches a point of saturation, so every person can hold only so much of honor. After the saturation point is reached, instead of the man's wearing the purple, the purple wears the man. It is always *after* the honor is accepted that the recipient moans in false humility: "Lord, I am not worthy."

But here, after the honor is received, Mary, instead of standing on her privilege, becomes a servant-nurse of her aged cousin and, in the midst of that service, sings a song in which she calls herself the Lord's handmaid—or better still the bondwoman of God, a slave who is simply His property and one who has no personal will except His own. Selflessness is shown as the true self. "There was no room in the inn" because the inn was filled. There was room in the stable because there were no egos there—only an ox and an ass.

God looked over the world for an empty heart—but not a lonely heart—a heart that was empty like a flute on which He might pipe a tune—not lonely like an empty abyss, which is filled by death. And the emptiest heart He could find was the heart of a Lady. Since there was no self there, He filled it with His very Self.

"Behold, from this day forward, all generations will count me blessed." These are miraculous words. How can we explain them, except by the Divinity of her Son? How could this country girl, coming from the despised village of Nazareth and wrapped in anonymity by Judean mountains, foresee in future generations how painters like Michelangelo and

Raphael, poets like Sedulius, Cynewulf, Jacopone da Todi, Chaucer, Thompson, and Wordsworth, theologians like Ephrem, Bonaventure, and Aquinas, the obscure of little villages, and the learned and the great would pour out their praise of her in an unending stream, as the world's first love, and say of their impoverished rhymes:

> *And men looked up at the woman made for the morning*
> *When the stars were young,*
> *For whom, more rude than a beggar's rhyme in the gutter,*
> *These songs are sung.*

Her Son will later give the law explaining her immortal remembrance: "He that humbleth himself, shall be exalted." Humility before God is compensated for by glory before men. Mary had taken the vow of virginity and, seemingly, thus prevented her beauty from passing on to other generations. And yet now—through the power of God—she sees herself as the mother of countless generations without ever ceasing to be a virgin. All generations who lost the favor of God by eating the forbidden fruit will now exalt her, because through her they enter once again into the possession of the Tree of Life. Within three months Mary has had her eight Beatitudes:

1. "Blessed art thou because full of grace," said the archangel Gabriel.
2. "Blessed art thou for thou shalt conceive in thy womb the Son of the Most High, God."
3. "Blessed art thou, Virgin Mother, for 'the Holy Spirit will come upon thee, and the power of the Most High shall overshadow thee'."
4. "Blessed art thou for doing God's will: 'Be it done unto me according to Thy Word.'"

5. "Blessed art thou for believing", said Elizabeth.
6. "Blessed is the fruit of thy womb (Jesus)", added Elizabeth.
7. "Blessed art thou among women."
8. "Blessed art thou, for the message that was brought to thee from the Lord shall have fulfillment."

Lowliness and exaltation are one in her: lowliness because, judging herself to be unworthy of being the Mother of Our Lord, she took the vow of virginity; exalted because God, looking upon what Mary believed was her nothingness, once more created a world out of "nothing".

Blessedness is happiness. Mary had everything that could make a person truly happy. For to be happy, three things are required: to have everything one wants, to have it united in one person who is loved with all the ardor of one's soul, and to know that this is possessed without sin. Mary had all three.

If her Divine Son had not intended that His Mother should be honored where He is adored, He would never have permitted these prophetic words of hers to have had fulfillment. He would have nudged the hands of the artists at their canvas, would have stopped the lips of the poets, and would have frozen our fingers as we told our beads.

How quickly the great men and women are forgotten, and how few of their names are remembered at all! A guidebook is necessary for us to identify the dead in Westminster Abbey; few are the citizens who know their world war heroes, after whom the streets were named. But here in Mary is a young girl, obscure and unknown, in an outpost of the Roman Empire; she who affirms that the law of forgetfulness will be suspended in her favor, and she prophesies it before a single Gospel has been written, before the Son of God has seen the light of day in the flesh.

He has mercy upon those who fear Him, from generation to generation; He has done valiantly with the strength of His arm driving the proud astray in the conceit of their hearts; He has put down the mighty from their seat, and exalted the lowly; He has filled the hungry with good things, and sent the rich away empty handed; He has protected His servant Israel, keeping His merciful design in remembrance, according to the promise which He made to our forefathers, Abraham and his posterity for evermore.

This part of the *Magnificat* is the most revolutionary document ever written, a thousand times more revolutionary than anything Karl Marx wrote. In relation to the preceding verses, it is suggestive to compare Mary's Revolution with the Revolution of Marx and Communism.

THE PHILOSOPHY OF REVOLUTION

Mary

Mary begins with the soul and God. "My soul magnifies the Lord; my spirit has found joy in God Who is my Savior." The whole universe revolves around these two realities: the soul aspiring to an infinity of happiness, which God alone can supply.

Marx

Marx ended the first of his books with the words: "I hate all the gods." For Communism there is only matter endowed with its own inner contradiction, which begets movement. Since there is only matter, there is no soul. The belief that each man has value "is founded", said Marx, "on the Christian illusion that every man has a soul".

There is no God, because a belief in God alienates man from himself and makes him subject to someone outside self. There is not God, but man. "Religion is the Opium of the people."

THE FUTURE OF REVOLUTION

Mary

"All generations will count me blessed." She will be an exception to the law of forgetfulness, because the Lord of History has willed that she be venerated through the centuries. History is providentially determined. The progress and fall of civilizations depend on the moral ordering of human life. Peace is the tranquility of order, and order implies justice to God and neighbor. Peace fails when each man seeks his own and forgets the love of God and neighbor.

Marx

History is dialectically determined. It is not God or the way men live that decides the progress and decay of civilization but a law of class conflict that continues until Communism takes over and classes no longer exist. The future is determined by matter. The present generation and all the past can look to a remote future where they will dance on the graves of their ancestors. Certain classes are destined to be the funeral pyre to light future generations, lifting clenched fists over the corpse of Lenin.

FEAR AND REVOLUTION

Mary

"He has mercy on those who fear Him, from generation to generation." Fear is here understood as filial, that is, a shrinking from hurting one who is loved. Such is the fear a son has for a devoted father and the fear a Christian has of Christ. Fear is here related to love.

Marx

Communism is founded not on *filial* but on *servile* fear, the kind of fear a slave has for a tyrant, a worker has for a dictator. The fear begotten by the revolution is a compulsion neurosis, born not of love but of power. A revolution that destroys filial fear of God always ends in the creation of servile fear of man.

TECHNIQUE OF REVOLUTION

Both Mary and Marx advocate the exaltation of the poor, the dethroning of the proud, the emptying of the rich in favor of the socially disinherited, but they differ in their technique.

Mary	*Marx*
Violence is necessary. "The Kingdom of Heaven suffereth violence." But the violence must be against self, against its selfishness, greed, lust, and pride.	Violence is necessary. But the violence must be against neighbor, against those who own, who believe in God and in democracy. Egotism must be disguised as social justice.
The sword that strikes must be thrust inward to rid oneself of all that would make one despise neighbor.	The sword that strikes must be thrust outward to rid society of all that would despise a revolution based on hate.
The transfer of wealth, which makes for the prosperity of the poor, is inspired by an inner charity that loves God and neighbor.	The transfer of wealth takes place through "violent confiscation" and the shifting of booty and loot from one man's pocket to another.
Man has nothing to lose but the chains of sin, which darkens his intellect and weakens his will. By throwing off sin through the merits of Christ, man becomes a child of God, an heir of Heaven, enjoying inner peace in this life and even amid its trials, and an ultimate and final ecstasy of love in Heaven.	Man has nothing to lose but the chains that bind him to God and to property. Thanks, then, to atheism and socialism, man will be restored to himself as the true god.

It is remarkable how Mary begins her *Magnificat* with her personal experiences and soon passes on to identify herself with the whole human race. She looks ahead and sees what the effect of the birth of her Son will be to the world, how it will improve the whole condition of human life, how it will free the oppressed, feed the hungry, and assist the helpless. And when she said these words, her Son was not yet born— although one would think, from the joy of the song, that He was already in her arms. She is singing here a song of pure faith about something certain to happen because *God* will make it come true, not predicting the mere revolution of blind material forces.

There is an intrinsic antagonism between her revolution and any other, because hers is based on the true psychology of human nature. Hers is based on the existence of an immense want, so serious and so imperative that every honest heart must crave for its satisfaction. Happy are they who experience, within themselves, the expelling of pride and egotism, and in whom spiritual hunger is fed—who discover, before it is too late, that they are poor, and naked, and blind, and who seek to clothe themselves with the raiment of grace that her Son brings.

4

When Did Belief in the Virgin Birth Begin?

In the study of law one of the most important subjects is *evidence*. One of the reasons why so few have arrived at a truth in which they believe absolutely is that they have forgotten the importance of *proof*. Evidence is one of the important divisions of theology. No belief can be accepted without proof or a "motive of credibility". One might say that the greatest sceptics are the Christians, for they will not believe in the Resurrection until they see the crucified and dead Man arise from the grave by the Power of God Himself. One could take any doctrine of Christianity as an example of proof and of evidence, but we will take one that the modern world has rejected for the last three hundred years (after believing in it for the first sixteen hundred years), namely, the virgin birth of Jesus from His Mother, Mary, who is a virgin.

Before adducing our evidence, it is important to realize that the Church, which is the Mystical Body of Christ, does not derive her belief from the Scriptures *alone*. This will come as a surprise to those who, whenever they hear of a particular Christian teaching, ask: "Is it in the Bible?" The Church was spread throughout the entire Roman Empire before a single book of the New Testament was written. There were already many martyrs in the Church before there were either Gospels or Epistles. An authoritative and recognized ministry was carrying on the Lord's work at His command, speaking in His name as *witnesses* of what they had seen, before anyone decided to write a single line of the New Testament.

To the early followers of Our Lord, and to us, the authority of the Apostles was equal to the authority of Christ, in the sense that it was the continuation of His teaching. Our Lord said: "He that heareth you, heareth me." The Apostles first taught and then later on, two—and only two—of the Twelve left a Gospel. To His Apostles, Our Lord said: "Going, therefore, teach ye all nations, baptizing them in the name of the Father, and of the Son, and of the Holy Ghost; teaching them to observe all things whatsoever I have commanded you; and behold I am with you all days even to the consummation of the world" (Mt 28:19, 20). And again He said : "As the Father hath sent me, I also send you" (Jn 20:21). The Apostles were the nucleus of the Church, the new Israel, the first visible manifestation of Christ's Mystical Body. That is why on Pentecost they chose one out of the community of 120 to take the place of Judas. The successor had to be an eyewitness of the Gospel events; that was the absolute condition of being an Apostle. The Church was an organic body of cohesion, the source of unity and authority, with Peter presiding because he was Divinely appointed. It would still be almost twenty-five years before the first of the Gospels would be written; hence those who isolate a single text from the Bible from this Apostolic tradition, or study it apart from it, are living and thinking in a vacuum. The Gospels need tradition as the lungs need air, and as the eyes light, and as the plants the earth! The Good Book was second, and not first. When finally the Gospels were written, they were the mere secretarial reports of what was already believed.

Pick up the Gospel of Luke, which was written sometime before the year 67, and read the opening lines: "For as much as many have taken hand to set forth in order, a narration of the things that have been accomplished among us: According as they have delivered them unto us, who from the beginning were eye-witnesses and ministers of the Word: It seemed good to me also, having diligently attained to all things from the beginning, to write to thee in order, most excellent Theophilus, that thou mayest know the verity of those words in which thou hast been instructed" (Lk 1:1–4). Luke did not write to Theophilus to tell him something brand new about someone who died over thirty-four years before. Theophilus, like every other member of the Apostolic Church in the Roman Empire, already knew about the miracle of the loaves and fishes, about the Resurrection and the Virgin Birth. It is similar to this. If we pick up a history book that tells us that in 1914 World War I began, it does not create that belief in us, it just confirms what we already know. So, too, the Gospels set down in a more systematic way what was already believed. If we had lived in the first twenty-five years of the Church, how would we have answered this question: "How can I know what I am to believe?" We could not have said, "I will look in the Bible." For there was no New Testament Bible then. We would have believed what the Apostolic Church was teaching, and, until the invention of printing, it would have been difficult for any of us to have made ourselves so-called infallible private interpreters of the book.

Never once did Our Lord tell these witnesses of His to write. He Himself wrote only once in His life, and that was on the sand. But He *did* tell them to preach in His name and to be witnesses to Him to the end of the earth, until the consummation of time. Hence those who take this or that text out of the Bible to prove something are isolating it from the historical atmosphere in which it arose and from the word of mouth that passed Christ's truth. If there are three persons in a room, there are also in it six legs and six arms—but they never create a problem because they are related to the physical organism. But if we found one arm outside the door, it would be a tremendous problem, because it is isolated from the organic whole. So it is with certain Christian truths that are isolated from the whole—for example, the doctrine of penance if it is isolated from Original Sin. It is only in the light of the circle of truth that the segments of the circle have a meaning.

When finally the Gospels were written, they recorded a tradition; they did not create it. It was already there. After a while men had decided to put in writing this living tradition and voice, which explains the beginning of the Gospel of Luke: "That thou mayest know the verity of those words in which thou hast been instructed." The Gospels did not start the Church; the Church started the Gospels. The Church did not come out of the Gospels; the Gospels came out of the Church.

The Church preceded the New Testament, not the New Testament the Church. First there was not a Constitution of the United States, and then Americans, who in the light of that Constitution decided to form a government and a nation. The Founding Fathers preceded the Foundation; so the Mystical Body of Christ preceded the reports written later by inspired secretaries. And incidentally, how do we know the Bible is inspired? It does not say so! Matthew does not conclude his Gospel saying: "Be sure to read Mark; he is inspired, too." Furthermore, the Bible is not a book. It is a collection of seventy-two books in all. It is worth opening a Bible to see if we have them all and have not been cheated. These widely scattered books cannot bear witness to their own inspiration. It is only by something outside the Bible that we know it is inspired. We will not go into that point now, but it is worth looking into.

When finally the Gospels were written, they did not prove what Christians believed, nor did they initiate that belief; they merely recorded in a systematic manner what they already knew. Men did not believe in the Crucifixion because the Gospels said there was a Crucifixion; they wrote down the story of the Crucifixion, because they already believed in it. *The Church did not come to believe in the Virgin Birth because the Gospels tell us there is a Virgin Birth*; it was because the living word of God in His Mystical Body already believed it that they set it down in the Gospels.

A second fact to be remembered is that this Mystical Body of Christ has a memory, as we have a memory. If our physical life extends back forty-five years, we can remember two world wars. We speak of them as a living witness, not from the books written but from having lived through them, and maybe through having fought in them. We may later on have read the books about these two world wars. Yet they are not the beginning of our knowledge but only a recalling or a deepening of what we already knew. In like manner, Our Lord is the Head of the new humanity, the new fellowship, or the spiritual organism that St. Paul calls His Mystical Body. To this Mystical Body Christ is associated, first in His Apostles, and then in all who believed in Him throughout the centuries. This Body, too, has a memory, reaching back to Christ. It knows that the Resurrection is true because she, the Church, was there. The cells of our body change every seven years, but we are the same personality. The cells of the Mystical Body, which we are, too, may change every fifty or sixty years; yet it is still Christ that lives in that Body.

The Church knows that Christ rose from the dead and that the Spirit descended on the Apostles on Pentecost because the Church *was there from the beginning*. The Church has a memory of over nineteen hundred years, and this memory is called tradition. The Apostles' Creed, which was an accepted formula in the Church around the year 100 and which summed up the Apostles' teaching, is as follows:

> I believe in God, the Father Almighty, the Creator of Heaven and earth; and in Jesus Christ, His only Son, Our Lord, Who was conceived by the Holy Ghost, born of the Virgin Mary, suffered under Pontius Pilate, was crucified, died and was buried. He descended into hell; the third day He arose again from the dead. He ascended into Heaven, sitteth at the right Hand of God, the Father Almighty, from whence He shall come to judge the living and the dead.
>
> I believe in the Holy Ghost, the Holy Catholic Church, the Communion of Saints, the forgiveness of sins, the resurrection of the body, and the life everlasting. Amen.

Note the words "conceived by the Holy Ghost, born of the Virgin Mary". The truths expressed in the Creed were essential for entrance into the Church. Everyone who was baptized early into Christ's Mystical Body believed in each of these truths. The Virgin Birth was as much an accepted Truth as the Resurrection in the first Christian centuries.

There is not *one* single quotation of the Gospels in the Creed. The early members of the Church were recording the early Christian tradition, of which the Gospels were only the literary expression. There are also several volumes of writings from within the first hundred years of the life of Our Lord; for example, the writing of St. Clement, one of the successors of St. Peter, who wrote in the year 92; and also Polycarp, the bishop of Smyrna, one of the successors of John the Evangelist; and Irenaeus, who names the twelve bishops of Rome; and Ignatius of Antioch, who said that he wanted to be "ground like wheat between the jaws of lions to be a living bread for His Savior".

Many of these writers do not quote the Gospels. We have fifteen hundred lines from Clement, and yet only two texts of his are from the New Testament; he was recording the Christian beliefs, accepted by the witnesses of Christ. Polycarp quotes the Gospel only three times, for he lived on familiar terms with many who had seen Our Lord, and he wrote what he knew and had learned from the Apostles. Ignatius of Antioch (who lived within seventy years of the life of Our Lord) wrote: "Our God, Jesus Christ, was conceived of the Holy Ghost . . . and was truly born of a virgin."

There is a double evidence from which we can draw, to learn true Christian teaching: one is the revealed Word of God in the Scriptures—the other is the continuous teaching of the Church from the very beginning, that is, her living memory. Just as lawyers, in proving a point, use not only the bare statement of law but also the way the courts have understood and interpreted that law, so too, the Scriptures are not a dead letter but are living and breathing in the beautiful context of a spiritual fellowship.

In the year 108, there were still many living who had been boys when Our Lord was crucified—who as young men saw and conversed with the Apostles before they were martyred—and who, in scattered parts of the Roman Empire, were already familiar with the Christian tradition passed on through the Church. Some of the other Apostles were not martyred until later—John did not die until the year 100. Some of these early writers were closer to John and other Apostles than we are to World War I. And this much is certain: if the Apostles, who lived with Our Lord and who heard Him speak on the open hills and in the temple—who listened to Him preach on the Kingdom of God forty days after His Resurrection—did not teach the Virgin Birth, *no one else would have taught it.* It was too unusual an idea for men to make up; it would have been ordinarily too difficult for acceptance *if it had not come from Christ Himself!*

The one man who might be most inclined to doubt the historical fact of the Virgin Birth on natural grounds (because he was a physician) was the second Evangelist, St. Luke. And yet he tells us the most about it. From the beginning Our Lord had many enemies. Certain aspects of His teaching were denied by heretics, but there was one teaching that no early heretic denied, and that was that He was born of a virgin. One would think that this should have been the doctrine first attacked, but the Virgin Birth was accepted by believers and early heretics alike. It would have been silly to try to convince anyone of the Virgin Birth if he did not already believe in the Divinity of Christ; that is why, probably, it would have been unwise for Mary to speak of it until after the Resurrection, although Joseph, Elizabeth, and probably John the Baptist already knew of it—and, need we say, the Son of God Himself, Who brought it all to pass.

"One-texters" say that the Bible speaks of Our Lord as having brethren; therefore, they conclude, He was not born of a virgin. But this claim can be answered. When a preacher in a pulpit addresses his congregation, "My dear brethren", it does not mean that everyone in the Church has the same mother. Secondly, the word "brother" is used in Sacred Scripture in the wide sense, to cover not only one's relatives but also one's friends; for example, Abraham calls Lot his brother: "Pray let us have no strife between us two, between my shepherds and thine; are we not brethren?" (Gen 13:8).

But Lot was not his brother. Thirdly, several who are mentioned as brothers of Christ, such as James and Joseph, are indicated elsewhere as the sons of another Mary, the sister of the mother of Jesus and wife of Cleophas! "And meanwhile his mother, and his mother's sister, Mary, the wife of Cleophas, and Mary Magdalen, had taken their stand beside the Cross of Jesus" (Jn 19:25). Fourthly, James, who is particularly mentioned as the brother of Jesus: "But I did not see any of the other apostles, except James, the Lord's brother" (Gal 1:19), is regularly named, in the enumeration of the Apostles, as the son of another father, Alphaeus (Mt 10:3; Mk 3:18; Lk 6:15).

The so-called brethren of Our Lord are nowhere mentioned in the Scripture as the sons and daughters of Joseph and Mary. Our Blessed Lord Himself used the term "brethren" in a large sense. "For one is your Master; and all you are brethren" (Mt 23:8). "And stretching forth His hand towards His Disciples He said: 'Behold . . . my brethren' " (Mt 12:49). Nowhere in Scripture is it said that Joseph had begotten brothers and sisters of Jesus, as nowhere does it say that Mary had other children besides her Divine Son.

The Gospel of St. John assumes the Virgin Birth. We humans can be born twice: once of our parents and once of the Holy Spirit, given to us by Our Lord in Baptism. This is what Our Lord meant when He told the old man Nicodemus that he must be born again, the first birth being of the flesh, the second of the spirit. What makes us Christian is this second birth through Baptism. But notice how it relates to the virgin birth of Our Lord. St. John, in the beginning of his Gospel, says that Our Lord gave us the "power to become the Sons of God". Then he tells us that this happens by a birth. But he immediately distinguishes, saying that it is not like a human birth, because there is in it neither blood, nor sex, nor human will, but solely the power of God. This statement of St. John assumes a common knowledge of the Virgin Birth. But how could any Christian understand such a birth, if it had not already happened? No one who at the end of the first century read the beginning of the Gospel of St. John was amazed that he should speak of a new generation without sex. For by this time, the whole Christian world knew that that is how Christianity had come into being. The Virgin Birth is God's idea, not man's. No one would have thought of it, if it had never happened. Pagan religions have no idea of it; their myths are of the union of gods with women, who bore children following a sexual union. All the love stories of Zeus and the other gods were of this anthropomorphic character. Nothing could be further from the truth than to represent these births as "virgin births".

St. Paul also implies the virgin birth of Christ by the use of a different word for "birth". Speaking of the earthly origin of the Son of the God, he writes: "That Gospel, promised long ago by means of His prophets in the holy Scriptures, tells us of his Son, *descended*, in respect of his human birth, from the line of David, but, in respect of the sanctified spirit that was His, marked out miraculously as the Son of God by His resurrection from the dead; Our Lord Jesus Christ" (Rom 1:14). "Then God sent out his Son on a mission to us. He *took birth* from a woman, *took birth* as a subject of the law, so as to ransom those who were subject to the law, and make us sons by adoption" (Gal 4:4–5). "He dispossessed Himself, and took the nature of a slave, fashioned in the likeness of men, and *presenting Himself* to us in human form" (Phil 2:7). Whenever St. Paul describes the early incarnation of Our Lord, he never uses the ordinary word to describe birth, which word is used in every other New Testament passage: namely, the verb *gennao*. But in the four instances where he touches on the temporal beginnings of the Son of God, he uses an entirely different word, *genemenos*, which comes from an entirely different verb, *ginomai*.

Never once does he employ the word *gennao* of Our Lord and His Mother, the word meaning "to be born", which is used throughout the New Testament; but when he speaks of the coming of Our Lord, he uses a form of the verb *ginomai* which means "to come into existence", "to become". In one passage (Gal 4:23, 24, 29) he uses the verb "to be born" three times, to describe the birth of Ismael and Jacob, but refuses to use it in the same chapter and context for the birth of Christ. The New Testament thirty-three times speaks of the birth of a child, and in each instance uses the word *gennao*, but it is never once used by St. Paul to describe the birth of Christ. St. Paul absolutely avoids saying Our Lord was born in the usual way. Our Lord was born *into* the human family; He was not born *of* it. God formed Adam, the first man, without the seed of a man, so why should we shrink from the thought that the new Adam would also be formed without the seed of a man? As Adam was made of the earth, into which God breathed a living soul, so the body of Christ was formed in the flesh of Mary by the Holy Spirit. So firmly rooted was the Virgin Birth in Christian tradition that none of the early apologists ever had to defend the Virgin Birth. It was believed in even by heretics, as surely as the Crucifixion, because it stood on the same footing as a historical fact.

There are two birth stories in the Gospel: those of Jesus and of John the Baptist. But notice the different stress in each story. The Gospel story of John the Baptist centers on the *father*, Zachary. The Gospel story of the birth of Jesus centers on the mother, Mary. In each instance, there were difficulties from the scientific point of view. Zachary was an old man, and his wife had long since passed the age of bearing children.

"And Zachary said to the angel: 'By what sign am I to be assured of this? I am an old man now, and my wife is far advanced in age'" (Lk 1:18). "But Mary said to the angel, 'How can that be, since I have no knowledge of man?'" (Lk 1:34). Mary was a virgin with the vow of virginity. The power of God had to operate in both cases, with Zachary doubting, and Mary accepting. For his doubt, Zachary was made dumb for a time.

No one ever makes a fuss against Zachary and Elizabeth bearing "the greatest man ever born of woman", but some do fuss about the Virgin Birth. This is not because of the human difficulties, for to God these are surmountable. The real reason for incredulity is that the attack on the Virgin Birth is a subtle attack on the Divinity of Christ. He who believes that Our Lord is true God and true man never is troubled with the Virgin Birth.

5

All Mothers Are Alike—Save One

No mother whose son has won distinction for himself, either in a profession or in the field of battle, believes that the respect paid her for being his mother detracts from the honor or dignity that is paid her son. Why, then, do some minds think that any reverence paid to the Mother of Jesus detracts from His Power and Divinity? We know the false rejoinder of those who say that Catholics "adore" Mary or make her a "goddess", but that is a lie. Since no reader of these pages would be guilty of such nonsense, it shall be ignored.

Where do this coldness, forgetfulness, and, at the least, indifference to the Blessed Mother start? From a failure to realize that her Son, Jesus, is the Eternal Son of God. The moment I put Our Divine Lord on the same level with Julius Caesar or Karl Marx, with Buddha or Charles Darwin, that is, as a mere man among men, then the thought of special reverence to His Mother as different from our mothers becomes positively repellent. Each famous man has his mother, too. Each person can say: "I have my mother, and mine is as good as or better than yours." That is why little is written of the mothers of any great men—because each mother was considered the best mother by her son. No one mother of a mortal is entitled to more love than any other mother. Therefore no sons and daughters should be required to single out someone else's mother as the Mother of mothers.

Our Lord described John the Baptist as "the greatest man ever born of woman". Suppose that a cult were started to honor his mother, Elizabeth, as superior to any other mother? Who among us would not rebel against it as excessive? Everything the critics would say of such exaggeration would be well taken, for the simple reason that John the Baptist is only a man. If Our Lord is just another man, or another ethical reformer, or another sociologist, then we share, even with the most bigoted, the resentment against thinking that the Mother of Jesus is different from any other mother.

The Fourth Commandment says: "Honor *thy* father and *thy* mother." It says nothing about honoring Gandhi's mother or Napoleon's father. But the Commandment to honor our fathers does not preclude adoring the Heavenly Father. If the Heavenly Father sends His Divine Son to this earth, then the Commandment to honor our earthly mothers does not preclude venerating the Mother of the Son of God.

If Mary were only the mother of another man, then she could not also be our mother, because the ties of the flesh are too exclusive. Flesh allows only one mother. The step between a mother and a stepmother is long, and few there are who can make it. But *Spirit* allows another mother. Since Mary is the Mother of God, then she can be the Mother of everyone whom Christ redeemed.

The key to understanding Mary is this: We do not start with Mary. We start with Christ, the Son of the Living God! The less we think of Him, the less we think of her; the more we think of Him, the more we think of her; the more we adore His Divinity, the more we venerate her Motherhood; the less we adore His Divinity, the less reason we have for respecting her. We could even resent hearing her name, if we had become so perverse as not to believe in Christ the Son of God. Never will it be found that anyone who really loves Our Lord as a Divine Savior dislikes Mary. Those who dislike any devotion to Mary are those who deny His Divinity or find fault with Our Lord because of what He says about hell, divorce, and judgment.

It is on account of Our Divine Lord that Mary receives special attention, and not on account of herself. Left to herself, her motherhood would dissolve into humanity. But when seen in the light of His Divinity, she becomes unique. Our Lord is God Who became man. Never before or since did Eternity become time in a woman, nor did Omnipotence take on the bonds of flesh in a maid. It is her Son who makes her motherhood different.

A Catholic boy from a parochial school was telling a university professor who lived next door about the Blessed Mother. The professor scoffed at the boy, saying: "But there is no difference between her and my mother." The boy answered: "That's what you say, but there's a heck of a lot of difference between the sons."

That is the answer. It is because Our Lord is so different from other sons that we set His Mother apart from all mothers. Because He had an Eternal Generation in the bosom of the Father as the Son of God and a temporal generation in the womb of Mary as the Son of Man, His coming created a new set of relationships. She is not a *private* person; all other mothers are. We did not *make* her different; we *found* her different. We did not choose Mary; *He did*.

But why was there a Virgin Birth? Because Christ is the Son of God, we cannot be as indifferent to the circumstances of His birth as we would be to the birth of the butcher or the baker. If Mary told the Apostles after Pentecost about His virgin birth, it must have made a difference; if the Apostles

put it in their Creed and teaching, it must have made a difference. Once Christ is accepted as the Son of God, there is
immediate interest not only in His prehistory, which John
describes in the Prologue of his Gospel, but also in His history and particularly in His birth.

Is the Virgin Birth fitting and becoming? The challenge to
our faith in the Virgin Birth is not related by anyone (except
in the Jewish Talmud) to sinfulness on Mary's part. The challenge concerns the physical possibility of a miraculous process
of life. By keeping His Mother absolutely stainless, He has
prevented the doubts about His Divine Paternity from being
such that they would wound her heart, her womanly heart. It
is impossible for us to imagine or feel, even to a slight degree,
the vast ocean of love of Christ for His Mother. Yet if even
we were faced with the problem of keeping the miasmic
breath of scandal from our own mothers, what would we not
do? And is it therefore hard to believe that the omnipotent
Son of God would do all in His power to protect His Own
Mother? With this in mind, there are many conclusions apparent.

No great triumphant leader makes his entrance into the
city over dust-covered roads when he could come on a
flower-strewn avenue. Had Infinite Purity chosen any other
port of entrance into humanity but that of human purity, it
would have created a tremendous difficulty—namely, how
could He be sinless if He was born of sin-laden humanity? If
a brush dipped in black becomes black, and if cloth takes on
the color of the dye, would not He, in the eyes of the world,
have also partaken of the guilt in which all humanity shared?
If He came to this earth through the wheatfield of moral
weakness, He certainly would have some chaff hanging on
the garment of His human nature.

Putting the problem in another way: How could God become man and yet be a sinless man and the Head of the new Humanity? First of all, He had to be a *perfect man* in order to act in our name, to plead our defense, and to pay our debt. If I am arrested for speeding, *you* cannot walk into the courtroom and say: "Judge, forget it, I will take the blame." If I am drowning, I cannot save anyone else who is drowning. Unless Our Lord is outside the sin-current of humanity, He cannot be Our Savior. "If the blind lead the blind, then both fall into the pit", said Our Lord. If He was to be the new Adam, the new Head of Humanity, the Founder of a new corporation or Mystical Body of regenerated humanity, as Adam was the head of fallen humanity, then He also had to be *different* from all other men. He had to be absolutely perfect, sinless, the Holy of Holies, all that God ever conceived man to be.

Such is the problem: How could God become man and yet be sinless man without Original Sin? How, in the language of St. Paul, could He "be like unto us in all things save sin"? How could He be a *man*, by being born of a *woman*? He could be a *sinless* man by being born of a *virgin*. The first statement is obvious: that He is born of a woman, then He shares in our humanity. But how would being born of a virgin make Him free from Original Sin?

Now, it must never be thought that the Incarnation would have been impossible without the Virgin Birth. Rash, indeed, would be the human mind to dictate to Almighty God the methods that He should use in coming to this earth. But once the Virgin Birth is revealed, then it is proper for us to inquire into its fitness, as we are now doing. The Virgin Birth is important because of its bearing upon the solidarity of the human race in guilt. The human race became incorporated to the first Adam by being born of the flesh; incorporation to the new Adam, Christ, is by being born of the spirit, or through a virgin birth. Thanks to it, we see how Our Blessed

Lord entered into the sinful race *from the outside*. Therefore, upon Him the curse did not rest, save as He freely bore it for those whom He redeemed by His blood. Nowhere do the New Testament writers argue from the Virgin Birth to the Godhead of the Virgin-born. Rather do they argue from it His sinless humanity.

To sum up: in order that Jesus Christ might be a descendant of Adam, he had to be born of a daughter of Adam. But the process of generation and birth of any individual is invisible. The only way to show that this process in the birth of Christ was miraculous was to have its invisible workings develop in a woman agreed by all to be incapable of having experienced the process—a virgin. Joseph, the just man, stood for all humanity when in his heart he questioned the fidelity of Mary. More than any other person he knew how cruel it was to place that doubt even in the face of the most incontrovertible evidence. He witnessed to Mary's immaculate life and her amiability even before her Son was born. His doubt was settled by Heaven itself. St. Joseph, more than any other human being on this earth, had a right to know the circumstances surrounding the birth of Jesus. And just as any husband is the prime witness of the fidelity of his wife, so, too, is Joseph in the case of Mary, his espoused; his testimony establishes for all men her virginity and the miraculous nature of the generation and birth of her Son.

As Father Joseph Tennant points out, there is a type of this miraculous birth in the story of Abraham and Sara. When they journeyed down to Egypt, Abraham asked Sara to say that she was his sister rather than his wife, lest the Egyptians kill him. The Pharaoh took her into his household. How long she lived with the Egyptian King is not indicated, but some space of time, and the Pharaoh and his household were punished with a sickness because of it. He finally dismissed both

Abraham and Sara from his palace. There is no expression of divine wrath reported in this case. But after God had promised that Sara would bear a son whose father would be Abraham, it was important that there be no doubt in Abraham's mind or in anybody else's about the paternity of Sara's son. Some time after the promise, in Gerara, there was danger that the King, Abimelech, would take her into his harem. With shameful cowardice Abraham permitted it to be done. (He was punished for this when God ordered him to sacrifice Isaac.) But God intervened immediately by appearing to Abimelech at night and threatening to wipe out his whole kingdom if he dared to touch Sara. "And Abimelech forthwith rising up in the night . . . called for Abraham and said to him, 'What hast thou done to us?' " It was not enough merely to have protected Sara. Abraham had to know from the lips of Abimelech himself that Sara was untouched, just as Joseph did in the case of Mary. And thus Isaac, the first of the "children of promise" (Gal 4:28) and of the miraculous seed of Abraham, was born.

Mary was not sinless because she was a virgin, but the best sign of her sinlessness was her virginity. Just as the Gospels prove the humble humanity of Christ by naming among his ancestors Lamech, the boastful murderer; Abraham, the coward; Jacob, the liar; Judas, the adulterer; Ruth, the pagan; David, the murderer and adulterer; and many idolatrous kings, showing that He was like to us in all things except sin, so, too, the same Gospels disassociate Mary from all sin in order to show her to be as much as possible "in the image and likeness of God". Mary was of the house of David, but Christ's relationship to that line is not given through Mary, but through Joseph, His foster father. And it had to be that the Mother of God was sinless in order that we might more easily believe that she had flung before the face of the world woman's greatest challenge to sin—the vow of virginity—and kept it and made it bear divine fruit.

We do not believe that Jesus is God because He was born of a virgin mother, as the Apostles and Evangelists did not believe it for that reason alone. We believe in the Divinity of Christ because of the evidence of the Resurrection, the marvel of the Gospel portrait, the growth of the Church, the miracles and prophecies of Christ, the consonance of His doctrine with the aspirations of the human heart. The Virgin Birth is rather related to the manhood of Christ and His separateness from the sin that affected all men who are born of the union of man and woman. Far from treating the Virgin Birth as the dazzling mark of Divinity, the *Te Deum* regards it as Our Lord's sublime condescension to the lowly conditions of humanity:

> When thou tookest upon Thee to deliver man:
> Thou didst not abhor the Virgin's womb.

The Virgin Birth is the safeguard of the sinlessness of the human nature that Our Blessed Lord assumed. The only salvation that is given to men on this earth is in the name of Him Who as God Himself entered the ranks of sinful men. That no one should ever deny He was a man, He was born like the rest of men from the womb of a woman—a fact that so scandalized Marcion that he said: "A babe wrapped in swaddling clothes is not the kind of a God that I will adore."

In the Incarnation, God the Son initiates the process of the re-creation of His own earlier and disordered creation by the method of clothing Himself with those very elements within it that had fallen into disarray. For the first time since the Fall of Man, a completely perfected unit of humanity is created in the world. This humanity is united substantially to the very Person of the Son of God.

What do all denials of the Virgin Birth testify? Generally, to the subtle attempt to pull down the new order of humanity and the race of the second Adam into the unredeemed world of the old Adam. If a human father supplied the human nature of Christ, then Christ is not the new Adam. The Virgin Birth keeps the Divine initiative of Redemption to God Himself. If the initiation of the new order is given to man, then it is taken from God. Without the Virgin Birth, Our Lord would be entangled in a sinful humanity. With it, He is incarnate in humanity without its sin. By getting rid of the Virgin Birth, one seeks to get rid of the Divine initiative within the race of the new Adam. The early heretics doubted the humanity of Our Lord, and so they denied that He had a human mother. Modern agnostics doubt the true Divinity, so they add a human father to His parentage.

There is never any danger that men will think too much of Mary; the danger is that they will think too little of Christ. Coldness toward Mary is a consequence of indifference to Christ. Any objection to calling her the "Mother of God" is fundamentally an objection to the Deity of Christ. The consecrated term *Theotokos*, "Mother of God," has ever since 432 been the touchstone of the Christian Faith. It was not that the Church then had the intention of expanding *Mariology*; it was rather that she was concerned with *Christological* orthodoxy. As John of Damascus said: "This name contains the whole mystery of the Incarnation." Once Christ is diminished, humanized, naturalized, there is no longer any use for the term "Mother of God". It implies a twofold generation of the Divine Word: one eternal in the bosom of the Father, the other temporal in the womb of Mary. Mary therefore did not bear a "mere man" but the "true God". No *new person* came into the world when Mary opened the portals of the flesh, but the Eternal Son of God was *made man*. All that came into being was a *new nature*, or a human nature to a Person Who existed from all eternity. It was the Word, the Second Person of the Blessed Trinity, Who became flesh and dwelt amongst us. *Theanthropos*, or God-Man, and *Theotokos*, or Mother of God, go together and fall together.

It will be discovered that so-called Christians who think they believe in the Divinity of Christ but do not believe in Mary as the Mother of God fall generally into four ancient heresies. They are *Adoptionists*, who believe that Christ was a mere man but after birth was adopted by God as His Son. Or they are *Nestorians*, who held that Mary gave birth to a man who had only a close union with Divinity. Or they are *Eutychians*, who denied the human nature of Christ and hence made Mary merely an instrument in a theophany. Or they are *Docetists*, holding that Christ's nature was only a phantom or an appearance. Those who are offended at reverence paid Mary, if they will analyze their thoughts, will discover that they are holding a Docetist or some similar ancient error. Even if they profess the Divinity of Christ in His earthly existence, such people shrink from affirming that His human nature is glorified with Him at the right hand of the Father, where He makes intercession for us. As some no longer think of Christ as God, so some no longer think of Christ as glorified Man. If He is no longer Man, then Mary is no longer His Mother. But if He is still Man, the relation of Mary to Him extends beyond Bethlehem and Calvary even to His Mystical Body the Church. No one, therefore, who thinks logically about Christ can understand such a question as: "Why do you speak so often of His Mother?"

The Virgin Birth, indeed, was a new type of generation. As our mind begets a thought without in any way destroying the mind, so Mary begot the Word within herself without in any way affecting her virginity. There are various ways of generating, but the three principal ways are carnal, intellectual, and Divine. The carnal is sexual, whether it be in animals or in humans. Second is the generation of a thought within the mind. I take the idea of "fortitude". That thought, or word (for it is a word even before I pronounce it), does not exist in the outside world. It has neither weight, nor color, nor longitude. Whence came it, then? It was begotten by the chaste generation of the mind. This intellectual generation is really a feeble image of the spiritual order of the Eternal Generation of the Son by the Father. "In the beginning was the Word, and the Word was with God, and the Word was God." God thinks a thought or a Word. But God does not think many thoughts or words. He thinks only one Word, which reaches to the abyss of all that is known or can be known. That Word is the perfect image of Himself as the Thinker. Because it has been eternally generated, God the Thinker is called the Father, as the principle of generation, and the Word is called the Son as the term of generation.

God willed that there be another kind of generation that would be neither wholly intellectual nor wholly carnal but, in the order of flesh, would reflect His eternal generation in time. God willed to take on a human nature like our own through a virgin, while conserving the virginity of His Mother, and showing precisely that He is the Word of God. As our mind does not alter or destroy itself in the begetting of a thought, so neither does the virginal body of Our Blessed Mother go through any alteration in begetting Him, as the Son of God made man. The Word of God willed that His generation in the order of the flesh and in time be elevated with as close a resemblance as possible to His Heavenly generation.

Christ is a Mediator between God and humanity; Mary is the Mediatrix between Christ and us. Our Lord is a Mediator between God and man. A mediator is like a bridge that unites two opposite banks of a river, except that here the bridge is between Heaven and earth. As you cannot touch the ceiling without a stepladder acting as a mediator, so sinful man could not in justice reach God, except by One Who mediated and was both God and man. As man, He could act in our name, take on our sins; as one of us, He redeems us on the Cross and gives us new life in His Resurrection. But as God, His words, miracles, and death have an infinite value, and therefore He restores more than we lost. God became man without ceasing to be either God or man and therefore is our Mediator, Our Savior, Our Divine Lord.

As we study His Divine life, seeing Him as the first refugee persecuted by a cruel government, working as a carpenter, teaching, and redeeming, we know that it all began when He took on our human nature and became man. If He had never taken on our human flesh, we would never have heard His Sermon on the Mount or have seen Him forgive those who dug His hands and feet with nails on the Cross. But the Woman gave Our Lord His human nature. He asked her to give Him a human life—to give Him hands with which to bless children, feet with which to go in search of stray sheep, eyes with which to weep over dead friends, and a body with which to suffer—that He might give us a rebirth in freedom and love.

It was through her that He became the bridge between the Divine and the human. If we take her away, then either God does not become man, or He that is born of her is a man and not God. Without her we would no longer have Our Lord! If we have a box in which we keep our money, we know that one thing we must always give attention to is the key; we never think that the key is the money, but we know that without the key we cannot get our money. Our Blessed Mother is like the key. Without her we can never get to Our Lord, because He came through her. She is not to be compared to Our Lord, for she is a creature and He is a Creator. But if we lose her, we cannot get to Him. That is why we pay so much attention to her; without her we could never understand how that bridge was built between Heaven and earth.

It may be objected: "Our Lord is enough for me. I have no need of her." But *He* needed her, whether we do or not. And, what is more important, Our Blessed Lord gave us His Mother as *our* Mother. On that Friday men call Good, when He was unfurled upon the Cross as the banner of salvation, He looked down to the two most precious creatures He had on earth: His Mother and His beloved disciple John. The night before, at the Last Supper, He had made His last Will and Testament, giving us that which on dying no man was ever able to give, namely, Himself in the Holy Eucharist. Thus He would be with us, as He said, "all days unto the consummation of the world". Now in the darkening shadows of Calvary, He adds a codicil to His will. There beneath the Cross, not prostrate, as the Gospel notes, "stood" His Mother. As a Son, He thought of His Mother; as a Savior, He thought of us. So He gave to us His Mother: "Behold thy mother."

At last we see illumined the Gospel's description of His birth, namely, that Mary "brought forth her first born and laid him in a manger". *Her first born.* St. Paul calls Him the "first born of all creatures". Does that mean that she was to have other children? Most certainly! But not according to the *flesh*, for Jesus was Her only Son. But she was to have other children by the *spirit*. Of these John is the first, born at the foot of the Cross, maybe Peter is the second, James, the third, and all of us the millionth and millionth of children. She gave birth in joy to Christ, Who redeemed us, then she gave birth in sorrow to us, whom Christ redeemed! Not by a mere figure of speech, not by a metaphor, but in virtue of Baptism did we become children of Mary and brothers of Our Lord, Jesus Christ.

Just as we do not shrink from the thought of God giving us His Father, so that we can pray: "Our Father," so neither do we rebel when He gives us His Mother, so that we can pray: "Our Mother". Thus the Fall of man is undone through another Tree, the Cross; Adam through another Adam, Christ; and Eve through the new Eve, Mary.

Born of the Virgin Mary: this is a true statement not only of Christ but also of every Christian, although in a lesser way. Every man is born of woman in the flesh as a member of the race of Adam. He is also born of the Woman in the Spirit if he is of the redeemed race of Christ. As she formed Jesus in her body, so she forms Jesus in our souls. In this one Woman are virginity and motherhood united, as if God willed to show us that both are necessary for the world. Things separated in other creatures are united in her. The Mother is the protector of the virgin, and the Virgin is also the inspiration of motherhood.

One cannot go to a statue of a mother holding a babe, hack away the mother, and expect to have the babe. Touch her and you spoil him. All other world religions are lost in myth and legend except Christianity. Christ is cut off from all the gods of paganism because He is tied to woman and to history. "Born of the Virgin Mary; suffered under Pontius Pilate". Coventry Patmore rightly calls Mary "Our only Saviour from an abstract Christ". It is easier to understand the meek and humble heart of Christ by looking at His Mother. She holds all the great Truths of Christianity together, as a piece of wood holds a kite. Children wrap the string of a kite around a stick and release the string as the kite climbs to the heavens. Mary is like that piece of wood. Around her we wrap all the precious strings of the great Truths of our holy Faith—for example, the Incarnation, the Eucharist, the Church. No matter how far we get above the earth, as the kite may, we always have need of Mary to hold the doctrines of the Creed together. If we threw away the stick, we would no longer have the kite; if we threw away Mary, we would never have Our Lord. He would be lost in the Heavens, like our runaway kite, and that would be terrible, indeed, for us on earth.

Mary does not prevent our honoring Our Lord. Nothing is more cruel than to say that she takes souls away from Christ. That could mean that Our Lord chose a mother who is selfish, He Who is Love itself. If she kept us from her Son, we would disown her! But is not she, who is the Mother of Jesus, good enough for us sinners? We would never have had Our Divine Lord if He had not chosen her.

We pray to the Heavenly Father, "Give us this day our daily bread." Though we ask God for our daily bread, we do not hate the farmer and the baker who help prepare it. Neither does the mother who gives the bread to her child dispense with the Heavenly Provider. If the only charge Our Lord has against us on Judgment Day is that we loved His Mother— then we shall be very happy!

As our love does not start with Mary, so neither does it stop with Mary. Mary is a window through which our humanity first catches a glimpse of Divinity on earth. Or perhaps she is more like a magnifying glass; she intensifies our love of her Son and makes our prayers more bright and burning.

God, Who made the sun, also made the moon. The moon does not take away from the brilliance of the sun. The moon would be only a burnt-out cinder floating in the immensity of space were it not for the sun. All its light is reflected from the sun. The Blessed Mother reflects her Divine Son; without Him, she is nothing. With Him, she is the Mother of Men.

On dark nights we are grateful for the moon; when we see it shining, we know there must be a sun. So in this dark night of the world when men turn their backs on Him Who is the Light of the World, we look to Mary to guide their feet while we await the sunrise.

6

The Virgin Mother

A woman can be a virgin in one of three ways: first, because she never had a chance to marry. This could be involuntary virginity (if she rebelled against her maidenhood), or it could be voluntary and meritorious (if she accepted it as God's holy will). No one is saved because of virginity alone—of the ten virgins in the Gospel, five were foolish women. There are virgins in hell, but there is no one in hell who is humble. A woman can be a virgin a second way—because she decided not to marry. This can be for social or economic reasons and, therefore, may have no religious value, but it can also be meritorious, if it is done for a religious motive—for example, the better to serve a sick member of a family or to dedicate oneself to neighbor for the love of God. Thirdly, a woman can be a virgin because she made a vow or a promise to God to keep herself pure for His sake although she has a hundred chances to marry.

Mary was a virgin in the third way. She fell in love at a very early age, and it was with God—one of those beautiful loves where the first love is the last love, and the last love is Eternal Love. She must have been very wise, as well as good, as a young girl of fifteen or sixteen, to have made such a choice. This alone made her very different from other women, who were anxious to bear children. When a married woman did not have children in that time, it was considered sometimes, but wrongly, that God was angry with her.

When Our Lady took the vow of virginity, she made herself "queer" to some people, for there will always be some material-minded people who cannot understand why some souls really love God. The Blessed Mother had a better chance than most women to become the Mother of God, for the Bible said that Our Lord would be born of the House of David, the great King who lived a thousand years before. And Mary belonged to that royal family. Without doubt Mary knew the prophecy of Isaias, which some had forgotten, namely, that the Messias would be born of a Virgin. But it is more likely, from what she said later, that she considered herself too lowly for such dignity and took the vow in the hope that, through her sacrifice and prayer, the coming of the Messias might be hastened.

How do we know that Mary took a vow? We know it from her answer to the angel Gabriel. Out from the great white throne of light came the angel to this beautiful girl kneeling in prayer. This visit of the angel to Mary is called the Annunciation because it announced the first really good news the earth had heard in centuries. Yesterday's news was about the fall of a man through a woman; today's news is about the regeneration of man through a woman.

An angel salutes a woman! This would be a perversion of Heaven's order, worse than men's worshipping animals, unless Mary had been destined by God to be even greater than the angels—aye, their very Queen! And so the angel, who was accustomed to be honored by men, now honors the Woman.

This ambassador of God gives no order but salutes her: "Hail, full of grace". "Hail" is our English translation for the Greek *Chaire* and probably is the equivalent of the old

Aramaic formula *Shalom*, which meant "Rejoice" or "Peace be to you." "Full of grace", the rare word in the Greek of the Gospel, signifies either "most gracious" or "full of virtue". It was almost like a proper noun in which God's emissary affirms that she is the object of His Divine pleasure.

It was less the flashing visit of the Heavenly messenger that troubled the humble maid than the startling greeting and the unexpected tone of Divine praise. A short time later, when she would visit her cousin Elizabeth, she would be asked: "How is it that the Mother of my God should come to me?" But now it is Mary's turn to ask: "Why should the angel of my God come to me?" The angel hastens to assure her of the reason of the visit. She is to fulfill within herself that which the prophet Isaias had announced seven centuries before: "A Virgin shall conceive, and bring forth a Son, and His name shall be called 'Emmanuel' (God with us)" (Is 7:14). Making clear allusion to that prophecy, the angel says: "Thou shalt conceive in thy womb, and shalt bring forth a son; and thou shalt call his name Jesus. He shall be great, and shall be called the Son of the Most High, and the Lord God shall give unto him the throne of David his father; and he shall reign in the house of Jacob forever" (Lk 1:30–33).

God was choosing her not just because she was a virgin but because of her humility. Later Mary herself declared this as the reason: "He looked upon the lowliness of his handmaid" (Lk 1:48). So Mary was troubled. Nothing troubles a humble soul like praise, and here the praise comes from an angel of God.

This great honor created a problem for Mary, who had vowed to give her body as well as her soul to God. Therefore she could never be a mother. As she put it: "I know not man. I have willed not to know man."

The Bible never speaks of marriage in terms of sex, but as

"knowledge", for example, "Joseph knew not Mary" (Mt 1:19); "Adam knew Eve and she conceived" (Gen 4:1). The reason it does this is in order to show how close a husband and wife should be: they are intended by God to be as close as your mind and that thing which you know. For example, you know that two plus two equals four, and you cannot think of anything coming between your mind and that. Your right arm is not united to your body so closely as anything that you know is united to your mind.

So Mary says: "How shall this be, seeing I know not man?" Mary did not say: "I will never marry; therefore I cannot become the Mother of Jesus." That would have been disobedient to the angel who asked her to become the Mother of Jesus. Neither did she say: "I do not want a husband, but let the will of God be fulfilled", for that would have been untrue to herself and her vow. Mary merely wanted to be enlightened concerning her duty. The problem was not her virginity. She was familiar enough with the prophecy of Isaias to know that God would be born of a virgin. Mary's only concern was—since up to this point in history motherhood and virginity had been irreconcilable—how will God arrange it? Her objection to the Virgin Birth was on the basis of science. The solution certainly cannot be natural; therefore it must be supernatural. God can do it, but how? Long before modern biology put a query to the Virgin Birth, Mary asked the scientific "How?" The angel answers that, in her case, birth will come without human love, but not without Divine Love, for the Third Person of the Blessed Trinity, the Holy Spirit, Who is the Love of God, will descend into her, and He that will be born of her will be "the Son of God".

Mary saw at once that this allowed her to keep her vow. All she wanted, anyway, was to love God. At this moment, when the Spirit of Love ravished her soul, so that she conceived the

Christ within, there must have come to her the fulfillment of
those ecstatic ravishments that creatures seek in the flesh but
that they never quite attain. The flesh in its peaks of love
when it becomes united to other flesh falls back upon itself
with satiety, but here in this union of human love with Divine
Love there is no throwback to self but only the sheer delight
of the ecstasy of the spirit. In flesh-love the ecstasy is first in
the body and then indirectly in the soul. In this Spirit-love it
was Mary's soul that was first ravished and then, not by human love, but by God. The love of God would so inflame her
heart, her body, her soul that when Jesus was born the world
could truly say of Him: "This is a Child of Love."

Being told how Divine Love will supplant human love
and how she can be a mother while remaining a virgin in the
great mystery of generation, Mary now gives her consent:
"Be it done unto me according to thy word", that is, as God
in His Wisdom wills it, so do I. And at that moment the
Word was conceived in her: "The Word became Flesh and
dwelt amongst us." Before the Fall, it was woman who came
from man in the ecstasy of sleep. Now it is man who comes
from a woman in the ecstasy of the Spirit.

One of the most beautiful lessons in the world emerges
from the Annunciation, namely, the vocation of woman to
supreme religious values. Mary is here recapturing woman's
vocation from the beginning, namely, to be to humanity the
bearer of the Divine. Every mother is this when she gives
birth to a child, for the soul of every child is infused by God.
She thus becomes a co-worker with Divinity; she bears what
God alone can give. As the priest in the order of Redemption, at the moment of Consecration, brings the crucified
Savior to the altar, so the mother in the order of creation
brings the spirit that issues from the Hand of God to the
cradle of earth. With such thoughts in mind, Léon Bloy once

said: "The more a woman is holy, the more she becomes a woman."

Why? It is not that women are naturally more religious than men. This statement is merely a rationalization made by men who have fallen from their ideals. Man and woman each have a specific mission under God to complement one another. Each, too, has its symbol in the lower order. Man may be likened to the animal in his acquisitiveness, mobility, and initiative. Woman may be likened to the flower, which is fixed between Heaven and earth; she is like the earth in her bearing of life; she is like Heaven in her aspirations to blossom upward to the Divine. The mark of man is initiative, but the mark of woman is cooperation. Man talks about freedom; woman about sympathy, love, sacrifice. Man cooperates with nature; woman cooperates with God. Man was called to till the earth, to "rule over the earth"; woman to be the bearer of a life that comes from God. The hidden wish of every woman in history, the secret desire of every feminine heart, is fulfilled in that instant when Mary says: "*Fiat*"—"Be it done unto me according to thy word."

Here is cooperation at its best. Here is the essence of womanhood—*acceptance, resignation, submission*: "Be it done unto me". Whether it be the unmarried daughter who cares for the mother with her *Fiat* of surrender to service, or the wife who accepts the husband in the unity of the flesh, or the saint who accepts little crosses proffered by her Savior, or this unique Woman whose soul submits to the Divine Mystery of mothering God made man—there is present in varying degrees the beautiful picture of woman in her sublimest vocation—making the Total Gift, accepting a Divine assignment, being submissive for Heaven's holy purposes. Mary calls herself *ancilla Domini*, the handmaid of the Lord. *Not* to be this for any woman lowers her dignity. Woman's unhappiest

moments are when she is unable to give; her most hellish
moments are when she refuses to give. Tragedy stalks when
woman is forced by economic or social circumstances to busy
herself in those materialities that hamper or dam up the out-
pouring of that specific quality of surrender to Divine Purpose that makes her a woman. Denied an outlet for the
bursting need of giving, she feels a deeper sense of emptiness
than a man, precisely because of the greater depths of her
fountain of love.

For a woman to be the Collaborator with the Divine—
whether it be helping the missions, visiting the sick after
business hours, freely offering services to hospitals, or mothering her children—is to enjoy that equilibrium of spirit
which is the essence of sanity. Liturgy speaks of woman as
fulfilling *mysterium caritatis*: the mystery of love. And love
does not mean to have, to own, to possess. It means to be
had, to be owned, to be possessed. It is the giving of self for
another. A woman may love God mediately through creatures, or she may love God immediately, as Mary did, but to
be happy she *must* bring the Divine to the human. The ex-
plosive revolt of woman against her alleged inequalities with
man is at bottom a protest against the restraints of a bourgeois civilization without faith, one that has chained her
God-given talents.

What every woman wants in the "mystery of love" is not
the bestial burst but the soul. Man is driven by love of pleasure; woman by the pleasure of love, by its meaning and the
enrichment of soul it grants. In this beautiful moment of the
Annunciation, woman reaches her sublimest fulfillment for
God's sake. As the earth submits to the exigency of the seed
for the sake of the harvest, as the nurse submits to the exigencies of the wounded for the sake of the healing, as the wife
submits to the exigencies of the flesh for the sake of the child,

so Mary submits to the exigencies of the Divine will for the sake of the Redemption of the world.

Closely allied with this submission is sacrifice. For submission is not passivity but action—the action of self-forgetfulness. Woman is capable of greater sacrifices than man, partly because her love is less intermittent, and also because she is unhappy without total and complete dedication. Woman is made for the sacred. She is Heaven's instrument on earth. Mary is the prototype, the pattern-woman who fulfills in herself the deepest aspirations of the heart of every daughter of Eve.

Virginity and maternity are not so irreconcilable as it would seem. Every virgin yearns to become a mother, either physically or spiritually, for unless she creates, mothers, nurses, and fosters life, her heart is as uneasy and awkward as a giant ship in shallow waters. She has the vocation of generating life, either in the flesh or in the spirit through conversion. There is nothing in professional life that necessarily hardens a woman. If such a woman does become hardened, it is because she is denied those specifically creative God-like functions without which she cannot be happy.

On the other hand, every wife and mother strives for spiritual virginity in that she would like to take back what she has given, that she might offer it all over again, only this time more deeply, more piously, more divinely. There is something incomplete about virginity, something ungiven, unsurrendered, kept back. There is something lost in all motherhood: something given, something taken—and something irrecoverable.

But in the Woman there was realized physically and spiritually what every woman desires physically. In Mary there was nothing unsurrendered, nothing lost; there was a harvest without the loss of the bud; an autumn in an eternal spring; a submission without a spoliation. Virgin and Mother! The only melody that fell from the violin of God's creation without the breaking of a string!

Woman has a mission to give life. The Life that is to be born of Mary comes without the spark of love of a human spouse but with the Flame of Love of the Holy Spirit. There can be no birth without love; but the meaning of the Virgin Birth is Divine Love acting without benefit of the flesh. As a result, He Whom the Heavens could not contain she now contains within herself. This was the beginning of the propagation of the faith in Christ Jesus Our Lord, for in her virgin body is celebrated, as in a new Eden, the nuptials of God and man.

Because in this one woman virginity and motherhood are united, it must be that God willed to show how both are necessary for the world. What are separated in other creatures are united in her. The Mother is the protectress of the virgin, and the Virgin is the inspiration of motherhood. Without mothers, there would be no virgins in the next generation; without the virgins, mothers would forget the sublime ideal that lies beyond the flesh. They complement one another, like the sun and the rain. Without the sun there would be no clouds, and without the clouds there would be no rain. The clouds, like mothers, surrender something in fecundating the earth; but the sun, like a virgin, recoups and recovers that loss by drawing the gentle drops back again into the heavens. How beautiful to think that He Who is generated without a mother in Heaven is now born without a father on earth! Can we imagine a little bird building the very nest in which it is to be hatched? It is clearly impossible, because the bird would have to exist before it could build its own nest. But that is what happened, in a sense, with God, when he chose Mary as His Mother: He thought of Her from all eternity—He made His Mother as the very nest from which He would be born.

We have often heard friends and relatives say of a child: "You look like your father" or "You look like your mother." Or, "You get your blue eyes from your mother's side" or "You get your smartness from your father's side." Well, Our Lord had no earthly father's side. Where did Our Lord get His beautiful face, His strong body, His clean blood, His sensitive mouth, His delicate fingers? He got them from His Mother's side. Where did He get His Divinity, His Divine mind that knows all things, even our most secret thoughts, and His Divine power over life and death? He got these from His Heavenly Father's side. It is a terrible thing for men not to know their father, but it is even more terrible not to know their Heavenly Mother. And the greatest compliment that can be paid to a true Christian is: "You took after your Father's side in grace, but in your humanity, you took after your Mother's side."

7

The World's Happiest Marriage

It is very difficult for the unspiritual-minded to think of a golden mean between marriage and being alone. They think either that a person is tied up with someone in wedded life or else that he lives in solitude. The two are not exclusive, for there is such a thing as a combination of marriage and solitude, and that is absolute virginity with wedded life, in which there is a union of the soul of one with another and yet an absolute separateness of body. Only the joys of the spirit are shared, never the pleasures of the flesh.

Today the vow of virginity is taken only outside of human espousals or marriage, but among some Jews and among some great Christian saints, the vow of virginity was sometimes taken along with espousals. Marriage then became the frame into which the picture of virginity was placed. Marriage was like a sea on which the bark of carnal union never sailed, but one from which one fished the sustenance for life.

There are some marriages where there is no unity of the flesh, because the flesh has already been sated and dulled. Some partners abandon passion only because passion has abandoned them. But there are also marriages wherein, after a unity of the flesh, couples have mutually pledged to God a sacrifice of the thrill of unity in the flesh for the sake of the greater ecstasies of the spirit. Beyond both of these, there is a true marriage where the exercise of the right to another's body is annulled—and even the desire of it; such is the marriage of two persons with the vow of virginity. It is one thing to give up the pleasures of married life because one is jaded with them, and quite another to give up the pleasures before they are ever experienced. Here the marriage is of the heart and not of the flesh; it is a marriage such as the stars have, whose light unites in the atmosphere although the stars themselves do not; a marriage like the flowers in the garden in springtime, which give forth perfume, although they themselves do not touch; a marriage like an orchestration, where a great melody is produced but where one instrument is without contact with the other. Such a marriage was actually the type of marriage that took place between the Blessed Mother and St. Joseph, one in which the right to another was surrendered for a higher purpose. The marriage bond does not necessarily imply carnal union. As St. Augustine says: "The basis of married love is the attachment of hearts."

First, then, we will inquire why there should have been a marriage at all, since both Mary and Joseph had taken the vow of virginity; and secondly, we will seek to understand the character of Joseph himself. The first reason for the espousal was that it kept the Blessed Mother covered with honor until the time came for her to reveal the Virgin Birth. We do not know exactly when she revealed the fact, but it is likely that it was done shortly after the Resurrection. There was no point in talking about the Virgin Birth until Our Lord had given the final proof of His Divinity. In any case, there were only a few who really knew it: the Mother herself, St. Joseph, Elizabeth, her cousin, and, of course, Our Blessed Lord. So far as public appearances went, it was thought that Our Blessed Lord was the son of Joseph. Thus the reputation of the Blessed Mother was conserved; if Mary had become a Mother without a spouse, it would have exposed the mystery of Christ's birth to ridicule and would have become a scandal to the weak.

A second reason for the marriage was that Joseph could bear witness to the purity of Mary. This involved, both for Mary and for Joseph, the greatest sorrow this side of Calvary. Every privilege of grace has to be paid for, and so Mary and Joseph had to pay for theirs. Mary did not tell Joseph that she was conceived by the Spirit of Love, because the angel did not bid her do so. The Blessed Mother once revealed to a saint: "Outside of Golgotha, I never suffered such intense agony as in those days when, despite myself, I brought worry to Joseph, who was so just." The sorrow of Joseph came from the inexplicable. On the one hand, he knew that Mary had taken the vow of virginity as he had done. It seemed impossible to believe her guilty, because of her goodness. But, on the other hand, because of her condition, how could he believe otherwise? Joseph suffered then what the mystics have called "the dark night of the soul". Mary had to pay for her honor, particularly at the end of her life, but Joseph had to pay for his at the beginning. Because Joseph had kept his vow, he was naturally surprised when he heard that Mary was with child. The surprise that Joseph felt was like that of Mary at the Annunciation: "How shall this be, seeing I know not man?" Mary wanted then to know how she could be both a virgin and a mother; Joseph wanted to know how he could be a virgin and a father. It took an angel to reassure them both that God had found a way. No human knowledge of science can explain such a thing. Only those who listen to angels' voices can pierce that mystery. As Joseph had a mind to put Mary away secretly, the Gospel lifts the veil of the mystery to him: "But hardly had the thought come to his mind, when an angel of the Lord appeared to him in a dream, and said, 'Joseph, son of David, do not be afraid to take thy wife Mary to thyself, for it is by the power of the Holy Ghost that she has conceived this child; and she will bear a son, whom thou shalt call Jesus, for he is to save his people from their sins'" (Mt 1:20–21).

Joseph's worries were overcome by a revelation of the dignity of Christ's Virgin Birth and of the nature of His mission—namely, to save us from our sins. The very words of the angel: "Do not be afraid to take thy wife Mary to thyself", seem to support the view that Joseph already believed that a miracle had taken place in Mary and that that was why he "feared" to bring her into his own house. It is unlikely that any man told of a Virgin Birth would ever have credited it if there had not already been in his heart a belief in the Messias, Christ, Who was to come. Joseph knew that the Messias would be born of the family of David, and he himself was of that family. He also knew of the prophecies concerning the Child, even the one of Isaias that He would be born of a Virgin. If Joseph had not already been described as a just man, the message of the angel and the honor that was to come to Mary would have been enough to have inspired great purity in him. For if a modern father were told that one day his son would be President of the United States, it would inspire a changed attitude toward his wife, the mother of the child. In like manner, all anxiety and anguish now leave Joseph, as his soul is filled with reverence and awe for the love of Mary's secret.

That brings us to the second interesting question concerning Joseph. Was he old or young? Most of the statues and pictures we see of Joseph today represent him as an old man with a gray beard, one who took Mary and her vow under his protection with somewhat the same detachment as a doctor would pick up a baby girl in a nursery. We have, of course, no historical evidence whatever concerning the age of Joseph. Some apocryphal accounts picture him as an old man; Fathers of the Church, after the fourth century, followed this legend rather rigidly. The painter Guido Reni did so when he pictured Joseph as an old man with white hair.

But when one searches for the reasons why Christian art should have pictured Joseph as aged, we discover that it was in order better to safeguard the virginity of Mary. Somehow, the assumption had crept in that senility was a better protector of virginity than adolescence. Art thus unconsciously made Joseph a spouse chaste and pure by age rather than by virtue. But this is like assuming that the best way to show that a man would never steal is to picture him without hands; it also forgets that old men can have unlawful desires, as well as young men. It was the old men in the garden who tempted Susanna. But more than that, to make Joseph out as old portrays for us a man who had little vital energy left, rather than one who, having it, kept it in chains for God's sake and for His holy purposes. To make Joseph appear pure only because his flesh had aged is like glorifying a mountain stream that has dried. The Church will not ordain a man to his priesthood who has not his vital powers. She wants men who have something to tame, rather than those who are tame because they have no energy to be wild. It should be no different with God.

Furthermore, it is reasonable to believe that Our Lord would prefer, for a foster father, someone who had made a sacrifice rather than someone who was forced to it. There is the added historical fact that the Jews frowned on a disproportionate marriage between what Shakespeare calls "crabbed age and youth"; the Talmud admits a disproportionate marriage only for widows or widowers. Finally, it seems hardly possible that God would have attached a young mother, probably about sixteen or seventeen years of age, to an old man. If He did not disdain to give His Mother to a young man, John, at the foot of the Cross, then why should He have given her an old man at the crib? A woman's love always determines the way a man loves: she is the silent educator of his virile powers. Since Mary is what might be called a "virginizer" of young men as well as women, and the greatest inspiration of Christian purity, should she not logically have begun by inspiring and virginizing the first youth whom she had probably ever met—Joseph, the Just? It was not by diminishing his power to love but by elevating it that she would have her first conquest, and in her own spouse, the man who was a *man*, and not a mere senile watchman!

Joseph was probably a *young* man, strong, virile, athletic, handsome, chaste, and disciplined; the kind of man one sees sometimes shepherding sheep, or piloting a plane, or working at a carpenter's bench. Instead of being a man incapable of loving, he must have been on fire with love. Just as we would give very little credit to the Blessed Mother if she had taken her vow of virginity after having been an old maid for fifty years, so neither could we give much credit to a Joseph who became her spouse because he was advanced in years. Young girls in those days, like Mary, took vows to love God uniquely, and so did young men, of whom Joseph was one so preeminent as to be called the "just". Instead, then, of being dried fruit to be served on the table of the king, he was rather a blossom filled with promise and power. He was not in the evening of life, but in its morning, bubbling over with energy, strength, and controlled passion.

Mary and Joseph brought to their espousals not only their vows of virginity but also two hearts with greater torrents of love than had ever before coursed through human breasts. No husband and wife ever loved one another so much as Joseph and Mary. Their marriage was not like that of others, because the right to the body was surrendered; in normal marriages, unity in the flesh is the symbol of its consummation, and the ecstasy that accompanies a consummation is only a foretaste of the joy that comes to the soul when it attains union with God through grace. If there are satiety and fed-up-ness in marriage, it is because it falls short of what it was meant to reveal, or because the inner Divine Mystery was not seen in the act. But in the case of Mary and Joseph, there was no need of the symbol of the unity of flesh, since they already possessed the Divinity. Why pursue the shadow when they had the substance? Mary and Joseph needed no consummation in the flesh, for, in the beautiful language of Leo XIII: "The consummation of their love was in Jesus." Why bother with the flickering candles of the flesh, when the Light of the World is their love? Truly He is *Jesu, voluptas cordium*. When He is the sweet voluptuousness of hearts, there is not even a thought of the flesh. As husband and wife standing over the cradle of their newborn life forget, for the moment, the need of one another, so Mary and Joseph, in their possession of God in their family, hardly knew that they had bodies. Love usually makes husband and wife one; in the case of Mary and Joseph, it was not their combined loves but Jesus Who made them one. No deeper love ever beat under the roof of the world since the beginning, nor will it ever beat, even unto the end. They did not go to God through love of one another; rather, because they went first to God, they had a deep and pure love, one for another. To those who ridicule such holiness, Chesterton wrote:

> *That Christ from this creative purity*
> *Came forth your sterile appetites to scorn.*
> *Lo! in her house Life without Lust was born*
> *So in your house Lust without Life shall die.*

THE WORLD'S HAPPIEST MARRIAGE

In a flesh-marriage, the body first leads the soul; and then, later, comes a more reposed state, when the soul leads the body. At this point, both partners go to God. But in a spirit-marriage, it is God Who possesses both body and soul from the beginning. Neither has a right to the other's body, for that belongs to the Creator through the vow. Mary and Joseph thus combined solitude and espousal through the spiritual magic of virginity along with togetherness. Joseph renounced paternity of the flesh and yet found it in the spirit, as the foster father of Our Lord; Mary renounced maternity and yet found it in her virginity, as the closed garden through which no one should pass except the Light of the World, Who would break nothing in His coming—any more than light breaks the window by coming into the room.

How much more beautiful Mary and Joseph become when we see in their lives what might be called the first Divine Romance! No human heart is moved by the love of the old for the young; but who is not moved by the love of the young for the young, when their bond is the Ancient of Days, Who is God? In both Mary and Joseph, there were youth, beauty, and promise. God loves cascading cataracts and bellowing waterfalls, but He loves them better, not when they overflow and drown His flowers, but when they are harnessed and bridled to light a city and to slake the thirst of a child. In Joseph and Mary, we do not find one controlled waterfall and one dried-up lake but rather two youths who, before they knew the beauty of the one and the handsome strength of the other, willed to surrender these things for Jesus.

Leaning over the manger crib of the Infant Jesus, then, are not age and youth but youth and youth, the consecration of beauty in a maid and the surrender of strong comeliness in a man. If the Ancient of Days turned back eternity and became young again—if the condition of entering Heaven is to be reborn and to become young again, then, to all young married couples: here is your model, your prototype, your Divine Imaginal. From these two spouses, who loved as no couple on earth has ever loved, learn that it takes not two to love, but three: you and you and Jesus. Do you not speak of "our love" as something distinct from the love of each one of you? That love, outside of both of you, and which is more than the addition of your two loves, is the love of God.

Married couples ought to say the Rosary together each night, for their common prayer is more than the separate prayers of each. When the child comes, they should say it before the crib, as Joseph and Mary prayed there. In this earthly trinity of Child, mother, and foster father, there were not two hearts with but a single thought but one great Heart into which the other two poured themselves out as confluent streams. As trustees of carnal wealth, husband and wife will see that the flames of love have been given to them not to scorch the flesh but to solder life. And children will ask: If He Who is the Son of God made Himself subject to His parents in reparation for the sins of pride, then how shall *they* escape the sweet necessity of obeying their parents who stand in the place of God? Democracy put man on a pedestal; feminism put woman on a pedestal. But neither democracy nor feminism could live a generation out unless a Child was put onto a pedestal. This is the significance of the marrying of Joseph and Mary.

8

Obedience and Love

On the eleventh day of February 1895, on the forty-first an-
niversary of the revelation of Our Lady at Lourdes, M. Jaurès
spoke as follows in the French Chamber of Deputies: "The
most priceless good conquered by man through all his sufferings and struggles, and despite all his prejudices, is the idea
that there is no sacred truth; that all truth that does not come
from us is a lie . . . if God Himself ever appeared before men,
the first duty of man would be to *refuse obedience* and to consider Him an equal with us, not a Master to Whom we should
submit."

This affirmation of man as against God is not new, except
in its verbiage. From the very beginning, man was a rebel
against his Divine destiny; consider the steward, who pre-
tends to be the master of the vineyard and then kills the mes-
sengers of the Lord—the prodigal son who demands his share
of the substance and then squanders it. Man has acted thus in
the past, and now the revolution is again in full swing. A
modern writer, explaining why he became a Communist,
answered that one must go back to the garden of Eden to
understand the real reason. There Satan tempted man, prom-
ising that "he would be like unto God". This desire of man to
deny his dependence on his Creator and to set himself up as

an absolute is the basic cause of men's becoming Communists. They are, fundamentally, already in revolt against God, and Communism gives the social pattern for that rebellion. The copy or the carbon then tries to be the original—but it could never strive to be the original unless it was already conscious that it was a carbon. Man is the shadow, who would be the substance; the pendulum, which would swing without being suspended from the clock; the painting, which would deny that an artist's hand ever touched it. The most daring of all sins is that of self-deification, and it is possible only because of a Divine Creation—for who would want to be God unless he had come from the hands of God? The human "I" was not made for the "I" alone, but for God's service. The man, therefore, who refuses to seek the perfection of his personality, namely, God, must do one of two things: he must either inflate himself into an infinity and identify himself in a fantastic swelling with the dimensions of God, or else he must suffer a terrible emptiness and void within his ego, which is the beginning of despair. Thus there is pride at one end of the mystical self and hopelessness at the other. The will that breaks away from God always becomes an assertive will that will tread anything, ruthlessly, underfoot. All that a will divorced from God cares about is power. Nietzsche's will-to-power is synonymous with atheism—not the mental atheism of the sophomore, who knows a smattering of science and of comparative religion, but an atheism of the will, which sets itself up as God. Through all the ages, and until the consummation of time, there will be those who will shriek before the Pilates of this world: "We will not have this Man rule over us!"

Behind this rebellion, or disobedience of God, there are two basic assumptions. The first is that the intelligence *invents* or *originates* truth and does not discover or find it. In the nine-

teenth century it was very common for materialists to believe
that they *originated* the laws of nature because they discovered
them. They forgot that the scientist is actually a proofreader
of the book of Nature and not its author. The second assumption is that subordination to another implies subjection.
This implies a denial of all degrees and hierarchy in nature
and in creation, as well as the reduction of mankind to an
egalitarianism in which each man is a god.

This philosophy of pride assumes that independence must
mean the want of any form of dependence. But independence is conditioned upon dependence. Our Declaration of
Independence affirms certain basic freedoms, such as the
right to life, to liberty, and to the pursuit of happiness. But in
a previous sentence it ascribes this independence to the fact
that all of these are the endowments of a Creator. Because
man is dependent on God, he is not dependent on a State.
But once dependence on God is lost, then the State takes over
the attributes of Divinity and, being material in its structure,
crushes the last vestige of the human spirit. To correct this
false deification of man, it is important once more to investi-
gate the meaning of obedience.

Obedience does not mean the execution of orders that are
given by a drill sergeant. It springs, rather, from the love of an
order, and love of Him who gave it. The merit of obedience
is less in the act than in the love; the submission, the devotion,
and the service that obedience implies are not born of servitude but are rather effects that spring from and are unified by
love. Obedience is servility only to those who have not understood the spontaneity of love.

To comprehend obedience, one must study it between two
great moments. The first moment was when a woman made
an act of obedience to the will of God: "Be it done unto me
according to thy word." The other moment was when a

woman asked man to be obedient to God: "Whatsoever He shall say to you, that do ye." Between these historical facts is the story told by Luke: "And after they had performed all things according to the law of the Lord, they returned into Galilee to their city Nazareth. And the Child grew and waxed strong, full of wisdom, and the grace of God was in him. . . . And he went down with them and came to Nazareth and was subject to them, and His mother kept all these words in her heart. Jesus advanced in wisdom and age and grace with God and men" (Lk 2:39, 40, 51, 52).

For the reparation of the pride of men, Our Blessed Lord humbled Himself in obedience to His parents: "And he was subject to them." It was God who was subject to man. God, Whom the principalities and powers obey, subjected Himself not only to Mary but to Joseph too, because of Mary. Our Blessed Lord Himself said that He came "not to be ministered unto, but to minister". Now He makes Himself the servant not only of His parents but even of the community, for later on the townspeople will speak of Him as the Son of the carpenter. This humility, abstraction made from His Divinity, was exactly contrary to what one would expect of a man destined to become the reformer of the human race. And yet, what did this carpenter do during these thirty years of His obscurity? He made a coffin for the pagan world; He fashioned a yoke for the modern world; and He fashioned a Cross upon which He would be adored. He gave the supreme lesson of that virtue which is the foundation of all Christianity—humility, submission, and a hidden life as a preparation for duty.

Our Lord spent three hours in redeeming, three years in teaching, and thirty years in obeying, in order that a rebellious, proud, and diabolically independent world might learn the value of obedience. Home life is the God-appointed training ground of human character, for from the home life of the child springs the maturity of manhood, either for good or for evil. The only recorded acts of Our Blessed Lord's childhood are acts of obedience—to God, His Heavenly Father, and also to Mary and Joseph. He thus shows the special duty of childhood and of youth: to obey parents as the vice-regents of God. He, the great God Whom the heavens and earth could not contain, submitted Himself to His parents. If He was sent on a message to a neighbor, it was the great Sender of the Apostles who delivered the message. If Joseph ever bade Him search for a tool that was lost, it was the Wisdom of God and the Shepherd in search of lost souls who was actually doing the seeking. If Joseph taught Him carpentry, He Who was taught was One Who had carpentered the universe and Who would one day be put to death by the members of His own profession. If He made a yoke for the oxen of a neighbor, it was He Who would call Himself a yoke for men—and yet a burden that would be light. If they bade Him work in a little plot of garden ground, to train the creepers or water the flowers, it was He Who was the great Dresser of the vineyard of His Church, Who took in hand the waterpot and the gardening tools. All men may ponder well the hint of a Child subject to His parents, that no Heavenly call is ever to be trusted that bids one neglect the obvious duties that lie near to hand.

There is an Oriental proverb that says: "The first deities the child has to acknowledge are his parents." And another says that "Obedient children are as ambrosia to the gods." The parent is to the child God's representative; and in order that parents may not have a responsibility that will be too heavy for them, God gives each child a soul, as so much clay that their hands can mold in the way of truth and love. Whenever a child is given to parents, a crown is made for it in Heaven;

and woe to those parents if that child is not reared with a sense of responsibility to acquire that crown!

Although the words "He was subject to them" apply especially to that period of Our Lord's life between the finding in the Temple and the Marriage Feast of Cana, nevertheless they are also a true description of His course in after years. His whole life was one of subjection and submission. He said that He had come to do His Father's will, and now He was obeying it, for it was His Father's will that He have Mary for a Mother and Joseph as a foster father. Later on, He submitted to receiving John's Baptism, although He had no need of it. He also submitted to paying the tax for the support of the Temple, although He, as the only-begotten Son of the Father, was rightfully exempt from that tax. He bade the Jews submit themselves to the Romans who had conquered them and to render unto Caesar the things that are Caesar's. He bade His Disciples observe and do all that the Scribes and Pharisees enjoined, because they sat in Moses' Chair and held a position of authority; finally, He became obedient under the sentence of death, drinking with the utmost meekness—even to the dregs—the cup of suffering that His Father had appointed to Him.

What adds particular emphasis to the fact of His obedience was that Our Blessed Lord was subject to parents so much His inferiors—even as a creature is far below a Creator. One day the sun in the heavens, in obedience to the voice of a Man, stopped in its course. So, obedient to the voice of Mary, the Light of the World submitted for thirty years—I might almost say that it stopped in full midday to illumine, embrace, and enrich her for all eternity.

The Apostles had the advantage of only three years' teaching to prepare themselves for the establishment of His Kingdom, but the Blessed Mother had the advantage of thirty years. When one tries to imagine how much insight and inspiration would come from catching only a momentary glimpse of Wisdom Incarnate, one is appalled to think how much inspiration and wisdom Mary must have received from the years of communing with her Divine Son. She must have been instructed in the Paternity of God and learned how the Person of the Father could not be born or proceed from others, but how He was rather the origin of all else. She must have understood, too, the eternal generation of the Son by the Father, as being not inferior but equal in Divinity and Eternity. She must have understood, too, how the Holy Spirit, the Third Person, proceeded from the Father and the Son as from one principle, by an act of will, equal to the other Persons in the Divine nature. If Our Blessed Lord after His Resurrection could so inspire the disciples of Emmaus in the interpretation of Scripture, then what must have been the thirty years' rehearsal of the Scriptures to His Mother, as He explained to her how she was to be the new Eve, and how she was to share in His work of redemption beginning at Cana and ending at the Cross? Let those who think that the Church pays too much attention to Mary give heed to the fact that Our Blessed Lord Himself gave ten times as much of His life to her as He gave to His Apostles.

If the mere touch of the hem of His garment could cure a woman suffering with an issue of blood, then the human mind can hardly contemplate what thirty years of residence with the eternal Logos of God must have done for a human mind. After the years of companioning with Philip, Our Blessed Lord said to him, somewhat impatiently, at the Last Supper: "Have I been with you all this time and still you do not understand?" How much greater an understanding of His mysteries He must therefore have expected of His Mother, who had suffered with Him during all His hidden life!

Returning again to the idea of His obedience: the Gospel indicates immediately three effects of Our Lord's submission and obedience, namely, growth in age and grace and wisdom. The first effect of obedience is age, or bodily perfection. The inverse of this truth is that disobedience to nature destroys bodily health—disobedience to God's law spoils spiritual health. By submitting Himself to the laws of human development, He consented to an unfolding that in childhood should exhibit a perfect child; in youth, a perfect youth; and in manhood, a perfect man. It was the unfolding of a perfect bud in a perfect flower. Whatever age one accepts as the one in which the body reaches its natural perfection, the fact is that it lasts only a short time, then begins the decline. As the moon begins to lessen as soon as it reaches its fullness, so too the human body grows to its peak of development and then begins its age. If thirty-three be taken as the age of full bodily growth and development, it would seem that Our Blessed Lord's ardent love for humanity waited until that age, when He had attained perfect growth and vigor, in order that He might offer His life in sacrifice at its very fullness. As the act of His will was total and complete, so the human nature that He would sacrifice on the Cross would not be wanting in anything for its perfect oblation. Obedience to the law of nature produces physical maturity; obedience to the law of parents produces mental maturity; obedience to the will of the Heavenly Father produces spiritual maturity. Our Blessed Lord, therefore, as the Lamb of God, submitted Himself to the shepherding of His Mother so that He might be physically perfect and without stain for the great day of His sacrifice on which He would be offered without opening His mouth.

The flower that is planted in the right place to absorb out of the earth and atmosphere the nutritive forces that it needs will grow. It toils not, neither does it spin, and yet its invisible machinery captures the sunbeams and converts them into flowers and fruit for the welfare of man. So children placed in the right environment grow in age, too. Place a waterwheel in a stream, and it turns; place it in the rocks, and it does not move. So long as we are in the wrong place, we cannot grow. The secret of the growth of Our Lord is that He started in the right place; He was bathed with the warmth and the light and the refreshment of a home that was dedicated to God. One cannot put a bomb under a child and make him a man. Each thing has its own appointed law of growth, provided its roots are properly fixed. All growth is silent, and there is not a word out of the home of Nazareth in these eighteen long years between the Finding in the Temple and the Marriage Feast. Thus, when nature is baptized in the fullness of the powers of spring, there is hardly a rustle. The whole movement takes place secretly and silently, for the new world comes up like the sound of a trumpet. The greatest moral structures grow from day to day without noise; God's kingdoms come without observation. So Our Blessed Lord stayed in His place, did His carpentry, was obedient to His parents, accepted the restraints of His position, met His cares with a transcendent disdain, drank in the sunlight of His Father's faith, possessed His soul in perfect patience, although urged by deep sympathy and a throbbing desire to save man. There was no hurry, no impatience, no quick maturing of power, no marring of strength by haste. When Perseus told Pallas Athena that he was ready to go forth, young as he was, against the fabled monster Medusa, the strange lady smiled and said: "Not yet; you are too young, and too unskilled, for this is Medusa, the mother of a monstrous brood. Return to your home and do the work that awaits you there. You must play the man in that before I can think you worthy to go in search of Medusa." If it is hurry that enfeebles us, it is the silent obedience to God's law that serves to strengthen us.

In addition to the growth in age, which is the fruit of obedience, the Gospel also indicates that there was a growth in grace and wisdom. These are both properties of the soul. As His human body grew in stature to fair and comely proportions, so His human intelligence and experimental knowledge unfolded gradually into full blossom. Growth in wisdom and grace or fervor for God imply that the person who grows is, at a more advanced age, wiser than when he was young— he knows something and he understands something he did not know and understand before. But how could this be in *His* case, since He is the Son of God? Was He not God even when He was a child? And how can God be ignorant of anything—or fail to understand anything? How could He grow in wisdom? Our Lord, even when He was a child, was Everlasting God, but it is also true that He was "manifest in the flesh". He became really and truly, and for our sake, an infant, a child, and a man. He did not merely *seem* to be human; He actually *was* human. In order that He might be really and truly a man, He consented, in His wonderful condescension, not to call into exercise those powers that He had as God. It is not too difficult for us to understand how a person, having strength, may refrain from using it. For example, a father can gently pick up a child, or a giant can turn the pages of a book. In like manner, a man may have strong and good eyesight, but he need not use it farther than he pleases. He may shut his eyes altogether; in that case he will see nothing. He may only half open the eyes—in that case he will see only dimly and confusedly. Or he may live in a dungeon, where there are only a few straggling rays of light to pierce the gloom.

So with Our Blessed Lord—He had in His Divine nature all wisdom and power; yet when He made His appearance among us as man, He did grow in that experimental knowledge which comes from living and doing certain things. He came into our dark nature, just as a free man might come out of the light of day into a dungeon and consent to be shut up. For a man in a prison may have the power to walk many miles, but the dungeon will permit him to walk only a few paces. He may have the power to see many miles, but his vision is limited to the prison walls. So Our Blessed Lord took a nature like ours in all things save sin and accommodated Himself to the feebleness of that nature—limited Himself, if we may use the expression, to the walls of it. That is why Our Blessed Lord never worked a miracle in His own behalf. Taking upon Himself a human nature, He subjected Himself to its limitations. But what is most interesting is that the subjection to His Blessed Mother is associated with growth in wisdom and favor with God. It is in His human nature that Our Blessed Lord gives us a perfect example of obedience.

This leads us to a forgotten aspect of obedience to law, namely, that *intelligence is related to obedience*. It is only by obedience that we grow in wisdom. A scientist who would know the laws of nature must sit passively before nature. He may not dictate to nature its laws, nor may he impose his own intelligence upon nature; rather, the more passive he is before nature, the more nature will reveal its secrets. And he who would play golf well must know how to hold the clubs aright, for here, too, wisdom is related to obedience. The more we obey the inherent laws of anything, the more that thing reveals itself to us. To obey God's laws because they are the ordinance of an All-wise and an All-loving God is the best means to discover the wisdom and the beauty of life. One whole Psalm of the Scriptures, Psalm 118 [119], is devoted to the idea that in obedience to the ordinance of God we grow in intelligence. Our Blessed Lord, developing this idea later on in His life, said: "If any man will do the will of my Father he shall know of the doctrine, whether it be of God or whether I speak of myself." Because obedience is the secret of perfection and wisdom (which Our Lord revealed by being subject to His parents), He insisted in His great upheaval of values that: "Unless you become converted and become as little children, you shall not enter the Kingdom of Heaven" (Mt 18:3). The great gates of the Kingdom, which are resistant to the poundings and the thumpings of the mighty, will swing back at the simple touch of a child. No old people ever enter the Kingdom of Heaven—certainly not those who have grown old in their own conceit. Childlikeness, with its accompanying obedience, is an indispensable qualification for membership in His community. Christianity began with the worship of a Babe, and only by the continued recognition of childlikeness will men be recognized as children of God. But childlikeness is not childishness. To be childish is to retain in maturity what should have been discarded at the threshold of manhood. Childlikeness, on the contrary, implies that with the mental breadth and practical strength and wisdom of maturity there are associated the humility, trustfulness, spontaneity, and obedience of the child. It is the proud and the prigs and the bullies who make social life difficult—the people who love the first places, who insist always on their own right, who refuse to serve unless they can be chairmen, who throw their weight around whether by fair means or by foul. Against all of these Our Blessed Lord sets Himself: first of all, by being obedient to His parents, and then, at the end of His life, by taking a towel and washing the feet of His disciples. "So it is that the Son of Man did not come to have service done him; he came to serve others, and to give his life as a ransom for the lives of many" (Mt 20:28).

What makes the obedience of this Child all the more impressive is that He is the Son of God. He Who is the general of humanity becomes a soldier in the ranks; the king steps from His throne and plays the role of peasant. If He Who is the Son of God makes Himself subject to His Mother and foster father in reparation for the sins of pride, then how shall children escape the sweet necessity of obedience to those who are their lawfully constituted superiors? The Fourth Commandment, "Thou shalt honor thy father and thy mother", has been broken by every generation since the dawn of man. At Nazareth, children were taught obedience by Him Who really is the Commandment. In this particular instance, where the Child is Divine, one might think that He at least would have reserved for Himself the right of "self-expression". Mary and Joseph, it seems, could have, with great propriety, opened the first "progressive school" in the history of Christianity—in which the child could do whatever He pleased: for the Child could never have displeased. And yet Our Lord says: "And He who sent me is with me: He has not left me all alone, since what I do is always what pleases Him" (Jn 8:29).

But there is no evidence that Jesus limited Mary and Joseph to the mere nominal right to command. The Gospel says: "He lived there in subjection to them." Two great miracles of humility and exaltation are involved—God obeying a woman, and a woman commanding her God. The very fact that He makes Himself subject endows her with power. By this long span of voluntary obedience, He revealed that the Fourth Commandment is the bedrock of family life. For, looking at it in a larger way, how could the primal sin of disobedience against God be undone except by the obedience in the flesh of the very God Who was defied? The first revolt in God's universe of peace was the thunderbolt of

Lucifer: "I will not obey!" Eden caught up the echo, and down the ages its infraction traveled, winging its way into the nook and crevices of every family where there were gathered a father, a mother, and a child.

By making Himself subject to Mary and Joseph, the Divine Child proclaims authority in the home and in public life to be a power granted by God Himself. From this follows the duty of obedience, for the sake of God and of one's conscience. As later on He would tell Pilate that the civil authorities exercised no power except that given them from above, so now by His obedience He bears witness to the solemn truth that parents exercise their authority in the name of God. Thus parents have the most sacred claim on their children, because their first responsibility is to God. "Every soul must be submissive to its lawful superiors; authority comes from God only, and all authorities that hold sway are of his ordinance" (Rom 13:1).

If the parents surrender their legitimate authority and primary responsibility to the children, the state takes up the slack. When obedience in conscience in the home vanishes, it will be supplanted by obedience by the force of the state. The glory of the ego, which infects the twentieth century, is so much social nonsense. The divine glory of the state that is now taking the ego's place is a social nuisance. Believers in ego consciousness and collective consciousness may regard humility and obedience as vices, but they are the stuff of which homes are made. When in the one family of the world where one might legitimately excuse "child worship", for here the child is God, one finds, on the contrary, child obedience, then let no one deny that obedience is the cornerstone of the home. Obedience in the home is the foundation of obedience in the commonwealth, for in each instance conscience submits to a trustee of God's authority. If it be true

that the world has lost its respect for authority, it is only because it lost it first in the home. By a peculiar paradox, as the
home loses its authority, the authority of the state becomes
tyrannical. Some moderns would swell their ego into infinity,
but at Nazareth Infinity stoops down to earth to shrink into
the obedience of a child.

9

The Marriage Feast at Cana

Everyone is interested in a marriage. If the human heart does not have enough love in its heart, it seeks out those who are in love. The most famous marriage in history was at Cana, because Our Blessed Lord was present there.

A marriage in the East was always a time of great rejoicing. The bridegroom went to the home of the bride, and in those days it was never the bride who kept the bridegroom waiting but rather the bridegroom, as in the parable, who kept the bride waiting. The bride was veiled, from head to foot, to symbolize her subjection as a wife. Both partners fasted the whole day before the marriage and confessed their sins in prayer as on the Day of Atonement. Ceremonies began at twilight, for it was a custom in Palestine, no less than in Greece:

> To bear away
> The bride from home at blushing shut of day.

The Cana marriage is the only occasion in Sacred Scripture where Mary, the Mother of Jesus, is mentioned before Him. It is very likely that it was one of her relatives who was being married, and possible that she was present at the wedding before Him. It is a beautiful and a consoling thought that Our

Blessed Lord, Who came to teach, sacrifice, and urge us to take up our cross daily, should have begun His public life by assisting at a marriage feast.

Sometimes these Eastern marriages lasted for seven days, but in the case of the poorer people, for only two. Whatever was the case at Cana, at some period of the entertainment the wine suddenly ran out. This was very embarrassing because of the passionate devotion of the Eastern people to hospitality and also because of the mortification it offered to the wedded pair. It is permitted us to conjecture why the wine should have failed. This was a wine country, and it is very likely that the host laid in an abundant supply. The explanation for the deficiency is probably the fact that Our Blessed Lord did not come alone. He brought with Him His Disciples, and this apparently threw a heavy burden upon the store of wine. Our Lord and His Disciples had already been journeying for three days and had covered a distance of ninety miles. The disciples were thus so hungry and so thirsty that it was a wonder that the food did not give out as well as the wine. Since wine was a symbol of mirth and health to the people, it was important that their need be filled—as an old Hebrew proverb put it: "Where wine is wanting, doctors thrive."

One of the most amazing features of this marriage is that it was not the wine servant, whose business it was to service the wine, who noticed the shortage, but rather Our Blessed Mother. (She notes our needs before we ourselves feel them.) She made a very simple prayer to her Divine Son about the empty wine pots when she said: "They have no wine." Hidden in the words was not only a consciousness of the power of her Divine Son but also an expression of her desire to remedy an awkward situation. Perhaps the Blessed Mother had already seen Our Lord work many miracles in secret—although He had not yet worked a single one in public. For if there had not already been a consciousness of the truth that He was the Son of the Omnipotent God, she would not have asked for a miracle. Some of the greatest miracles of the world have similarly been done through the influence of a mother: "The hand that rocks the cradle is the hand that rules the world."

The answer of Our Blessed Lord was, "Woman, what is that to me? My hour is not yet come."

Note that Our Lord said: "My hour is not yet come." Whenever Our Blessed Lord used that expression "hour", it was in relation to His Passion and His death. For example, the night that Judas crossed the brook of Cedron to blister His lips with a kiss, Our Lord said: "This is your hour and the powers of darkness." A few hours before, when seated at His Last Supper on earth and anticipating His death, He said: "Father, the hour is come. Glorify Thy Son with the glory that He had with Thee before the foundations of the world were laid." Earlier, when a crowd attempted to take His life by stoning, Scriptures say: "His hour was not yet come." Our Blessed Lord was obviously, at Cana, saying that the hour in which He was to reveal Himself had not yet come according to His Father's appointment. And yet, implicit in Mary's statement was a request that He actually begin it. Scriptures tell us: "So in Cana of Galilee, Jesus began His miracles, and made known the glory that was within Him, so that His disciples learned to believe in Him" (Jn 2:11). In our own language, Our Lord was saying to His Blessed Mother:

"My dear Mother, do you realize that you are asking me to proclaim my Divinity—to appear before the world as the Son of God and to prove my Divinity by my works and my miracles? The moment that I do this, I begin the royal road to the Cross. When I am no longer known among men as the son of the carpenter, but as the Son of God, that will be my first step toward Calvary. My hour is not yet come; but would you have me anticipate it? Is it your will that I go to the Cross? If I do this, your relationship to me changes. You are now my mother. You are known everywhere in our little village as the 'Mother of Jesus'. But if I appear now as the Savior of men and begin the work of redemption, *your* role will change, too. Once I undertake the salvation of mankind, you will not only be my mother, but you will also be the mother of everyone whom I redeem. I am the Head of humanity; as soon as I save the body of humanity, you, who are the Mother of the Head, become also the Mother of the body. You will then be the universal Mother, the new Eve, as I am the new Adam.

"To indicate the role that you will play in Redemption, I now bestow upon you that title of universal motherhood; I call you—*Woman*. It was to you that I referred when I said to Satan that I would put enmity between him and the Woman, between his brood of evil and your seed, which I am. That great title of Woman I dignify you with now. And I shall dignify you with it again when my hour comes and when I am unfurled upon the Cross, like a wounded eagle. We are in this work of redemption together. What is yours is mine. From this hour on, we are not just Mary and Jesus, we are the new Adam and the new Eve, beginning a new humanity, changing the water of sin into the wine of life. Knowing all this, my dear Mother, is it your will that I anticipate the Cross and that I go to Calvary?"

Our Blessed Lord was presenting to Mary not merely the choice of asking for a miracle or not; rather He was asking if she would send Him to His death. He had made it quite plain that the world would not tolerate His Divinity—that if He turned water into wine, someday wine would be changed into blood. The answer of Mary was one of complete co-operation in the redemption with Our Blessed Lord, as she spoke for the last time in Sacred Scripture. Turning to the wine steward she said, "Whatsoever He shall say to you, that do ye" (Jn 2:5). What a magnificent valedictory! As Our Blessed Lord had said that He had come on earth to do His Father's will, so Mary bade us do the will of her Divine Son. "Whatsoever He shall say to you, that do ye." The waterpots are filled, are brought to Our Blessed Lord, and then, in the magnificent line of the poet Richard Crashaw, "The unconscious waters saw their God, and blushed."

The first lesson from Cana is: "Aid yourself, and Heaven will aid you." Our Lord could have produced wine out of nothing, as He had made the world from nothing, but He willed that the wine servants bring their pots and fill them with water. We must not expect God to transform us without our bringing something to be transformed. In vain do we say: "O Lord, help me overcome my evil habits or let me be sober, pure, and honest." What good are these prayers unless we bring at least our own efforts? God will, indeed, make us peaceful and happy again, but only on condition that we bring the water of our own feeble efforts. We are not to remain passive, while awaiting the manifestation of God's power; there must be the indispensable gesture of our own liberty, even though it brings to God something as unspirited as the routine waters of our insipid lives! Collaboration with God is essential if we are to become the sons of God.

The second lesson of Cana is that Mary intercedes to gain us what we need, without our always knowing our needs. Neither the wine steward nor the diners knew that the wine was failing; therefore, they could not ask for help. In like manner, if we do not know what our soul needs, how can we put such needs in our prayers? Often we do not know what is vital to our lives: St. James tells us that we do not ask aright but seek to satisfy only our carnal and egotistic desires.

Surely we could go to Our Lord, as the wine steward, as the diners could have gone to Our Lord. But they did not go, and some of us would not go at all; or, if we did go, we would not always ask for the right thing. There are so few of us who know the reason for our unhappiness. We pray for wealth, to "break the bank", to win the Irish Sweepstakes; we ask for peace of mind and then dash off to a psychoanalytic couch— when we should ask for peace of soul, be on our knees bemoaning our sins and asking pardon. So few of us know that we need God. We are at the end of our strength and even of our hope; and we do not know that we ought to be asking for Divine strength and Divine love.

That is where devotion to Mary comes in. The people at the table did not know what they needed to maintain the joy of the marriage feast, even when the Lord was in their midst. There are many of us who would not come to Our Lord unless we had someone who knows our needs better than we know ourselves and who will ask Our Lord for us. This role of Mary makes her acceptable to everyone. Those at the marriage table did not need to know she was the Mother of the Son of God in order to receive the benefit of her Divine Son. But one thing is certain—no one will ever call on her without being heard or without being finally led to her Divine Son, Jesus Christ, for Whose sake she alone exists—for Whose sake she was made pure—and for Whose sake she was given to us.

The Marriage Feast of Cana also reveals how Mary makes up for our battered and weak wills; she does this by substituting herself for us. It is very hard for us to receive a Divine favor unless we desire it. Until we love and serve God, we are inert and dead. It is impossible for most of us to ask for a soul healing, for so few of us know that we are wounded. Mary comes into this crisis of life to substitute for us in the same way that a mother substitutes for a sick child. The child cannot tell the mother his need. There may be a pin pricking him, he may be hungry, or he may be sick. The child may cry, but it is as vague a complaint as are our own adult cries when we are unhappy and fearful, worried and frustrated. The mother in such a circumstance carries the child to the doctor. The mother thus puts herself in the place of the child, who does not have the knowledge to know what is best or cannot will to do anything to help himself. She "doubles", as it were, for the freedom of the child. Thus does the mother dispose the child to receive what is best. And as the mother knows the needs better than the babe, so the Blessed Mother understands our cries and worries and knows them better than we know ourselves. As the baby needs the doctor, so the Blessed Mother knows we need her Divine Son. As Our Lord mediates between us and the Heavenly Father, so the Blessed Mother mediates between us and Our Divine Lord. She fills our empty pots, she supplies the elixir of life, she prevents the joys of life from ebbing away. Mary is not our salvation—let us not be absurd on that. The mother is not the doctor, and neither is Mary the Savior. But Mary brings us to the Savior!

Three years now pass, and all that Our Blessed Lord told His Mother at Cana is fulfilled. The hour is come; the wine has changed to blood. He has worked His miracles, and men have crucified Him. Unfurled on either side of Him, as if to put Him in their class, are two thieves. The world will allow only the mediocre to live. It hates the very wicked, like the thieves, because they disturb its possessions and security. It also hates the Divinely Good, it hates Our Blessed Lord, because He disturbs its conscience, its heart, and its evil desires.

Our Blessed Lord now looks down from His Cross to the two most beloved creatures that He has on earth, John and His Blessed Mother. He picks up the refrain of Cana and addresses Our Blessed Mother with the same title He gave her at the marriage feast. He calls her "Woman". It is the second Annunciation. With a gesture of His dust-filled eyes and His thorn-crowned head, He looks longingly at her, who had sent Him willingly to the Cross, who is now standing beneath it as a cooperator in His Redemption, and He says: "Behold thy son." Then, turning to John, He does not call him John; to do that would have been to address him as the son of Zebedee and no one else. But, in his anonymity, John stands for all of us—Our Lord thus says to His beloved Disciple: "Son, behold thy mother."

Here is the answer, after all these years, to the mysterious words in the Gospel of the Incarnation that stated that Our Blessed Mother laid her "first born" in the manger. Did that mean that Our Blessed Mother was to have other children? It certainly did, but not according to the flesh. Our Divine Lord and Savior Jesus Christ is the only Son of Our Blessed Mother by the flesh. But Our Lady was to have other children, not according to the flesh, but according to the spirit!

10

Love and Sorrow

Pleasure is the bait God uses to make creatures recognize their destiny, whether it be that of eating for the sake of the individual health or mating for the sake of society. God also puts a limit on pleasure: one of these is a "fed-up-ness", which comes from nature; the other is that of the woman, who is most reasonable when man is most irrational. In this domain of the flesh, man is liberty; woman, the law.

If, then, a woman is not taught carnal pleasure by the man, two effects will follow: first, her restraining power will create continency and purity. Since pleasure is outgoing, she will become more inward and self-possessed, as if hugging a great secret to her heart. Desire is anticipation, pleasure is participation, but purity is emancipation. The second effect is just the opposite, namely, sorrow. She who lives without pleasure not only gives up something but also receives something—it may be the hatred of those who see in her the enemy of the flesh, whether they be man or woman. Such is the story of virgins like Agatha, Cecilia, Susanna, and, in our day, Maria Goretti. As the sun hardens mud, so purity provokes those who are already sinners to hardness of heart, persecution, and violence.

The day Mary declared: "I know not man", she not only

affirmed that she was untaught by pleasures, but she also brought her soul to such a focused inwardness for God's sake that she became a virgin—not only through the absence of man but also through the presence of God. The secret that she kept was no other than the Word! Bereft of the pleasures of the body but not of all joys, she could sing to her cousin Elizabeth: "My soul doth rejoice in the Lord."

On the other hand, Mary was also a Woman of Sorrow. To love God immediately and uniquely makes a woman hated. The day she brought her Babe, her Divine Love, to the Temple, the old priest Simeon told her that a sword her soul would pierce. The hour the Roman sergeant ran the spear into the Heart of Christ, he pierced two hearts with one blow—the heart of the God-Man for Whom Mary gave up the knowledge of pleasure, and the heart of Mary, who gave her beauty to God and not to man.

No one in the world can carry God in his heart without an inner joy and an outer sorrow, without singing a *Magnificat* to those who share the secret, and without feeling the thrust of a sword from those who want freedom of the flesh without the law. Love and sorrow often go together. In carnal love, the body swallows the soul; in spiritual love, the soul envelops the body. The sorrow of the first is never to be satisfied; one who wants to drink the ocean of love is unhappy if limited to a mere cup with which to drink. The sorrow of the second love is never being able to do enough for the beloved.

In the human love of marriage, the joys of love are a pre-payment for its duties, responsibilities, and, sometimes, its sorrows. Because the crosses lie ahead in human love, there is the Transfiguration beforehand, when the face of love seems to shine as the sun and the garments are as white as snow. There are those who, like Peter, would wish to capitalize the joys and to make a permanent tabernacle of love on the mountaintops of ecstasy. But there is always the Lord, speaking through the conscience and saying that to capture love in a permanent form one *must* pass through a Calvary. The early transports of love are an advance, an anticipation, of the real transports that are to come when one has mounted to a higher degree of love through the bearing of a cross.

What most human love forgets is that love implies responsibility; one may not fool with the levers of the heart in the vain hope of escaping duties, fidelity, and sacrifice for the beloved. So-called birth control, which assists in neither birth nor control, is based on the philosophy that love is without obligations. The real problem is how to make humans realize the sacredness of love—how to induce mothers to see a Messiahship in the begetting of children. The best way to achieve this would surely be to bring forward the example of a *woman who would accept the responsibilities of love without the prepayment of pleasure*—one who would say: "I will do it all for nothing! I will accept the bearing of a child, the responsibility of His education, a share in His world mission", without even asking for the ecstasies of the flesh. Such is the role of the Blessed Mother. She undertook marriage, birth, a share in the Agony, all for the love of God, not asking the initial joys to prepare her for those trials. The best way to convince mankind that it must take the medicine that cures is to take it oneself and without the sugar coating, yet never wince because of its bitterness. The Sisters of Charity in the poor sections of our cities, the missionaries caring for the victims of leprosy—these give inspiration to all social workers. The former do their work for nothing except the love of God, and thus they keep before the world the ideal of a disinterested affection for the hungry and the sick.

In the Annunciation, God told Mary, through an angel, that she would conceive without the benefit of human affection and its joys—that is, with no payment of pleasure to herself. She thus dissociated carnal joys and social responsibilities. Her sacrifice was a rebuke to those who would snare the music by breaking the lute, pick up the violins of life and never produce a tune, lift a chisel to marble and yet never bring forth a statue. But it also gave courage to those whose burdens are heavier than their pleasures—to those who have children destined for death when they are hardly launched on the sea of life, to those who find their love's surrender betrayed and even despised. If Our Lord allowed Mary to suffer the trials that even the most grieved mother could suffer—such as to have her Son pursued by the totalitarian soldiers at two years of age, to be a refugee in a foreign country, to point to a Father's business that would end in death, to be arrested falsely, to be condemned by His own people, and to suffer the taking-off in the prime of life—it was in order to convince mothers with sorrows that trials without pleasures can be overcome and that the final issues of life are not solved here below. If the Father gave His Son a Cross and the Mother a sword, then somehow sorrow does fit into the Divine plan of life. If Divine Innocence and His Mother, who was a sinless creature, both underwent agonies, it cannot be that life is a snare and a mockery, but rather it is made clear that love and sorrow often go together in this life and that only in the next life is sorrow left behind.

Christians are the only people in history who know that the story of the universe has a happy ending. The Apostles did not discover this until after the Resurrection, and then they went through the ancient world shouting and screaming the excitement of the good news. Mary knew it for a long time, and in the *Magnificat* sang about it, even before Our Lord was born.

Great is the sorrow of a woman when her husband aban-

dons his responsibility to her and seeks what he calls "freedom" from what is his own flesh and blood. What the woman
feels in such abandonment is akin to what the Church feels in
heresy. Whenever, through history, those who are the members of her Mystical Body isolate themselves from her flesh
and blood, not only do they suffer in their isolation, but the
Church suffers still more. The irresponsibility of love is the
source of life's greatest tragedies, and as the Church suffers
more than the heretic, so the woman probably suffers more
than the erring man. She stands as the "other half" of that
man, a constant reminder to him and to society that what
God joined together has, by a perverse will, been rent asunder. The husband may have left his spouse to teach another
woman pleasure; but the wife remains as the unfinished symphony, clamoring for spiritual understanding. A civilization
that no longer stands before God in reverence and responsibility has also renounced and denounced the dignity of
woman, and the woman who submits and shares in such a
divorce of responsibility from love stands in such a civilization
either as a mirage or a pillar of salt.

The world is not shocked at seeing love and sorrow linked
arm in arm when love is not perfect; but it is less prepared to
see immaculate love and sorrow in the same company. The
true Christians should not be scandalized at this, since Our
Lord is described as the Man of Sorrows. He Who came to
this earth to bear a Cross might conceivably drag it through
His Mother's heart. Scripture suggests that He schooled and
disciplined her in sorrow. There is an expression used today,
always in a bad sense, but which, if used in the right sense,
could apply to the relations between Our Lord and His
Blessed Mother, and that is "alienation of affections". He
begins detaching Himself from His Mother, seemingly alien-
ating His affections with growing unconcern—only to reveal

at the very end that what He was doing was introducing her through sorrow to a new and deeper dimension of love.

There are two great periods in the relations of Jesus and Mary, the first extending from the Crib to Cana, and the second, from Cana to the Cross. In the first, she is the Mother of Jesus; in the second, she begins to be the Mother of all whom Jesus would redeem—in other words, to become the Mother of men.

From Bethlehem to Cana, Mary has Jesus as a mother has a son; she even calls Him familiarly, at the age of twelve, "Son", as if that were her usual mode of address. He is with her during those thirty years, fleeing in her arms to Egypt, living at Nazareth, and being subject to her. He is hers, and she is His, and even at the very moment when they walk into the wedding feast, her name is mentioned first: "Mary, the Mother of Jesus, was there."

But from Cana on, there is a growing detachment, which Mary helps to bring on herself. She induced her Son to work His first miracle, as He changed her name from Mother to Woman, the significance of which will not become clear until the Cross. Readers of Genesis will recall how God promised that Satan would be crushed through the power of a woman. When Our Lord tells Mary that they are both involved in the manifestation of His Divinity, she practically sends Him to the Cross by asking for the first of the miracles and, by implication, His Death. A year or more later, as a devoted mother, she follows Him in His preaching. It is announced to Our Lord that His Mother is seeking Him. Our Lord, with seeming unconcern, turns to the crowd and asks: "Who is my Mother?" (Mt 12:48). Then, revealing the great Christian mystery that relationship is dependent not on flesh and blood but on union with Divine Nature through grace, He adds: "If anyone does the will of my Father who is in heaven, he is my brother, and sister, and mother" (Mt 12:50).

The ties that bind us to one another are less of race than of obedience to the will of God. From that text originated the titles of "Father", "Mother", "Brother", and "Sister", as used throughout the Church to imply that our relations are in Christ rather than in human generation. He Who called His Mother "Woman" is now telling us and her that we can enter a new family with her, as He has already taught us to enter into new bonds with His Own Heavenly Father. If we can call God "our Father", then we can call her "our Mother", if we do the will of the Father.

The mystery comes to an end at Calvary when, from the Cross, Our Lord now hearkens back to Cana and again uses the word "Woman", the title of universal motherhood. Speaking to her of all of us who will be redeemed by His Precious Blood, He says: "Behold thy Son." Finally, to John, who, unnamed, stood for us, He said: "Behold thy Mother." She becomes our Mother the moment she loses her Divine Son. The mystery is now solved. What seemed an alienation of affection was in reality a deepening of affection. No love ever mounts to a higher level without death to a lower one. Mary dies to the love of Jesus at Cana and recovers Jesus again at Calvary with His Mystical Body, whom He redeemed. It was, for the moment, a poor exchange, giving up her Divine Son to win us; but in reality, she did not win us apart from Him. On that day when she came to Him preaching, He began to merge the Divine Maternity into the new motherhood of all men; at Calvary, He caused her to love men as He loved them.

It was a new love, or perhaps the same love expanded over the wider area of humanity. But it was not without its sorrow. It cost Mary something to have us as sons. She could beget

Jesus in joy in a stable, but she could beget us only on Calvary, only in labors great enough to make her Queen of Martyrs. The *Fiat* she pronounced when she became the Mother of God now becomes another *Fiat*, like unto Creation in the immensity of what she brought forth. It was also a *Fiat* that so enlarged her affections as to increase her pains. The bitterness of Eve's curse—that she would bring forth her children in sorrow—is now fulfilled, and not by the opening of a womb, but by the piercing of a heart, as Simeon had foretold. It was the greatest of all honors to be the Mother of Christ; but it was also a great honor to be the Mother of Christians. There was no room in the inn for that first birth, but Mary had the whole world for her second.

Here, at last, is the answer to the query, "Did Mary have other children besides Jesus?" She certainly did. Millions and millions of them! But not according to the flesh. He alone was born of her flesh; the rest of us were born of her spirit. As the Annunciation tied her up with Divinity before the coming of her Divine Son, so this word from the Cross tied her up with all humanity until His Second Coming. She was a child of that chosen section of humanity called "the seed of Abraham", the scion of that long line of royalty and kings who hand on to her Divine Son the "throne of His Father David". But, as the new Eve, she hands on to her Son the heritage of the whole human race, from the day of Adam until now; and through her Son she breaks the boundaries of that limited blessing to the seed of Abraham and pours it out upon every nation, race, and peoples. Her moment in history was the "fullness of time"; this phrase meant that the human race had at last produced a representative worthy of becoming the chosen vessel of the Son of God. "One who comes into his property while he is still a child has no more liberty than one of the servants, though all the estate is his" (Gal 4:1).

Our Lord is not immersed in history, but Mary is. He comes to earth from outside time; she is within time. He is the suprahistorical; she, the historical. He is the Eternal in time; she is the House of the Eternal in time. She is the final meeting place of all humanity and all history. Or, as Coventry Patmore says:

> *knot of the cord*
> *Which binds together all and all unto their Lord.*

At the end of the story of love and sorrow, we see that love needs a constant purification, and this happens only through sorrow. Love that is not nourished on sacrifice becomes trite, banal, and commonplace. It takes the other for granted, makes no more professions of love because it has sounded no new depths. Our Lord would not have His Mother's love on one plane of ecstasy while on this earth; He would universalize it, expand it, make it catholic. But to do this, He had to send Her seven swords of sorrow, which enlarged her love from the Son of Man to the sons of men.

Without this deepening, love falls into one of two dangers: *contempt* or *pity*—*contempt* because the other no longer pleases the ego, *pity* because the other is worthy of some consideration without love. Had Our Divine Lord not called Mary into the fellowship of His suffering, had she been dispensed from Calvary because of her Majesty as His Mother, she would have had *contempt* for those who took the life of her only Son, and only *pity* for us who had no such blessing. But because He first identified Himself with our human nature at Bethlehem, later with our daily tasks at Nazareth and with our misunderstandings at Galilee and Jerusalem, and finally with our tears and blood and agonies at Calvary, He gave to us His Mother and, to all of us, the lesson that love must embrace mankind or suffocate in the narrowness of its ego. Summoned by Him to share His daily Cross, her love expanded with His own and reached such a peak of universal identification that His Ascension was paralleled by her Assumption. He, Who inspired her to *stand* at the foot of the Cross as an active participant in its redemption, would not be remiss in crowning such love with union with Him where love would be without sorrow, or where sorrow would be swallowed up in joy.

Love never becomes a cult without a death. How often does even human love come into the full consciousness of the other's devotedness, until the death of the partner? History becomes legend after death, and love becomes adoration. One no longer keeps any memory of the other's faults, or what was left undone; all is surrounded in an aureole of praise. The ennui of life fades away; the quarrels that hurt evaporate or else they are transformed into souvenirs of affection. The dead are always more beautiful than the living.

In the case of Mary, we have no memories of her imperfections fading away, for she was "blessed among women"; but we do have such a deepening of love as to produce a cult. He, Who sacrificed Himself for us, thought so much of His death that He left a Memorial of it and ordered its re-enactment in what is today known as the Mass. His love, which died, became adoration in the Eucharist. Why, then, should not she, who gave Him that body with which He could die and that blood which He could pour forth, be remembered, not in adoration, but in veneration, and as long as time endures? But if, along with the God Who is the Man of Sorrows and Who entered into His glory, there is a creature, a Woman of Sorrows who accompanied Him into that glory, then we all have an inspiration to love *through* a cross and *with* it, that we too may reign with Christ.

11

The Assumption and the Modern World

The definition of the Immaculate Conception was made when the modern world was born. Within five years of that date, and within six months of the apparition of Lourdes where Mary said, "I am the Immaculate Conception", Charles Darwin wrote his *Origin of Species*, Karl Marx completed his Introduction to the *Critique of the Philosophy of Hegel* ("Religion is the opium of the people"), and John Stuart Mill published his *Essay on Liberty*. At the moment the spirit of the world was drawing up a philosophy that would issue in two world wars in twenty-one years and the threat of a third, the Church came forward to challenge the falsity of the new philosophy. Darwin took man's mind off his Divine origin and fastened it on an unlimited future when he would become a kind of God. Marx was so impressed with this idea of inevitable progress that he asked Darwin if he would accept a dedication of one of his books. Then, following Feuerbach, Marx affirmed not a bourgeois atheism of the intellect but an atheism of the will, in which man hates God because man is God. Mill reduced the freedom of the new man to license and the right to do whatever he pleases, thus preparing a chaos of conflicting egotisms, which the world would solve by totalitarianism.

If these philosophers were right and if man is naturally good and capable of deification through his own efforts, then it follows that everyone is immaculately conceived. The Church arose in protest and affirmed that only one human person in all the world is immaculately conceived, that man is prone to sin, and that freedom is best preserved when, like Mary, a creature answers *Fiat* to the Divine will.

The dogma of the Immaculate Conception wilted and killed the false optimism of the inevitable and necessary progress of man without God. Humbled in his Darwinian-Marxian-Millian pride, modern man saw his doctrine of progress evaporate. The interval between the Napoleonic and Franco-Prussian Wars was fifty-five years; the interval between the Franco-Prussian War and World War I was forty-three years; the interval between World Wars I and II, twenty-one years. Fifty-five, forty-three, twenty-one, and a Korean War five years after World War II are hardly progress. Man finally saw that he was not naturally good. Once having boasted that he came from the beast, he now found himself to be acting as a beast.

Then came the reaction. The Optimistic Man who boasted of his immaculate conception now became the Pessimistic Man who could see within himself nothing but a bundle of libidinous, dark, cavernous drives. As in the definition of the Immaculate Conception the Church had to remind the world that perfection is not biologically inevitable, so now in the definition of the Assumption she has to give hope to the creature of despair. Modern despair is the effect of a disappointed hedonism and centers principally on sex and death. To these two ideas, which preoccupy the modern mind, the Assumption is indirectly related.

The primacy of sex is to a great extent due to Sigmund Freud, whose basic principle in his own words is: "Human actions and customs derive from sexual impulses, and fundamentally, human wishes are unsatisfied sexual desires. . . . Consciously or unconsciously, we all wish to unite with our mothers and kill our fathers, as Oedipus did—unless we are female, in which case we wish to unite with our fathers and murder our mothers." The other major concern of modern thought is death. The beautiful philosophy of being is reduced to *Dasein*, which is only *in-der-Welt-sein*. There is no freedom, no spirit, and no personality. Freedom is for death. Liberty is contingency threatened with complete destruction. The future is nothing but a projection of death. The aim of existence is to look death in the eye.

Jean-Paul Sartre passes from a phenomenology of sexuality to that which he calls "nausea", or a brazen confrontation of nothingness, toward which existence tends. Nothing precedes man; nothing follows man. Whatever is opposite him is a negation of his ego, and therefore nothingness. God created the world out of nothingness; Sartre creates nothingness out of the world and the despairing human heart. "Man is a useless passion."

Agnosticism and pride were the twin errors the Church had to meet in the Doctrine of the Immaculate Conception; now it is the despair resulting from sex and death she has to meet in this hour. When the agnostics of the last century came in contact with the world and its three libidos, they became libertines. But when pleasure diminished and made hungry where most it satisfied, the agnostics, who had become libertines by attaching themselves to the world, now began in disgust to withdraw themselves from the world and became philosophers of existentialism. Philosophers like Sartre, Heidegger, and others are born of a detachment from the world, not like the Christian ascetic, because he loves God, but because they are disgusted with the world. They become contemplatives, not to enjoy God, but to wallow in their despair, to make a philosophy out of it, to be brazen about their boredom, and to make death the center of their destiny. The new contemplatives are in the monasteries of the jaded, which are built not along the waters of Siloe but along the dark banks of the Styx.

These two basic ideas of modern thought, sex and death, are not unrelated. Freud himself hinted at the union of Eros and Thanatos. Sex brings death, first of all because in sex the other person is possessed, or annihilated, or ignored for the sake of pleasure. But this subjection implies a compression and a destruction of life for the sake of the Eros. Second, death is a shadow that is cast over sex. Sex seeks pleasure, but since it assumes that this life is all, every pleasure is seasoned not only with a diminishing return but also with the thought that death will end pleasure forever. Eros is Thanatos. Sex is death.

From a philosophical point of view, the doctrine of the Assumption meets the Eros–Thanatos philosophy head-on, by lifting humanity from the darkness of sex and death to the light of Love and Life. These are the two philosophical pillars on which rests the belief in the Assumption.

1. *Love*. The Assumption affirms not sex but love. St. Thomas in his inquiry into the effects of love mentions ecstasy as one of them. In ecstasy one is "lifted out of his body", an experience that poets and authors and orators have felt in a mild form when, in common parlance, "they were carried away by their subject". On a higher level, the spiritual phenomenon of levitation is the result of such an intense love of God that saints are literally lifted off the earth. Love, like fire, burns upward, since it is basically desire. It seeks to become more and more united with the object that is loved. Our sensate experiences are familiar with

the earthly law of gravitation, which draws material bodies to the earth. But in addition to terrestrial gravitation, there is a law of spiritual gravitation, which increases as we get closer to God. This "pull" on our hearts by the Spirit of God is always present, and it is only our refusing wills and the weakness of our bodies as a result of sin that keep us earth-bound. Some souls become impatient with the restraining body; St. Paul asks to be delivered from its prison house.

If God exerts a gravitational pull on all souls, given the intense love of Our Lord for His Blessed Mother that descended and the intense love of Mary for her Lord that ascended, there is created a suspicion that love at this stage would be so great as "to pull the body with it". Given further an immunity from Original Sin, there would not be in the body of Our Lady the dichotomy, tension, and opposition that exist in us between body and soul. If the distant moon moves all the surging tides of earth, then the love of Mary for Jesus and the love of Jesus for Mary should result in such an ecstasy as "to lift her out of this world".

Love in its nature is an ascension in Christ and an assumption in Mary. So closely are love and the Assumption related that a few years ago the writer, when instructing a Chinese lady, found that the one truth in Christianity that was easiest for her to believe was the Assumption. She personally knew a saintly soul who lived on a mat in the woods, whom thousands of people visited to receive her blessing. One day, according to the belief of all who knew the saint, she was "assumed" into Heaven. The explanation the convert from Confucianism gave was: "Her love was so great that her body followed her soul." One thing is certain: the Assumption is easy to understand if one loves God deeply, but it is hard to understand if one loves not.

Plato in his *Symposium*, reflecting the Grecian view of the elevation of love, says that love of the flesh should lead to love of the spirit. The true meaning of love is that it leads to God. Once the earthly love has fulfilled its task, it disappears, as the symbol gives way to reality. The Assumption is not the killing of the Eros but its transfiguration through Agape. It does not say that love in a body is wrong, but it does hold that it can be so right, when it is Godward, that the beauty of the body itself is enhanced.

Our Age of Carnality, which loves the Body Beautiful, is lifted out of its despair, born of the Electra and Oedipus incests, to a body that is beautiful because it is a temple of God, a gate through which the Word of Heaven passed to earth, a tower of ivory up which climbed Divine Love to kiss upon the lips of His Mother a Mystic Rose. With one stroke of an infallible dogmatic pen, the Church lifts the sacredness of love out of sex without denying the role of the body in love. Here is one body that reflects in its uncounted hues the creative love of God. To a world that worships the body, the Church now says: "There are two bodies in Heaven, one the glorified human nature of Jesus, the other the assumed human nature of Mary. Love is the secret of the Ascension of one and of the Assumption of the other, for love craves unity with its beloved. The Son returns to the Father in the unity of Divine Nature, and Mary returns to Jesus in the unity of human nature. Her nuptial flight is the event to which our whole generation moves.

2. *Life*. Life is the second philosophical pillar on which the Assumption rests. Life is unitive; death is divisive. Goodness is the food of life, as evil is the food of death. Errant sex impulses are the symbol of the body's division from God as a result of Original Sin. Death is the last stroke of that division. Wherever there is sin, there is multiplicity: the Devil says,

"My name is Legion; there are many of us" (Mark 5:9). But life is immanent activity. The higher the life, the more immanent is the activity, says St. Thomas. The plant drops its fruit from a tree, the animal drops its kind for a separate existence, but the spiritual mind of man begets the fruit of a thought that remains united to the mind, although distinct from it. Hence intelligence and life are intimately related. *Da mihi intellectum et vivam.* God is perfect life because of perfect inner intellectual activity. There is no extrinsicism, no dependence, no necessary outgoing on the part of God.

Since the imperfection of life comes from remoteness to the source of life and because of sin, it follows that the creature who is preserved from Original Sin is immune from that psychological division which sin begets. The Immaculate Conception guarantees a highly integrated and unified life. The purity of such a life is threefold: a physical purity, which is integrity of body; a mental purity, without any desire for a division of love, which love of creatures apart from God would imply; and finally, a psychological purity, which is immunity from the uprising of concupiscence, the sign and symbol of our weakness and diversity. This triple purity is the essence of the most highly unified creature whom this world has ever seen.

Added to this intense life in Mary, which is free from the division caused by sin, there is still a higher degree of life because of her Divine Motherhood. Through her portals Eternity became young and appeared as a Child; through her, as to another Moses, not the tables of the Law, but the Logos was given and written on her own heart; through her, not a manna that men eat and die, but the Eucharist descends, of which, if a man eats, he will never die. But if those who commune with the Bread of Life never die, then what shall we say of her who was the first living Ciborium of that Eucharist, and who on Christmas day opened it at the communion rail of Bethlehem to say to Wise Men and Shepherds: "Behold the Lamb of God Who taketh away the sins of the world"?

Here there is not just a life free from the division that brings death but a life united with Eternal Life. Shall she, as the garden in which grew the lily of Divine sinlessness and the red rose of the passion of redemption, be delivered over to the weeds and be forgotten by the Heavenly Gardener? Would not one communion preserved in grace through life ensure a Heavenly immortality? Then shall not she, in whose womb was celebrated the nuptials of eternity and time, be more of eternity than time? As she carried Him for nine months, there was fulfilled in another way the law of life: "And they shall be two in one flesh."

No grown men and women would like to see the home in which they were reared subjected to the violent destruction of a bomb, even though they no longer lived in it. Neither would Omnipotence, Who tabernacled Himself within Mary, consent to see His fleshly home subjected to the dissolution of the tomb. If grown men love to go back to their homes when they reach the fullness of life, and become more conscious of the debt they owe their mothers, then shall not Divine Life go back in search of His living cradle and take that "flesh-girt paradise" to Heaven with Him, there to be "gardenered by the Adam new"?

In this doctrine of the Assumption, the Church meets the despair of the world in a second way. She affirms the beauty of life as against death. When wars, sex, and sin multiply the discords of men, and death threatens on every side, the Church bids us lift up our hearts to the life that has the immortality of the Life that nourished it. Feuerbach said that a man is what he eats. He was more right than he knew. Eat the food of earth, and one dies; eat the Eucharist, and one lives eternally. She, who is the mother of the Eucharist, escapes the decomposition of death.

The Assumption challenges the nothingness of the Mortician philosophers in a new way. The greatest task of the spiritual leaders today is to save mankind from despair, into which sex and fear of death have cast it. The world that used to say, "Why worry about the next world, when we live in this one?" has finally learned the hard way that, by not thinking about the next life, one cannot even enjoy this life. When optimism completely breaks down and becomes pessimism, the Church holds forth the promise of hope. Threatened as we are by war on all sides, with death about to be rained from the sky by Promethean fires, the Church defines a truth that has Life at its center. Like a kindly mother whose sons are going off to war, she strokes our heads and says: "You will come back alive, as Mary came back again after walking down the valley of Death." As the world fears defeat by death, the Church sings the defeat of death. Is not this the harbinger of a better world, as the refrain of life rings out amidst the clamors of the philosophers of death?

As Communism teaches that man has only a body, but not a soul, so the Church answers: "Then let us begin with a Body." As the mystical body of the anti-Christ gathers around the tabernacle doors of the cadaver of Lenin, periodically filled with wax to give the illusion of immortality to those who deny immorality, the Mystical Body of Christ bids the despairing to gaze on the two most serious wounds earth ever received: the empty tomb of Christ and the empty tomb of Mary. In 1854 the Church spoke of the Soul in the Immaculate Conception. In 1950 her language was about the Body: the Mystical Body, the Eucharist, and the Assumption. With deft dogmatic strokes the Church is repeating Paul's truth to another pagan age: "Your bodies are meant for the Lord." There is nothing in a body to beget despair. Man is related to Nothingness, as the philosophers of decadentism teach, but only in his origin, not in his destiny. They put nothingness as the end; the Church puts it at the beginning, for man was created *ex nihilo*. The modern man gets back to nothingness through despair; the Christian knows nothingness only through self-negation, which is humility. The more that the pagan "nothings" himself, the closer he gets to the hell of despair and suicide. The more the Christian "nothings" himself, the closer he gets to God. Mary went so deep down into Nothingness that she became exalted. *Respexit humilitatem ancillae suae.* And her exaltation was also her Assumption.

Coming back to the beginning . . . to Eros and Thanatos: sex and death, said Freud, are related. They are related in this sense: Eros as egotistic love leads to the death of the soul. But the world need not live under that curse. The Assumption gives Eros a new meaning. Love does lead to death. Where there is love, there is self-forgetfulness, and the maximum in self-forgetfulness is the surrender of life. "Greater love than this no man hath, that he lay down his life for his friends" (Jn 15:13). Our Lord's love led to His death. Mary's love led to her transfixion with seven swords. Greater love than this no woman hath, that she stand beneath the Cross of her Son to share, in her own way, in the Redemption of the world.

Within three decades the definition of the Assumption will cure the pessimism and despair of the modern world. Freud, who did so much to develop this pessimism, took as his motto: "If I cannot move the Gods on high, I shall set all hell in an uproar." That uproar which he created will now be stilled by a Lady as powerful as an "army drawn up in battle array". The age of the "body beautiful" will now become the age of the Assumption.

In Mary there is a triple transition. In the Annunciation we pass from the holiness of the Old Testament to the holiness of Christ. At Pentecost we pass from the holiness of the historical Christ to the holiness of the Mystical Christ or His Body, which is the Church. Mary here receives the Spirit for a second time. The first overshadowing was to give birth to the Head of the Church; this second overshadowing is to give birth to His Body as she is in the midst of the Apostles abiding in prayer. The third transition is the Assumption, as she becomes the first human person to realize the historical destiny of the faithful as members of Christ's Mystical Body, beyond time, beyond death, and beyond judgment.

Mary is always in the vanguard of humanity. She is compared to Wisdom, presiding at Creation; she is announced as the Woman who will conquer Satan, as the Virgin who will conceive. She becomes the first person since the Fall to have a unique and unrepeatable kind of union with God; she mothers the infant Christ in Bethlehem; she mothers the Mystical Christ at Jerusalem; and now, by her Assumption, she goes ahead like her Son to prepare a place for us. She participates in the glory of her Son, reigns with Him, presides at His Side over the destinies of the Church in time, and intercedes for us, to Him, as He, in His turn, intercedes to the Heavenly Father.

Adam came before Eve chronologically. The new Adam, Christ, comes after the new Eve, Mary, chronologically, although existentially He preceded her as the Creator a creature. By stressing for the moment only the time element, Mary always seems to be the advent of what is in store for man. She anticipates Christ for nine months, as she bears Heaven within her; she anticipates His Passion at Cana and

His Church at Pentecost. Now, in the last great doctrine of the Assumption, she anticipates Heavenly glory, and the definition comes at a time when men think of it least.

One wonders if this could not be the last of the great truths of Mary to be defined by the Church. Anything else might seem to be an anticlimax after she is declared to be in Heaven, body and soul. But actually there is one other truth left to be defined, and that is that she is the Mediatrix, under her Son, of all graces. As St. Paul speaks of the Ascension of Our Lord as the prelude to His intercession for us, so we, fittingly, should speak of the Assumption of Our Lady as a prelude to her intercession for us. First, the place, Heaven; then, the function, intercession. The nature of her role is not to call her Son's attention to some need, in an emergency unnoticed by Him, nor is it to "win" a difficult consent. Rather it is to unite herself to His compassionate Mercy and give a human voice to His Infinite Love. The main ministry of Mary is to incline men's hearts to obedience to the will of her Divine Son. Her last recorded words at Cana are still her words in the Assumption: "Whatsoever He shall say to you, that do ye." Added to these is the Christian prayer written by Francis Thompson to the daughter of the ancient Eve:

> *The celestial traitress play,*
> *And all mankind to bliss betray;*
> *With sacrosanct cajoleries,*
> *And starry treachery of your eyes,*
> *Tempt us back to Paradise.*

PART II

The World the Woman Loves

12

Man and Woman

In human love there are two poles: man and woman. In Divine love there are two poles: God and man. From this difference, finite in the first instance, infinite in the second, arise the major tensions of life. The difference in the God–man relationship between Eastern religions and Christianity is that in the East, man moves toward God; in Christianity, God moves first toward man. The Eastern way fails because man cannot lift himself by his own bootstraps. Grass does not become a banana through its own efforts. If carbon and phosphates are to live in man, man must come *down* to them and elevate them to himself. So if man is to share the Divine Nature, God must come down to man. This is the Incarnation.

The first difference in the man–woman relationship can be understood in terms of a philosophical distinction between *intelligence* and *reason*, which St. Thomas Aquinas makes, and which has saved his followers from falling into errors like those of Henri Bergson. Intelligence is higher than reason. The angels have intelligence, but they have no reason. *Intelligence* is immediacy of understanding and, in the domain of knowledge, is best explained in terms of "seeing". When a mind says, "I see", he means that he grasps and comprehends. *Reason*, however, is slower. It is mediate rather than immediate. It makes no leap but takes steps. These steps in a reasoning process are threefold: major, minor, conclusion.

Applying the distinction to man and woman, it is generally true that man's nature is more rational, and woman's, more intellectual. The latter is what is generally meant by intuition. The woman is slower to love, because love, for her, must be surrounded by a totality of sentiments, affections, and guarantees. The man is more impulsive, wanting pleasures and satisfactions, sometimes outside of their due relationship. For the woman, there must be a vital bond of relationship between herself and the one she loves. The man is more on the periphery and rim and does not see her whole personality involved in his pleasures. The woman wants unity; the man, pleasure.

On the more rational side, the man often stands completely bewildered at a "woman's reasons". They are difficult for him to follow because they are not capable of being broken down, analyzed, torn apart. They come as a "whole piece"; her conclusions obtrude without any apparent basis. Arguments seem to leave her cold. This is not to say who is right, for either approach could be right under different circumstances. In the trial of Our Blessed Lord the intuitive woman, Claudia, was right, and her practical husband, Pilate, was wrong. He concentrated on public opinion as a politician; she concentrated on justice, for the Divine Prisoner was in her eyes a "just man". This immediacy of conclusion can often make a woman very wrong, as it did in the case of the wife of Zebedee, when she urged Our Lord to allow her sons to sit at his right and left sides when He came into the Kingdom. Little did she see that a chalice of suffering had to be drunk first, for Divine Reason and Law has dictated that "no one would be crowned unless he had struggled".

A second difference is between reigning and governing. The man governs the home, but the woman reigns. Government is related to justice; reigning is related to love. Instead of man and woman being opposites, in the sense of contraries, they more properly complement one another as their Creator intended when He said: "It is not good for man to be alone." In the old Greek legend referred to by Plato, he stated that the original creature was a composite of man and woman and, for some great crime against God, this creature was divided, each going its separate way but neither destined to be happy until they were reunited in the Elysian fields.

The Book of Genesis reveals that Original Sin did create a tension between man and woman, which tension is solved in principle by man and woman in the New Testament becoming "one flesh" and a symbol of the unity of Christ and His Church. This harmony, then, should exist between man and woman, in which each fills up, at the store of the other, his or her lacking measure in quiet and motion.

The man is normally more serene than the woman, more absorbent of the daily shocks of life, less disturbed by trifles. But, in contrast, in great crises of life, it is the woman who, because of her gentle power of reigning, can give great consolation to man in his troubles. When he is remorseful, sad, and disquieted, she brings comfort and assurance. As the surface of the ocean is agitated and troubled, but the great depths are calm, so in the really great catastrophes that affect the soul, the woman is the depth, the man the surface.

The third difference is that the woman finds less repose in mediocrity than man. The more a person is attached to the practical, the concrete, the monetary, and the material, the more his soul becomes indifferent to great values and, in particular, to the Tremendous Lover. Nothing so dulls the soul as counting, and only what is material can be counted. The woman is more idealistic, less content over a long period of time with the material, and more quickly disillusioned about the carnal. She is more *amphibious* than man, in the sense that she moves with great facility in the two zones of matter and spirit. The oft-repeated suggestion that woman is more religious than man has some basis in truth, but only in the sense that her nature is more readily disposed toward the ideal. The woman has a greater measure of the Eternal, and man a greater measure of Time, but both are essential for an incarnational universe, in which Eternity embraces Time in a stable of Bethlehem. When there is descent into an equal degree of vice, there is always a greater scandal caused by a woman than by a man. Nothing seems more a profanation of the sacred than a drunken woman. The so-called double standard, which does not exist and which has no ethical foundation, is actually based on the unconscious impulse of man to regard woman as the preserver of ideals, even when he fails to live up to them.

There never can be a giver without a gift. This suggests the fourth difference: man is generally the giver, woman the gift. The man *has*; the woman *is*. Man has a sentiment; woman is sentiment. Man is afraid of dying; woman is afraid of not living. She is unhappy unless she makes the double gift: first of herself to man, then of herself to posterity in the form of children. This quality of immolation, because it involves the wholeness of self, makes a woman seem less heroic than a man. The man concentrates his passions of love into great focal points. When there is a sudden outburst of love, such as on a battlefield, he is immediately crowned the hero. The woman, however, identifies love with existence and scatters her self-oblation through life. By multiplying her sacrifices, she seems to be less of a hero. Her daily dissipation of vital energies in the service of others makes no one act seem outstanding. It may well be that the woman is capable of greater sacrifice than man, not only because she is gift, which is the same as surrender, but also because seeing ends rather than means and destinies rather than the present, she sees the pearl of great price for which lesser fields may be sacrificed.

These differences are not irreconcilable opposites; rather, they are complementary qualities. Adam needed a helpmate, and Eve was made—"flesh of his flesh and bone of his bone". The functional differences corresponded with certain psychic and character differences, which made the body of one in relation to another like the violin and the bow, and the spirit of one to another like the poem and meter.

There is no such problem as "Which is the more valuable?" for in the Scriptures husband and wife are related, one to another, as Christ and His Church. The Incarnation meant Christ's taking unto Himself a human nature as a spouse and suffering and sacrificing Himself for it, that it might be unspotted and holy; so husband and wife are bound together in a union unbreakable except by death. But there is a problem that is purely relative, namely, *"Which stands up better in a crisis—man or woman?"* One can discuss this in a series of historical crises, but without arriving at any decision. The best way to arrive at a conclusion is to go to the greatest crisis the world ever faced, namely, the Crucifixion of Our Divine Lord. When we come to this great drama of Calvary, there is one fact that stands out very clearly: *men failed*. Judas, who had eaten at His table, lifted up his heel against Him, sold Him for thirty pieces of silver, and then blistered His lips with a kiss, suggesting that all betrayals of Divinity are so terrible that they must be prefaced by some mark of esteem and affection. Pilate, the typical time-serving politician, afraid of incurring the hatred of his government if he released a man whom he already admitted was innocent, sentenced Him to death. Annas and Caiaphas resorted to illegal night trials and false witnesses, and rent their garments as if scandalized at His Divinity. The three chosen Apostles who had witnessed the Transfiguration and therefore were thought strong enough to endure the scandal of seeing the Shepherd struck, slept in a moment of greatest need, because they were unworried and untroubled. On the way to Calvary, a stranger, interested only in the drama of a man going to execution was forced and compelled to offer Him a helping hand. On Calvary itself, there is only one of the twelve Apostles present, John, and one wonders if even he would have been there had it not been for the presence of the Mother of Jesus.

In contrast, there is not a single instance of a woman's failing Jesus. At the trial, the only voice that is raised in His defense is the voice of a woman. Braving the fury of court officials, she breaks into the Judgment Hall and bids her husband, Pilate, not to condemn the "just man". On the way to Calvary, although a man is forced to help carry the Cross, the pious women of Jerusalem, ignoring the mockery of the soldiers and bystanders, console Him with words of sympathy. One of them wipes His face with a towel and forever after has the name of Veronica, which means "true image", for it was His image the Savior left on her towel. On Calvary itself, there are three women present, and the name of each is Mary: Mary of Magdala, who is forever at His feet and will be there again on Easter morn; Mary of Cleophas, the mother of James and John; and Mary, the Mother of Jesus—the three types of souls forever to be found beneath the Cross of Christ: penitence, motherhood, and virginity.

This is the greatest crisis this earth ever staged, and women did not fail. May not this be the key to the crisis of our hour? Men have been ruling the world, and the world is still collapsing. Those very qualities in which man, apparently, shone are the ones that today seem to be evaporating. The first of his peculiar powers, *reason*, is gradually being abdicated, as philosophy rejects first principles, as law ignores the Eternal Reason behind all ordinances and legislation, and as psychology substitutes for reason the dark, cavernous instincts of the subterranean *libido*. The second of his powers, *governing*, is gradually vanishing, as democracy becomes arithmocracy, as numbers and polls decide what is right and wrong, and as *people* degenerate into *masses* who are no longer self-determined personalities but groups moved by alien and extrinsic forces of propaganda. The third of his powers, *dedication to the temporal and the material*, has become so perverted that the material, in the shape of an atom, is used to annihilate the human and even to bring the world to a point where time itself may cease in the dissolution of the world as "an unsubstantial pageant faded". His fourth attribute, that of being the *giver*, has in its forgetfulness of God made him the *taker*; assuming that this world is all, he feels he ought to get all he can out of it before he dies like an animal.

This does not mean that woman has kept her qualities of soul untarnished; she would be the first to admit that she too has failed to live up to her ideals. When the bow is broken, the violin cannot give forth its chords. Woman has been insisting on "equality" with man, not in the spiritual sense, but only as the right to be a *competitor* with him in the economic field. Admitting, then, only one difference, namely, the procreation of species, which is often stifled for economic reasons, she no longer receives either minor or major respect from her "equal"—man. He no longer gives her a seat in the crowded train; since she is his equal in doing a man's work, there is no reason why she should not be an Amazon and fight with man in war and be bombed with man in Nagasaki.

Totalitarian war, which makes no distinction of combatant and civilian, of soldier and mother, is a direct consequence of a philosophy in which woman abdicated her peculiar superiority and even the right to protest against the demoralization. This is not to condemn women's place in economic life, but only to condemn the failure to live up to those *creative* and *inspiring* functions that are specifically feminine.

In this time of trouble, there must be a hearkening back to a woman. In the crisis of the Fall of man, it was to a Woman and her seed that God promised relief from the catastrophe; in the crisis of a world when many, blessed with revelation, forgot it and the Gentiles abandoned reason, it was to a Woman that an angel was sent, to offer the fulfillment of the promise that the seed would be Word made flesh, Our Divine Lord and Savior, Jesus Christ. It is a historical fact that, whenever the world has been in danger of collapse, there has been re-emphasis of devotion to the Woman, who is not salvation but who renders it by bringing her children back again to Christ.

More important still, the modern world needs, above all things else, the restoration of the *image of man*. Modern politics, from monopolistic capitalism through socialism to communism, is the destruction of the image of man. Capitalism made man a "hand" whose business it was to produce wealth for the employer; communism made man a "tool" without a soul, without freedom, without rights, whose task it was to make money for the state. Communism, from an economic point of view, is rotted capitalism. Freudianism reduced the Divine image of man to a sex organ, which explained his mental processes, his taboos, his religion, his God, and his super-ego. Modern education denied, first, that he had a soul, then, that he had a mind, finally, that he had a consciousness.

The major problem of the world is the restoration of the *image of man*. Every time a child is born into the world, there is a restoration of the *human image*, but only from the *physical* point of view. The surcease from the tragedy can come only from the restoration of the *spiritual* image of man, as a creature made to the image and likeness of God and destined one day, through the human will in cooperation with God's grace, to become a child of God and an heir of the Kingdom of Heaven. The image of man that was first ruined in the revolt against God in Eden was restored when the Woman brought forth a Man—a perfect man without sin, but a man personally united with God. He is the pattern of the new race of men, who would be called Christians. If the image of man was restored through a Woman, in the beginning, then shall not the Woman again be summoned by the Mercy of God to recall us once again to that original pattern?

This would seem to be the reason for the frequent revelations of the Blessed Mother in modern times at Salette, Lourdes, and Fatima. The very emergence of woman into the political, economic, and social life of the world suggests that the world needs a continuity that she alone can supply; for while man is more closely related to things, she is the protector and defender of life. She cannot look at a limping dog, a flower overhanging a vase, without her heart and mind and soul going out to it, as if to bear witness that she has been appointed by God as the very guardian and custodian of life. Although contemporary literature associates her with frivolity and allurement, her instincts find repose only in the preservation of vitality. Her very body commits her to the drama of existence and links her in some way with the rhythm of the cosmos. In her arms, life takes its first breath, and in her arms, life wants to die. The word most often used by soldiers dying on the battlefields is "Mother". The woman with her children is "at home", and man is "at home" with her.

Woman restores the *physical* image, but it is the *spiritual* image that must be restored, for both man and woman. This can be done by the *Eternal Feminine*: the Woman who is blessed above all women. Through the centuries woman has been saying: "My hour is not yet come", but now "The hour is come." Mankind will find its way back again to God through the Woman, who will gather up and restore the broken fragments of the image. This she will do in three ways.

By restoring constancy in love. Love today is fickle, although it was meant to be permanent. Love has only two words in its vocabulary: "You" and "Always". "You", because love is unique. "Always", because love is enduring. Love never says, "I will love you for two years and six days." Divorce is inconstancy, infidelity, temporality, the very fragmentation of the heart. But how shall constancy return except through woman? A woman's love is less egotistic, less ephemeral than a man's. Man has to struggle to be monogamous; a woman takes this for granted. Because every woman promises only what God can give, man is prone to seek the Infinite in a multiplication of the finite. The woman, on the contrary, is more devoted and faithful to the one she loves on human terms. But modern woman too often fails to give an example of this constancy; either she lets her love degenerate into a jealous possessiveness, or she learns infidelity from law courts and psychiatrists. There is need of the *Woman*, whose love was so constant that the *Fiat* to physical union with love in the Annunciation became celestial union with it in the Assumption. The Woman, who leads all souls to Christ and who attracts only to "betray" them to her Divine Son, will teach lovers that "what God hath joined together let no man put asunder".

By restoring respect for personality. Man generally speaks of things; woman generally speaks of persons. Since man is made to control nature and to rule over it, his principal concern is with *some thing.* Woman is closer to life and its prolongation; her life centers more on personality. Even when falling from feminine heights, her gossip is about people. Since the whole present political and economic world is gauged to the destruction of personality, God in His Mercy is trumpeting once more the *Woman* to "make a man", to re-make personality. The twentieth-century resurgence of devotion to Mary is God's way of pulling the world away from the primacy of the economic to the primacy of the human, from the things to life and machines to men. The praise from the woman in the crowd who heard Our Lord preaching and exclaimed: "Blessed is the womb that bore Thee and the breasts that nursed Thee" (Lk 11:27) was typically feminine. And the answer of Our Lord was equally significant: "Yea! Blessed rather are those who hear the Word of God and keep it" (Lk 11:27) This, then, is what devotion to Mary does in this troubled hour: it restores personality by inspiring it to keep the Word of God.

By infusing the virtue of purity into souls. A man teaches a woman pleasure; a woman teaches a man continence. Man is the raging torrent of the cascading river; woman is the bank that keeps it within limits. Pleasure is the bait God uses to induce creatures to fulfill their Heavenly infused instincts— pleasure in eating, for the sake of the preservation of the individual; pleasure in mating, for the sake of the preservation of the species. But God puts a limit to each to prevent the riotous overflow. One is satiety, which comes from nature itself and limits the pleasure of eating; the other is the woman, who rarely confuses the pleasure of mating with the sanctity of marriage. During the weakness of human nature, the liberty

of man can degenerate into license, infidelity, and promiscuity—as the love of woman can decay into tyranny, possessiveness, and insane jealousy.

Since the abandonment of the Christian concept of marriage, both man and woman have forgotten their mission.
Purity has become identified with repression instead of being
seen as it really is—the reverence for preserving a mystery of
creativeness until God sanctions the use of that power. While
man is outgoing in his pleasure, womanly purity keeps hers
inward, channeled, or even self-possessed, as if a great secret
had to be hugged to the heart. There is no conflict between
purity and carnal pleasure in blessed unions, for desire, pleasure, and purity each has its place.

Since woman today has failed to restrain man, we must
look to the Woman to restore purity. The Church proclaims
two dogmas of purity for the Woman: one, the purity of soul
in the Immaculate Conception, the other, the purity of body
in the Assumption. Purity is not glorified as ignorance, for
when the Virgin Birth was announced to Mary, she said, "I
know not man." This meant not only that she was untaught
by pleasures; it implied also that she had so brought her soul to
focus on inwardness that she was a virgin, not only through
the *absence of man* but also through the *presence of God*. No
greater inspiration to purity has the world ever known than
the *Woman*, whose own life was so pure that God chose her as
His Mother. But she also understands human frailty and so is
prepared to lift souls out of the mire into peace, as at the Cross
she chose as her companion the converted sinner Magdalen.
Through all the centuries, to those who marry to be loved,
Mary teaches that they should marry to love. To the unwed,
she bids them all keep the secret of purity until an Annunciation, when God will send them a partner; to those who, in
carnal love, allow the body to swallow the soul, she bids that

the soul envelop the body. To the twentieth century, with its
Freud and sex, she bids man to be made again to the God-like
image through herself as the *Woman*, while she, in turn, with
"traitorous trueness and loyal deceits", betrays us to Christ—
Who in His turn delivers us to the Father, that God may be all
in all.

13

The Seven Laws of Love

The Blessed Mother is recorded as speaking only seven times in Sacred Scripture. These seven words are here used to illustrate the seven laws of love.

1. *Love is a choice.* Every act of love is an affirmation, a preferment, a decision. But it is also a negation. "I love *you*" means that I do not love *her*. Because love is a choice, it means detachment from a previous mode of life, a breaking with old bonds. Hence the Old Testament law: "A man, therefore, will leave his father and mother and will cling to his wife" (Gen 2:24). Along with detachment, there is also a deep sense of attachment to the beloved. The desire in one is met by a response on the part of the other. Courting love never asks why one is loved. The only question love asks is "How?" Love is never free from difficulties: "How shall we live? How can we support ourselves?"

God loves man even in his sin. But He would not intrude upon human nature with His Love. So He woos one of the creatures to detach herself, by an act of her will, from sinful humanity and to attach herself to Him so intimately that she might give Him a human nature to begin the new humanity. The first woman made a choice that brought ruin; the New Woman is asked to make a choice for man's restoration. But there was one difficulty standing in the way: "How shall this be, seeing I know not man?" But since Divine Love is doing the courting, Divine Love shall also supply the means of embodying Itself: He that is born of her will be conceived by the Spirit of God's Love.

2. *Choice ends in identification with the beloved*. All love craves unity, the supplying of the lack of the self at the store of the other. Once the will makes the choice, surrender follows, for freedom is ours only to give away. "My will is mine to make it thine", is on the lips of every lover. Freedom exists for the sweet slavery of love. All love is passing from potency to act, from choice to possession, from desire to unity, from courtship to marriage. Since the very beginning, love was spoken of as making man and woman "two in one flesh". One soul passes into another soul, and the body follows the soul to such unity as it can achieve. The difference between prostitution and love is that in the former there is the offering of the body without the soul. True love demands that the will to love should precede the act of possession.

After God had courted the soul of a creature and asked her to supply Him with a human nature, and when all difficulties of *how* her virginity could be preserved were cleared away, there came the great act of surrender. *Fiat*. "Be it done unto me . . ."—surrender, resignation, and the celebration of the Divine Nuptials. In another sense, there were now two in one flesh: the Divine and human natures of the Person of Christ lived in the womb of Mary, God and man made One. In no person in this world was there ever such unity of God and man as Mary experienced within her during the nine months in which she bore Him whom Heaven could not contain. Mary, who was already one with Him in mind, was now one with Him in body, as Love reached its peak in mothering the wandering Word.

3. *Love requires a constant de-egotization.* It is easy for love to take the beloved for granted and to assume that what was freely offered for life needs no repurchasing. But love can be treated either as an antique that needs no care or as a flower that needs pruning. Love could become so possessive that it would hardly be conscious of the rights of others: lest love so degenerate into a mutual exchange of egotisms, there must be a constant going out to others, an exteriorization, an increased searching for the formation of an "us". Love of God is inseparable from love of neighbor. Words of love must be translated into action, and they must go beyond the mere boundary of the home. The needs of neighbor may become so imperative that one may have to sacrifice one's own comfort for another. Love that does not expand to neighbor dies of its own too-much.

Mary obeys this third law of love, even in her pregnancy, by visiting a pregnant relative, an elderly woman who is already six months with child. From that day to this, no one who boasts of his love of God may claim exemption from the law to love his neighbor too. Mary hastens—*Maria festinans*—across the hills to visit her cousin Elizabeth. Mary is present at a birth at this Visitation, as she will later attend a marriage at Cana and a death on Calvary: the three major moments in the life of a neighbor. Now, no sooner does an angel visit her than she makes a visit to a woman in need. A woman is best helped by a woman, and the one woman who bears Love Divine within her casts such a spell over another woman with child that John the Baptist leaps with joy in her womb. The bearing of Christ is inseparable from the service of Christ. God the Son had come to Mary not for her sake alone but also for the sake of the world. Love is social, or it ceases to be love.

4. *Love is inseparable from joy.* A woman's greatest joy is when

she brings a child into the world. The father's joy is changing a woman into a mother. Love cannot endure without joys, although these are sometimes given as prepayments for later responsibilities. The joy of love goes out in two directions: one is horizontal, through the extension of love in the family; the other is vertical, a mounting to God with our thanks because He is the source of all love. The miser is devoured by his gold, the saint by his God.

In moments of ecstasy, lovers ask where their love will end. Will it run out as feeble drops of rain upon the parched sands of the desert without joy, or will it run like rivers to the sea and back again unto God? Love must seek an explanation for its ecstasies and joys; it asks, "If the spark of love is so great, what must be the flame?"

Where the ecstasy of love comes from God, it is only natural that its joy should break out into song, as it does in the *Magnificat* of Mary. Somehow Mary knows that her love will have a happy ending, even though there will be revolutions dethroning the mighty and unseating the proud. This Queen of Song now sings a song different from that of all other mothers. All mothers sing to their babes, but here is one mother who sings before the Babe is born. She says only a *Fiat* to an angel, she says nothing to Joseph, but she chants verse upon verse of a song to God, Who looked down on the humility of His handmaid. As the infant leaped in the womb of Elizabeth, so a song leaped to Mary's lips; for if a human heart can so thrill to ecstasy, what joy did she know, who was in love with the Great Heart of God!

5. *Love is inseparable from sorrow.* Because love, which demands the eternal for satisfaction, is compassed by time, it always knows some inadequacy and discontent. Trials, bereavements, and even the changes and rhythms of love itself prove a strain even to the most devoted lover. Even when love

is most intense, it often throws the lover back upon himself, and he becomes conscious that, despite his desire to be one with the beloved, he is still distinct and separate. There is a limit to the total possession of another in his life. Every marriage promises what God alone can give. The saints have the Dark Night of the soul, but all lovers have the Dark Night of the body.

If Mary is to feel the sorrow of love, she must feel the separation from the Beloved that comes during the three days' loss. Despite the will to be one with the Christ-love, there comes an estrangement, a separation, a change in moods as she asks: "Son, why hast thou done so to us? Knowest thou not that we have sought thee sorrowing?" The course of true love never runs smooth. Not even the most spiritual love is exempt from aridity, spiritual dryness, and a feeling that one has lost the Divine Presence. In humans the superabundance of love sometimes destroys love, so that after a while love becomes a duty. In Divine Love the richness of Divinity and its superabundance create a need, so that the absence of God, even for three days, causes the soul the greatest agony it can endure in this vale of tears.

6. *All love, before it mounts to a higher level, must die to a lower one.* There are no plains in the kingdom of love. One is either going uphill or coming down. There is no certainty of increasing ecstasy. If there is no purification, the fire of passion becomes the flicker of the sentiment and finally only the ashes of habit. No one is thirsty at the border of a well. There is no such thing as loving too much; one either loves madly or too little. Some wonder, in their satiety, if love itself is a snare and a delusion. The truth is that the law of love must always operate: love that does not mount perishes. The joys and the ecstasies, unless they are freshened by sacrifice, become mere friendships. Mediocrity is the penalty of all those who refuse

to add sacrifice to their love, and thus to prepare it for a wider horizon and a higher peak.

At the Marriage Feast of Cana, Mary had an opportunity to keep the love of her Son to herself alone. She had the choice of continuing to be only the Mother of Jesus. But she knew that she must not keep that love for herself alone under the penalty of never enjoying love to the fullest. If she would save Jesus, she must lose Him. So she asked Him to work His first miracle, to begin His public life, and to anticipate the *hour*—and that means His Passion and Death. At that moment, when she asked water to be changed into wine, she died to love of Jesus as her Son and began to mount to that higher love for all whom Jesus would redeem when He died on the Cross. Cana was the death of the mother–Son relationship and the beginning of that higher love involved in the Mother–humanity, Christ-redeemed relationship. And by giving up her Son for the world, she eventually got Him back—even in the Assumption and the Coronation.

7. *The end of all human love is doing the will of God.* Even the most frivolous speak of love in terms of eternity. Love is timeless. As true love develops, there are at first two loves facing one another, seeking to possess one another. As love progresses, the two loves, instead of seeking one another, seek an object outside both. They both develop a passion for unity outside themselves, namely, in God. That is why, as a pure Christian love matures, a husband and spouse become more and more religious as time goes on. At first the happiness consisted in doing the will of the other; then the happiness consisted in doing the will of God. True love is a religious act. If I love you as God wills that I love you, it is the highest expression of love.

The last words of Mary that were spoken in Sacred Scripture were the words of total abandonment to the will of God.

"Whatsoever He shall say to you, that do ye." As Dante said: "In His will is our peace." Love has no other destiny than to obey Christ. Our wills are ours only to give away. The human heart is torn between a sense of emptiness and a need of being filled, like the waterpots of Cana. The emptiness comes from the fact that we are human. The power of filling belongs only to Him Who ordered the waterpots filled. Lest any heart should fail in being filled, Mary's last valedictory is: "Whatsoever He shall say to you, that do ye." The heart has a need of emptying and a need of being filled. The power of emptying is human—emptying in the love of others; the power of filling belongs only to God. Hence all perfect love must end on the note: "Not my will, but Thine be done, O Lord!"

14

Virginity and Love

Those who live by what Our Lord calls the "spirit of the world" are radically incapable of understanding anything done by others out of the spirit of Christ, Who said, "I have taken you out of the world, therefore the world will hate you" (Jn 15:19). When the world hears of a young girl entering the convent, it asks: "Was she disappointed in love?" The best answer to that inanity is: "Yes! But it was not a man's love that disappointed her, but the world's love." Actually, a young girl enters the convent because she has fallen in love: she is in love with Love Itself, namely, God. The world can understand why one should love the sparks, but it cannot understand why one should love the Flame. It is comprehensible that one should love the flesh that fades and dies, but incomprehensible that one should love, with "passionless passion and wild tranquility" the Love that is Eternal.

Anyone who knows the real philosophy of love should not be confused at such a noble loving. There are three stages of love, and few there are who ever arrive at the third stage. The first love is *digestive* love, the second is *democratic* love, and the third is *sacrificial* love. *Digestive* love centers in the person whom one loves. It assimilates persons, as the stomach assimilates food, using them as means to either its own pleasure or its own utility. Mere physical or sex love is digestive; it flatters the other person for his possession, as the farmer fattens livestock for the market. Its proffered gifts are only "baits", used as Trojan horses to win the other person over at the moment of its devouring. Those marriages that last only a few years and end in divorce and remarriage are founded on a love that is purely organic and glandular. Such love is a Moloch that devours its victims. If the partners survive digestion, it is only the carcass that is dismissed with the melancholy words: "We are no longer in love, but we are still good friends."

Above digestive love is *democratic* love, in which there is a reciprocal devotion founded on natural honor, justice, common likes, and a sense of decency. Here the other person is treated with becoming respect and dignity. This stage deserves the name of love, which the first does not.

Over and above this is what might be called *sacral* or *sacrificial* love, in which the lover sacrifices himself for the beloved, counts himself most free when he is a "slave" to the object of his love, and desires even to immolate self so that the other might be glorified. Gustave Thibon beautifully describes these three loves. He calls them indifference, attachment, detachment.

Indifference. As far as I am concerned, you do not exist.

Attachment. You exist, but this existence is based on our reciprocal relations. You exist in the measure that I possess you; and the moment I dispossess you, you no longer exist.

Detachment. You exist for me absolutely, quite independent of my personal relations with you and beyond anything you could do for me. I adore you as a reflection of the Divinity, which can never be taken from me. And I have no need to possess in order that you have existence for me.

Consecrated virginity is the highest form of *sacral* or *sacrificial* love; it seeks nothing for itself but only the will of the beloved. Pagans reverenced virginity, but they regarded it as almost the exclusive power of woman, for purity was seen only in its mechanical and physical effects. Christianity, on the contrary, looks upon virginity as a surrender of sex and of human love for God.

The world makes the mistake of assuming that virginity is opposed to love, as poverty is opposed to wealth. Rather, virginity is related to love as a university education is related to a grammar-school education. Virginity is the mountain peak of love, as marriage is its hill. Simply because virginity is often associated with asceticism and penance, it is thought to mean only the *giving up* of something. The true picture is that asceticism is only the fence around the garden of virginity. A *guard* must always be stationed around the Crown Jewels of England, not because England loves soldiers but because it needs them to protect the jewels. So the more precious the love, the greater the precautions to guard it. Since no love is more precious than that of the soul in love with God, the soul must ever be on the watch against lions who would overrun its green pastures. The grating in a Carmelite monastery is not to keep the sisters in but to keep the world out.

Married love, too, has its moments of renouncement, whether they be dictated by nature or by the absence of the beloved. If nature imposes sacrifices and asceticism on married love by force, why should not grace freely suggest a virgin love? What one does out of the exigencies of time, the other does out of the exigencies of eternity. Every act of love is an engagement for the future, but the virgin's vow centers more on eternity than on time.

As virginity is not the opposite of love, neither is it the opposite of generation. The Christian blessing on virginity did not abrogate the order of Genesis to "increase and multiply", for virginity also has its generation. Mary's consecration

of virginity was unique in that it resulted in a physical generation—the Word made flesh. But it also set the pattern of
spiritual generation, for she begot the Christ-life. In like
manner, virgin love must not be barren but, like Paul, must
say: "I have begotten you as most dear children in Christ."
When the woman in the crowd praised the Mother of Our
Lord, He turned the praise to spiritual motherhood and said
that she who did the will of His Father in Heaven was His
mother. Relationship was here lifted from the level of the
flesh to the spirit. To beget a body is blessed; to save a soul is
more blessed, for such is the Father's will. An idea thus can
transform a vital function, not by condemning it to sterility
but by elevating it to a new fecundity of the spirit. There
would, therefore, seem to be implied in all virginity the necessity of apostleship and the begetting of souls for Christ.
God, Who hated the man who buried his talent in the
ground, will certainly despise those who pledge themselves to
be in love with Him and yet show no new life—converts or
souls saved through contemplation. Birth control, whether
undertaken by husband and wife or by a virgin dedicated to
Christ, is reprehensible. On Judgment Day, God will ask all
the married and all virgins the same question: "Where are
your children? Where are the fruits of your love, the torches
that should be kindled by the fires of your passion?" Virginity
is meant for generation as much as married love is; otherwise
the Model-Virgin would not have been the Mother of
Christ, giving an example to others to be the mothers and
fathers of Christians. It is only love that can gain victory over
love; only the soul in love with God can overcome the body–
soul in love with another body–soul.

There is an intrinsic relation between virginity and intelligence. There is no doubt that, as St. Paul says, "The flesh
militates against the spirit." The sex-mad individual is always

under psychological necessity to "rationalize" his conduct, which is so obviously contrary to the dictates of conscience. But this psychic tendency to "justify oneself" by making a creed to suit one's immoral behavior necessarily destroys reason. Furthermore, passion harms reason, even when it does not quote Freud to justify adultery. By its very nature, the concentration of vital energies in the centrality of the flesh necessarily implies a diminution of those energies in the higher realms of the spirit. In a more positive way, we may say that the purer the love, the less the disturbances of the mind. But since there can be no greater love than that of the soul in union with the Infinite, it follows that the mind free from anxieties and fear should have the greatest clearness of intellectual insights. The concentration on *spiritual* fecundity should by its very nature produce a high degree of intellectual fecundity. Here one speaks not of knowledge *about things*, for that depends on effort, but of judgment, counsel, decision, which are the marks of a keen intelligence. One finds a suggestion of this in Mary, whose virginity is associated with wisdom in the highest degree, not only because she owned it in her new right but also because she begot Intelligence Itself in her flesh.

If God in His wisdom chose, in one woman, to unite virginity and motherhood, it must be that one is destined to illumine the other. Virginity illumines the homes of the married, as marriage pays back its debt with the oblation of virgins. Again, if marriage is ever to realize its dreams, it must proceed from the impulsion of instinct to those lofty ideals of love that virginity maintains. Married love that begins with the flesh guiding the spirit, under the inspiration of virginity, is elevated to a point at which the spirit guides the body. Carnal love, which by its nature implies no inner purification, would never mount above exhaustion and disgust, were there not that sacrificial oblation which virgins keep fresh in the world. And even when people do not live up to such ideals, they love to know that there are some who do. Though many married people tear up the photographs of what married love should be, it is a consolation to know that the sacrificial virgins are keeping the blueprints.

As sex-love centers in the ego, there is hope for happiness as long as virgins still center their love in God. While fools love what is only an image of their own desire, the redeemers of humanity are loving Him, of Whom all love ought to be an image. When the sated hits bottom and believes there is nothing more in the world worth loving, it is encouraging to know that Madonna-love can point to them and say: "You have hit only the bottom of your own egotism, but not the bottom of real love."

The virgin-love of Christianity teaches the disillusioned lovers that, instead of trying to make the infinite out of a succession of finite loves, they should take the one finite love they have and, by selflessness and charity, capture the Infinite already hidden within it. Promiscuity may be regarded as a misguided search for the Infinite, which is God. As the avaricious soul wants "more and more", hoping that by adding zeroes he can make the Infinite, so the carnal man wants another wife or another husband, vainly believing that what one lacks the other will supply. In vain does one change violins to prove the melody; in vain does one think that the infinity of desire with which all love begins is anything but God, with Whose love the virgin started and ended.

No human being can live without dreams. He who dreams only of the human and the carnal must one day be prepared either to see his dream die, or else he must die to the dream. Nothing is more pitiable than to see the thrice-divorced read romances, hoping to discover on a printed page what they

know they never found in life itself. The virgin dies to all
dreams but one, and as time goes on her dream comes more
and more true, until finally she wakes up to find herself in the
arms of the Beloved. It has been said of Mary that she
dreamed of Christ before she conceived Him in her body.
When Christianity called Him the "Word made flesh", it
meant that He was the Dream come true, Love becoming the
Beloved. In a noble married love, one must love the other as
the messenger of a transcendent love, that is, as a dream and
an ideal. The child born of that love is looked upon as the
messenger from another world. But all this is a reflection of
that virgin-love, modeled in Mary, which surrenders all
earthly loves, until the Messenger is One sent by the Father,
Whose name is Christ. This is not barrenness but fecundity—
not the absence of love but its very ecstasy—not disappoint-
ment in love but its sweet ecstasy. And from that hour, when
a Virgin held Love Itself in her arms, all lovers will instinctively peer through stable doors to catch a glance of what all
virgins envy most: falling in love with a First Love that is the
Alpha and the Omega—Christ, the Son of the Living God.

As breathing requires atmosphere, so love requires a
Christosphere and a Mariasphere. That ideal love we see beyond all creature love, and to which we instinctively turn
when flesh-love fails, is the same ideal that God had in His
Heart from all eternity—the Lady Whom He would call our
Blessed "Mother". She is the one every man loves when he
loves a woman—whether he knows it or not. She is what
every woman wants to be when she looks at herself. She is the
woman every man marries in his ideal; she is hidden as an
ideal in the discontent of every woman with the carnal aggressiveness of man; she is the secret desire every woman has
to be honored and fostered. To know a woman in the hour of
possession, a man must first have loved her in the exquisite

hour of a dream. To be loved by man in the hour of possession, a woman must first want to be loved, fostered, and honored as an ideal. Beyond all human love is another love; that
"other" is the image of the possible. It is that "possible" which
every man and woman love when they love one another.
That "possible" becomes real in the blueprint Love of Him
Whom God loved before the world was made, and in that
other love which we all love because she brings Christ to us
and brings us to Christ: Mary, the Immaculate Virgin, the
Mother of God.

15

Equity and Equality

The two basic errors of both communism and historical liberalism on the subject of women are: (1) that women were never emancipated until modern times, since religion particularly kept them in servitude; (2) that equality means the right of a woman to do a man's work.

It is not true that women began to be emancipated in modern times and in proportion to the decline of religion. Woman's *subjection* began in the seventeenth century, with the breakup of Christendom, and took on a positive form at the time of the Industrial Revolution. Under the Christian civilization women enjoyed rights, privileges, honors, and dignities that have since been swallowed up by the machine age. No one has better dissipated the false idea than Mary Beard in her scholarly work *Woman as Force in History*. She points out that, of eighty-five guilds in England during the Middle Ages, seventy-two had women members on an equal basis with men, even in such professions as barbers and sailors. They were probably as outspoken as men, for one of the rules of the guilds was that "the sistern as well as the brethren" may not engage in disorderly or contumacious debates. In Paris, there were fifteen guilds reserved exclusively for women, while eighty of the Parisian guilds were mixed. Nothing is more erroneous historically than the belief that it was our modern age that recognized women in the professions. The records of these Christian times reveal the names of thousands upon thousands of women who influenced society and whose names are now enrolled in the catalogue of saints— Catherine of Siena alone having left eleven large volumes of her writings. Up to the seventeenth century in England, women engaged in business, and perhaps even more so than today; in fact, so many wives were in business that it was provided by law that the husbands should not be responsible for their debts. Between 1553 and 1640, 10 percent of the publishing in England was done by women. Because the homes had their own weaving, cooking, and laundry, it has been estimated that women in pre-industrial days were producing half the goods required by society. In the Middle Ages, women were as well educated as men, and it was not until the seventeenth century that women were barred from education. Then, at the time of the Industrial Revolution, all the activities and freedom of women were curtailed, as the machine took over the business of production and men moved into the factory. Then came a loss of legal rights by women, which reached its fullness in Blackstone, who pronounced woman's "civil death" in law.

As these disabilities continued, woman felt the loss of her freedom, and rightly so, because she felt she had been hurt by man and robbed of her legal rights; and she fell into the error of believing that she ought to proclaim herself equal with men, forgetful that a certain superiority was already hers because of her functional difference from man. Equality then came to mean, negatively, the destruction of all privileges enjoyed by specific persons or classes and, positively, absolute and unconditioned sex equality with men. These ideas were incorporated into the first resolution for sex equality passed in

Seneca Falls, New York, in 1848: "Resolved that woman is man's equal, was intended to be so by the Creator, and the highest good of the race demands that she be recognized as such."

This brings us to the second error in the bourgeois-capital-istic theory of women, namely, the failure to make a distinction between mathematical and proportional equality. Mathematical equality implies exactness of remuneration— for example, that two men who work at the same job at the same factory should receive equal pay. Proportional equality means that each should receive this pay according to his function. In a family, for example, all children should be cared for by the parents, but this does not mean that, because sixteen-year-old Mary gets an evening gown with an organdy trim, the parents should give seventeen-year-old Johnnie the same thing. Women, in seeking to regain some of the rights and privileges they had in Christian civilization, thought of equality in mathematical terms or in terms of sex. Feeling themselves overcome by a monster called "man", they identi-fied freedom and equality with the right to do a man's job. All the psychological, social, and other advantages that were peculiar to women were ignored until the inanities of the bourgeois world reached their climax in communism, under which a woman is emancipated the moment she goes to work in a mine. The result has been that woman's imitation of man and her flight from motherhood have developed neuroses and psychoses that have reached alarming proportions. The Christian civilization never stressed equality in a mathemati-cal sense, but only in the proportional sense, for equality is wrong when it reduces the woman to a poor imitation of a man. Once woman became man's mathematical equal, he no longer gave her a seat in a bus and no longer took off his hat in an elevator. (In a New York subway recently a man gave a woman his seat, and she fainted. When she revived, she thanked him, and *he* fainted.)

Modern woman has been made equal with man, but she has not been made happy. She has been "emancipated", like a pendulum removed from a clock and now no longer free to swing, or like a flower that has been emancipated from its roots. She has been cheapened in her search for mathematical equality in two ways: by becoming a victim to man and a victim to the machine. She became a victim to man by becoming only the instrument of his pleasure and ministering to his needs in a sterile exchange of egotisms. She became a victim to the machine by subordinating the creative principle of life to the production of nonliving things, which is the essence of communism.

This is not a condemnation of a professional woman, because the important question is not whether a woman finds favor in the eyes of a man but whether she can satisfy the basic instincts of womanhood. The problem of a woman is whether certain God-given qualities, which are specifically hers, are given adequate and full expression. These qualities are principally devotion, sacrifice, and love. They need not necessarily be expressed in a family or even in a convent. They can find an outlet in the social world, in the care of the sick, the poor, the ignorant—in the seven corporal works of mercy. It is sometimes said that the professional woman is hard. This may in a few instances be true, but if so it is not because she is in a profession but because she has alienated her profession from contact with human beings in a way to satisfy the deeper cravings of her heart. It may very well be that the revolt against morality and the exaltation of sensuous pleasure as the purpose of life are results of the loss of the spiritual fulfillment of existence. Having been frustrated and disillusioned, such souls first become bored, then cynical, and finally suicidal.

The solution lies in a return to the Christian concept, wherein stress is placed not on *equality* but on *equity*. Equality is law. It is mathematical, abstract, universal, indifferent to conditions, circumstances, and differences. Equity is love, mercy, understanding, sympathy—it allows the consideration of details, appeals, and even departures from fixed rules that the law has not yet embraced. In particular, it is the application of law to an individual person. Equity places its reliance on moral principles and is guided by an understanding of the motives of individual families that fall outside the scope of the rigors of law. In the old English law of Christian days the subjects, in petitioning the court for extraordinary privileges, asked them "for the love of God and in the way of charity". For that reason, the heads of courts of equity were the clergy, who drew their decisions from Canon Law, and in vain did civil lawyers, with their exact prescriptions, argue against their opinions. The iron ring outside a cathedral door, which a pursued criminal might grasp, gave him what is known as the "right of sanctuary", and, while giving him immunity from the prescriptions of civil law, it made him subject to the more merciful law of the Church.

Applying this distinction to women: it is clear that *equity* rather than *equality* should be the basis of all the feminine claims. Equity goes beyond equality by claiming superiority in certain aspects of life. Equity is the perfection of equality, not its substitute. It has the advantages of recognizing the specific difference between man and woman, which equality does not have. As a matter of fact, men and women are not equal in sex; they are quite unequal, and it is only because they are unequal that they complement one another. Each has a superiority of function. Man and woman are equal inasmuch as they have the same rights and liberties, the same final goal of life, and the same redemption by the Blood of Our

Divine Savior—but they are different in function, like the lock and the key.

One of the greatest of the Old Testament stories reveals this difference. While the Jews were under Persian captivity, Aman, the prime minister of King Assuerus, asked his master to slay the Jews because they obeyed the law of God rather than the Persian law. When the order went out that the Jews were to be massacred, Esther was asked to approach the wicked King to plead for her people. But there was a law that no one should enter the King's presence, under the penalty of death, unless the King extended his sceptre as a permission to approach the throne. That was the law. But Esther said: "I will go in to the King, against the law, not being called, and expose myself to death and to danger" (Esther 4:16). Esther fasted and prayed and then approached the throne. Would the sceptre be lowered? The King held out the golden sceptre, and Esther drew near and kissed the top of it, and the King said to her: "What wilt thou, Queen Esther? What is thy request?" (Esther 5:3).

This story has been interpreted through the Christian ages as meaning that God will reserve to Himself the reign of justice and law, but to Mary, His Mother, will be given the reign of mercy. During the Christian ages, Our Blessed Mother bore a title that has since been forgotten, namely, Our Lady of Equity. Henry Adams describes the Lady of Equity in the Cathedral of Chartres. Stretching through the nave of the church are two sets of priceless stained-glass windows, the one given by Blanche of Castile, the other by her enemy, Pierre de Dreux, which seem to "carry on war across the very heart of the cathedral". Over the main altar, however, sits the Virgin Mary, the Lady of Equity, with the Holy Child on her knees, presiding over the courts, listening serenely to pleas for mercy in behalf of sinners. As Mary Beard beautifully put it: "The Virgin signified to the people moral, human or humane power, as against the stern mandates of God's law." And we might add, this is the woman's special glory—mercy, pity, understanding, and the intuition of human needs. When women step down from the role of the Lady of Equity and her prototype Esther and insist only on equality, they lose their greatest opportunity to change the world. Law has broken down today. Jurists no longer believe in a Divine Judge behind the law. Obligations are no longer sacred. Even peace is based upon the power of great nations, rather than on the justice of God. The choice before women in this day of the collapse of justice is whether to equate themselves with men in rigid exactness or to rally to equity, to mercy and love, giving to a cruel and lawless world something that equality can never give.

If women, in the full consciousness of their creativeness, say to the world: "It takes us twenty years to make a man, and we rebel against every generation snuffing out that manhood in war", such an attitude will do more for the peace of the world than all the covenants and pacts. Where there is equality there is justice, but there is no love. If man is the equal of woman, then she has rights—but no heart ever lived only on rights. All love demands inequality or superiority. The lover is always on his knees; the beloved must always be on a pedestal. Whether it be man or woman, the one must always consider himself or herself as undeserving of the other. Even God humbled Himself in His Love to win man, saying He "came not to be ministered unto, but to minister". And man, in his turn, approaches that loving Savior in Communion with the words: "Lord, I am not worthy."

As we said, professional careers do not of themselves defeminize women; otherwise the Church would not have raised political women to sainthood, as in the cases of St.

Elizabeth and St. Clotilde. The unalterable fact is that no woman is happy unless she has someone for whom she can sacrifice herself—not in a servile way but in the way of love. Added to the devotedness is her love of creativeness. A man is afraid of dying, but a woman is afraid of not living. Life to a man is personal; life to a woman is otherness. She thinks less in terms of perpetuation of self and more in terms of perpetuation of others—so much so, that in her devotedness she is willing to sacrifice herself for others. To the extent that a career gives her no opportunity for either, she becomes defeminized. If these qualities cannot be given an outlet in a home and a family, they must nevertheless find other substitutions in works of charity, in the defense of virtuous living, and in the defense of right, as other Claudias enlighten their political husbands. Then woman's work as a money earner becomes a mere prelude and a condition for the display of equity, which is her greatest glory.

The level of any civilization is the level of its womanhood. This is because there is a basic difference between knowing and loving. In knowing something, we bring it down to the level of our understanding. An abstract principle of physics can be understood by an ordinary mind only by examples. But in loving, we always go up to meet the demand of the one loved. If we love music, we submit to its laws and disciplines. When man loves woman, it follows that the nobler the woman, the nobler the love; the higher the demands made by the woman, the more worthy a man must be. That is why woman is the measure of the level of our civilization. It is for our age to decide whether woman shall claim equality in sex and the right to work at the same lathe with men, or whether she will claim equity and give to the world that which no man can give. In these pagan days, when women want only to be equal with men, they have lost respect. In Christian days, when men were strongest, woman was most respected. As the author of Mont St. Michel and Chartres puts it:

> The twelfth and thirteenth centuries were a period when men were at their strongest; never before or since have they shown equal energy in such varied directions, or such intelligence in the direction of their energy; yet these marvels of history—these Plantagenets; these Scholastic philosophers; these architects of Rheims and Amiens; these Innocents, and Robin Hoods, and Marco Polos; these crusaders who planted their enormous fortresses all over the Levant; these monks who made the wastes and barrens yield harvests—all, without apparent exception, bowed down before the woman.

Explain it who will! Without Mary, man has no hope except in atheism, and for atheism the world was not ready. Hemmed back on that side, men rushed like sheep to escape the butcher and were driven to Mary—only too happy in finding protection and hope in a being who could understand the language they talked and the excuses they had to offer. Thus, society invested in her care nearly its whole capital, spiritual, artistic, intellectual, and economic, even to the bulk of its real and personal estate. As Abelard said of her: "After the Trinity you are our only hope . . . you are placed there as our advocate; all of us who fear the wrath of the Judge, fly to the Judge's Mother, who is logically compelled to intercede for us and stands in the place of a mother to the guilty."

Christianity does not ask the modern woman to be exclusively a Martha or a Mary; the choice is not between a professional career and contemplation, for the Church reads the Gospel of Martha and Mary for Our Lady to symbolize that she combines both the speculative and the practical, the serving of the Lord and the sitting at His Feet. If woman wants to be a revolutionist, then the *Woman* is her guide, for she sang the most revolutionary song ever written—the *Magnificat*, the

burden of which was the abolition of principalities and powers and the exaltation of the humble. She breaks the shell of
woman's isolation from the world and puts woman back into
the wide ocean of humanity. She, who is the Cosmopolitan
Woman, gives us the Cosmopolitan Man, for which giving all
generations shall call her blessed.

She was the inspiration to womanhood, not because she
claimed there was equality in sex (peculiarly enough, this was
the one equality she ignored), but because of a transcendence
in function that made her superior to a man, inasmuch as she
could encompass a man, as Isaias foretold. Great men we
need, like Paul with a two-edged sword to cut away the
bonds that tie down the energies of the world—and men like
Peter, who will let the broad stroke of their challenge ring
out on the shield of the world's hypocrisy—great men like
John, who, with a loud voice, will arouse the world from the
sleek dream of unheroic repose. But we need women still
more: women like Mary of Cleophas, who will raise sons to
lift up white hosts to a Heavenly Father; women like Magdalen, who will take hold of the tangled skeins of a seemingly wrecked and ruined life and weave out of them the
beautiful tapestry of saintliness and holiness; and women,
above all, like Mary, the Lady of Equity, who will leave the
lights and glamors of the world for the shades and shadows of
the Cross, where saints are made. When women of this kind
return to save the world with equity, then we shall toast
them, we shall salute them, not as "the modern woman,
once our superior and now our equal" but as the Christian
woman closest to the Cross on Good Friday and first at the
Tomb on Easter morn.

16

The Madonna of the World

From the Bantu tribes of Congo Africa comes this story. A Bantu mother believed that the evil spirits were disturbing her child, although the child actually had only whooping cough. It never entered the mind of the woman to call on the name of God—although the Bantus had a name for God, *Nzakomiba*. God was utterly foreign to these people and was presumed to be totally disinterested in human woes. Their big problem was how to avoid evil spirits. This is the basic characteristic of missionary lands: pagan peoples are more concerned with pacifying devils than with loving God.

The missionary Sister, who is a doctor and who treated and cured the child, tried in vain to convince the woman that God is love. Her answer was an entirely different word: *Eefee*. The missionary Sister then said: "But God's love is like that: *Nzakomb' Acok'*—*Eefee*. God has the same feeling of love for us that a mother has for her children." In other words, mother-love is the key to God's love. St. Augustine, who was so devoted to his mother, St. Monica, must have had something like this in mind when he said: "Give me a man who has loved and I will tell him what God is."

That brings up the question: Can religion do without motherhood? It certainly does not do without fatherhood, for one of the most accurate descriptions of God is that of the Giver and Provider of good things. But since motherhood is as necessary as fatherhood in the natural order—perhaps even more so—shall the devoted religious heart be without a woman to love? In the animal kingdom, mothers are the fighters for their offspring, whom paternity often abandons. On the human level, life would indeed be dull if through every beat of its existence one could not look back in gratitude to a mother who threw open the portals of life to give life and then sustained it by the one great, irreplaceable love of each child's universe.

A wife is essentially a creature of time, for even while she lives she can become a widow; but a mother is outside time. She dies, but she is still a mother. She is the image of the eternal in time, the shadow of the infinite on the finite. Centuries and civilizations dissolve, but the mother is the giver of life. Man works on this generation: a mother on the next. A man uses his life; a mother renews it.

The mother, too, is the preserver of equity in the world, as man is the guardian of justice. But justice would degenerate into cruelty if it were not tempered by that merciful appeal to excusing circumstances which only a mother can make. As man preserves law, so woman preserves equity or that spirit of kindness, gentleness, and sympathy which tempers the rigors of justice. Virgil opened his great poem by singing of "arms and a man"—not of women. When women are reduced to bear arms, they lose that specific quality of femininity; then equity and mercy vanish from the earth.

Culture derives from woman—for had she not taught her children to talk, the great spiritual values of the world would not have passed from generation to generation. After nourishing the substance of the body to which she gave birth, she then nourishes the child with the substance of her mind. As guardian of the values of the spirit, as protectress of the morality of the young, she preserves culture, which deals with purposes and ends, while man upholds civilization, which deals only with means.

It is inconceivable that such love should be without a prototype Mother. When one sees tens of thousands of reprints of Murillo's *Immaculate Conception*, one knows that there had to be the model portrait from which the copies derived their impression. If fatherhood has its prototype in the Heavenly Father, Who is the giver of all gifts, then certainly such a beautiful thing as motherhood shall not be without some original Mother, whose traits of loveliness every mother copies in varying degrees. The respect shown to woman looks to an ideal beyond each woman. As an ancient Chinese legend puts it: "If you speak to a woman, do it in pureness of heart. Say to yourself: 'Placed in this sinful world, let me be pure as the spotless lily, unsoiled by the mire in which it grows.' Is she old? Regard her as your mother. Is she honorable? Regard her as your sister. Is she of small account? As your younger sister. Is she a child? Then treat her with reverence and politeness."

Why did all pre-Christian people paint, sculpture, lyricize, and dream of an ideal woman if they did not really believe that such a one *ought* to be? By making her mythical and legendary, they surrounded her with a mystery that took her out of the realm of time and made her more Heavenly than earthly. In all people is a longing of the heart for something motherly and divine, an ideal from which all motherhood descends like the rays from the sun.

The full hope of Israel has been realized in the coming of the Messias; but the full hope of the Gentiles has not yet been fulfilled. The prophecy of Daniel that Christ would be the *Expectatio Gentium* is so far fulfilled only in part. As

Jerusalem had the hour of its visitation and knew it not, so every people and race and nation has its appointed hour of grace. Just as God in His Providence hid the continent of America from the Old World for almost fifteen hundred years after His birth and then allowed the veil that hung before it to be pierced by the ships of Columbus, so He has kept a veil before many nations of the East so that in this hour His ships of grace might finally pierce their veil and reveal, in this late hour, the undying strength of the Incarnation of the Son of God. The present crisis of the world is the opening of the East to the potency of the Gospel of Christ. The practical West, having lost faith in the Incarnation, has begun to believe that man does everything and God does nothing; the impractical contemplative East, which has believed that God does everything and man does nothing, is soon to have its day of discovery that man can do all things in the God Who strengthens him.

But it is impossible to conceive that the East will have its own peculiar advent or coming of Christ without the same preparation that Israel once had in Mary. As there would have been no advent of Christ in the flesh in His first coming without Mary, so there can be no coming of Christ in spirit among the Gentiles without Mary's again preparing the way. As she was the instrument for the fulfillment of the hope of Israel, so she is the instrument for the fulfillment of the hope of the pagans. *Her role is to prepare for Jesus.* This she did physically by giving Him a body that could conquer death, by giving Him hands with which He could bless children and feet with which He could seek out the lost sheep. But as she prepared His body, so she now prepares souls for His coming. As she was in Israel before Christ was born, so she is in China, Japan, and Oceania before Christ is born. She *precedes* Jesus— not ontologically but physically—in Israel, as His Mother, and spiritually, among the Gentiles, as the one who readies His tabernacle among men. There are not many who can say "Our Father" in the strict sense of the term, for that implies that we are partakers in the Divine Nature and brothers with Christ. God is not Our Father by the mere fact that we are creatures; He is only our Creator. Fatherhood comes only by sharing in His nature through sanctifying grace. A liturgical manifestation of this great truth is found in the way in which the Our Father is recited in most of the ceremonies of the Church. It is recited aloud in the Mass, because *there* it is assumed that all present are already made sons of God in Baptism. But where the ceremony is one in which sanctifying grace cannot be presumed among those present, the Church recites the Our Father silently.

Thus pagans, who have not yet been baptized either by water or desire, cannot say the Our Father, but they *can* say the Hail Mary. As there is a grace that prepares for grace, so there is in all the pagan lands of the world the influence of Mary, preparing for Christ. She is the spiritual "Trojan horse" preparing for the assault of love by her Divine Son, the "Fifth Column" working within the Gentiles, storming their cities from within, even when their Wise Men know it not, and teaching muted tongues to sing her *Magnificat* before they have known her Son.

The David of old spoke of her as preparing for Israel the first advent of Christ:

> *The queen stood on thy right hand, in gilded clothing; surrounded with variety.*
> *Hearken, O daughter, and see, and incline thy ear: and forget thy people and thy father's house.*
> *And the king shall greatly desire thy beauty; for He is the Lord thy God, and Him they shall adore.*

And the daughters of Tyre with gifts, yea, all the rich among
the people, shall entreat thy countenance.
All the glory of the king's daughter is within in golden
borders, clothed round about with varieties.
After her shall virgins be brought to the king: her neighbors
shall be brought to thee.
They shall be brought with gladness and rejoicing: they shall
be brought into the temple of the king.

From an unexpected quarter comes an equally poetic tribute to "The Veiled Glory of this Lampless Universe", in the words of Percy Bysshe Shelley:

Seraph of heaven! too gentle to be human,
Veiling beneath that radiant form of Woman
All that is insupportable in thee
Of light, and love, and immortality!
Sweet Benediction in the eternal Curse!
Veiled glory of this lampless Universe!
Thou Moon beyond the clouds! Thou living Form
Among the Dead! Thou Star above the Storm!
Thou Wonder, and thou Beauty, and thou Terror!
Thou Harmony of Nature's art! thou Mirror
In whom, as in the splendour of the Sun,
All shapes look glorious which thou gazest on!
Ay, even the dim words which obscure thee now
Flash, lightning-like, with unaccustomed glow;
I pray thee that thou blot from this sad song
All of its much mortality and wrong,
With those clear drops, which start like sacred dew
From the twin lights thy sweet soul darkens through,
Weeping, till sorrow becomes ecstasy:
Then smile on it, so that it may not die.

There is a beautiful legend of Kwan-yin, the Chinese goddess of mercy, to whom so many pleadings have gone from Chinese lips. According to legend, this princess lived in China hundreds of years before Christ was born. Her father, the King, wished her to marry. But, resolving upon a life of virginity, she took refuge in a convent. Her angry father burned the convent and forced her to return to his palace. Given the alternative of death or marriage, she insisted on her vow of virginity, and so her father strangled her. Her body was brought to hell by a tiger. It was there she won the title "goddess of mercy". Her intercession for mercy was so great, and she so softened the hard hearts of hell, that the very devils ordered her to leave. They were afraid she would empty hell. She then returned to the island of Pluto off the coast of Chekiang where, even to this day, pilgrims travel to her shrine. The Chinese have at times pictured her as wearing on her head the image of God, to Whose Heaven she brings the faithful, although she herself refuses to enter Heaven so long as there is a single soul excluded.

Western civilization, too, has its ideals. Homer, a thousand years before Christ, threw into the stream of history the mystery of a woman faithful in sorrow and loneliness. While her husband, Ulysses, was away on his travels, Penelope was courted by many suitors. She told them she would marry one of them when she finished weaving a garment. But each night she undid the stitches she had put in it during the day, and thus she remained faithful until her husband returned. No one who sang the song of Homer could understand why he glorified this sorrowful mother, as they could not understand why, in another poem, he glorified a defeated hero. It was not for a thousand years, until the day of a defeated hero on a Cross and a sorrowful Mother beneath it, that the world understood the mysteries of Homer.

The instinct of all men to look for a mother in their religion is conspicuous, even in modern times, among non-Christian peoples. Our missionaries report the most extraordinary reaction of these peoples as the Pilgrim statue of Our Lady of Fatima was carried through the East. At the edge of Nepal, three hundred Catholics were joined by three thousand Hindus and Moslems, as four elephants carried the statue to the little church for Rosary and Benediction. At Rajkot, which has hardly any faithful, unbelieving ministers of state and high-ranking government officials came to pay veneration. The mayor of Nadiad read a speech of welcome and stressed how proud he was to welcome the statue. For twelve hours the crowds, almost exclusively non-Christian, passed through the church as Masses continued from two o'clock in the morning until nine-thirty. As one old Indian put it: "She has shown us that your religion is sincere; it is not like ours. Your religion is a religion of love; ours is one of fear."

At Patna, the Brahman Hindu governor of the province visited the church and prayed before the statue of Our Lady. In one tiny village of Kesra Mec, more than twenty-four thousand people came to see the statue. The Rajah sent 250 rupees, and his wife sent a petition of prayers. Greetings were read in six languages at Hy Derabid Sind. At Karachi an exception was made by the Moslems to favor her. Whenever the Christians there hold a procession, they are obliged to cease praying whenever they pass a mosque—but on this occasion they were permitted by the Moslems to pray before any mosque along their way.

In Africa, the Mother plays an important role in tribal justice. In northwestern Uganda, where the White Fathers labor with astounding zeal and success, every major decision, even the celebration of the coronation of the King, must be submitted to the Queen Mother. Anything she disapproves is put aside; her judgment is final. This is based on the assumption that she knows her son: she knows what will please or displease him. When the Queen Mother comes to the palace of her son, the King, she rules in his stead. One of the reasons why there were not two more martyrs among the famous martyrs of Uganda in Africa is because the pagan Queen Mother interceded for them. When the son becomes King, the son must sit on her lap before leaving for the ceremony, as if to bear witness to the fact that he is her child. The Queen Mother of the Batusti people in Rwanda is so influential among her people that the colonial government tries to keep her at a distance from her son, King Mutari II; both are converts to the Faith.

India, too, has had its history in which woman played her role. Its peoples are descended from the Dravidians, the early barbaric tribes who intermingled with Aryan invaders about fifteen hundred years before Christ. In the Dravidic hymns, virgins, like the Durgas and Kalis, were venerated. Hinduism became polytheistic, and a multiplicity of gods were adored; among the Hindus the virgins were almost simultaneously symbols of sweetness and terror, a combination that is not too difficult to understand. There is sweetness where there is love; there are also fear and terror, because that love is for the highest alone and is intolerant of all that surrenders to less than divinity.

Because of the want of authority and also because of the tolerant pantheism in religion in India, the feminine principle degenerated into something that seemed stupid to the Western mind, namely, the veneration of the sacred cow. Even in this decay of the feminine principle, there is to be detected a grain of truth. The cow to the Hindu fulfills many functions. Religiously, she is the symbol of the best gift that one can give to the Brahmans; to kill a cow is one of the Hindu's worst sins and can rarely be atoned by penance and purification. To the prince and peasant alike, the cow is his holy mother. He would even have the cow present when he dies, so that he may hold her tail as he breathes his last. Looking back on his life, he is indebted to her for her milk and butter; for his warmth, since it was her dung that was used as fuel, and her dung that coated the walls of his dwelling; and for his sustenance, since it was the cow, again, that pulled his cart and plow.

As one of the learned Hindu members said in the legislative assembly: "Call it prejudice, call it passion, call it the height of religion, but this is an undoubted fact, that in the Hindu mind nothing is so deep-rooted as the sanctity of the cow. Though the Western world makes fun of this symbol of religion, it is nevertheless a kind of glorification of motherhood and femininity in religion. When the Hindus come to a knowledge of how much the feminine principle in religion actually prepared for Christianity, they will reclaim the cow as the symbol of the feminine, as the Jews use the lily and the dove and the ray of light. In one of the beautiful paintings of the Nativity by Alfred Thomas of Madras, India, a Madonna Mother is pictured in her saffron sari as she sits crosslegged upon the earth. There is a straw roof over her head, supported from a growing tree trunk to which the sacred cow is tethered. Other nations of the earth have used the lion and the eagle as the symbols of their ideals; the Hindu people have taken the cow as the symbol of their religion, not fully understanding its meaning until Christianity gives them the true feminine principle: the Mother of God. If a lamb can be used by the Holy Spirit as the symbol of Christ, Who sacrificed Himself for the world, then one is wrong to frown upon the Indian for taking, as the symbol of his faith, an animal who gave him all that he needed for his life.

Japan, too, has its feminine principle of religion. For centuries, the goddess of mercy called Kwanon has been venerated. It is interesting that the Buddhists, who already know this goddess of mercy and who have come to learn of the Blessed Mother, have seen the first as the preparation for the second. Upon becoming Christian, there is no need for such Buddhists to turn their back on Kwanon as evil; rather, they accept her as the far-off foreshadowing of the woman who was not a goddess but the Mother of Mercy Itself. Very becomingly, the Japanese artist Takahira Toda, who came from a family of Buddhist priests, became a member of Christ's Mystical Body after seeing the similarity between Kwanon and the Virgin Mary. In his picture *The Visitation of Mary* he reveals the typical Japanese Virgin, demure and solitary, who has just felt within herself the full meaning of the words she pronounced to the angel, "Be it done unto me according to Thy word." A painting of the Nativity by the Japanese artist Teresa Kimiko Koseki pictures the babyhood of Our Lord, and here only one characteristic distinguishes the Japanese Madonna from the countless other mothers of Japan—and that is the halo of light above her head. In a very extraordinary painting by Luke Hasegawa, the Blessed Mother appears standing, surrounded by a wire fence, which may signify either a fenced-in missionary compound or, perhaps, a home, where motherhood is best understood. From this enclosure the Madonna, towering almost as high as the mountains in the background, looks down with affection upon the city and the harbor and the world of commerce—not yet conscious, perhaps, that she is the true Kwanon for whom the Japanese have been longing for centuries.

Wherever the people are primitive, in the right sense of the term, there is devotion to motherhood. The so-called "dark continent" of Africa has been close to nature and, therefore, to birth; when Christianity began to reveal the fullness of the mystery of birth and life, Africa interpreted the Madonna and the Child in terms of its own native culture. Mary, who had predicted that all generations would call her blessed, must have had it in mind that one day there would be a literal fulfillment of the words that are used of her in the liturgy: *Nigra sum sed formosa*—"I am black but beautiful!" There is a legend to the effect that one of the Three Wise Men was black. If this be so, then he who adored the Virgin and her Babe under a flaming Orient star now recovers the glory of his race in seeing the Mother and the Child portrayed as their own. Well indeed may the mothers of Africa (who during the days of colonial expansion saw their young sons snatched from their hands to become slaves in another land) look forward to a Madonna who might save them as she would save her own Son. A poetess has put upon the lips of a black Madonna this evening prayer:

> *Unanswered yet, but not yet unheard,*
> *O God, my prayer to You unfurled—*
> *He's just a Negro boy they say,*
> *Common, cheap and unlearned.*
> *What difference if he never does return?*
> *But, God, he is my only son.*
>
> *He knew a Bethlehem like your Son, God!*
> *No home like other little boys,*
> *With now and then a precious toy.*
> *He was unwanted like your only Son,*
> *And lots of Herods sought the life*
> *Of my little black son.*
>
> *He knew a flight like your son, God!*
> *A flight from hunger and starvation,*

Sometimes from sickness and disease.
He knew abuse, distress, want and fear.
He knew the love of a Madonna, too,
Just like your little Son.

Must he, too, know a dark Gethsemane?
A Golgotha and a Calvary too?
If so then I like the Madonna Mary
Must help him bear his cross.
Help me to pray: "not mine, but thine"
Just like your only Son.

But no one has better than Gilbert K. Chesterton glorified the Black Virgin, who is as much the Africans' mother as any other peoples' under the sun, and even more their mother than of those who would look upon the people of Africa as less noble than themselves.

In all thy thousand images we salute thee,
Claim and acclaim on all thy thousand thrones
Hewn out of multi-colored rocks and risen
Stained with the stored-up sunsets in all tones—
If in all tones and shades this shade I feel
Come from the black cathedrals of Castille
Climbing these flat black stones of Catalonia,
To thy most merciful face of night I kneel.[1]

Thus, whether one studies world history before or after Christ, there is always revealed a yearning in every human breast for ideal motherhood. Reaching out from the past to Mary, through ten thousand vaguely prophetic Judiths and Ruths, and looking back through the mists of the centuries,

---

[1] G. K. Chesterton, "The Black Virgin", from *I Sing of a Maiden*.

all hearts come to rest in her. This is the ideal woman! She is *the Mother*. No wonder that an aged woman, seeing her beauty cross the threshold, cried out: "Blessed art thou amongst women." And this young expectant Mother, far from repudiating this high estimate of her privilege, goes beyond it by anticipating the judgment of all time: "All generations shall call me blessed." Surveying the future, this ideal Mother has no hesitation in proclaiming that the distant ages will ring with her praise. Women live only for a few years, and the vast majority of the dead are not remembered at all. But Mary is confident that she is the real exception to this rule. Daring to predict that the law of forgetfulness will be suspended in her favor, she proclaims her eternal remembrance, even before the Child by Whom she will be remembered has been born. Our Lord has not yet worked a miracle; no hand of His had been lifted over palsied limbs—He was but scarcely veiled from the Heavenly glory and had only for a few months been tabernacled within her, and yet this Woman looks down the long corridors of time. Seeing there the unknown people of Africa, Asia, China, Japan, she proclaims with absolute assurance: "From henceforth, all generations shall call me blessed." Julia, the ill-used daughter of Augustus and wife of Tiberius; Octavia, the sister of Augustus whom Anthony divorced to marry Cleopatra—names once familiar to a people and a world—today receive no tribute of praise. But this lovely maiden, who lived in a little town in the far reaches of the Roman Empire, a town that was associated with reproach, is at this hour more honored and oftener borne in mind by civilized man than any other member of her sex who ever lived. And she knew the reason why: "Because He that is Mighty has done great things to me, and Holy is His Name."

As one searches for the reasons for this universal love of Mary among peoples who do not even know her Son, it is to be found in four instincts deeply embedded in the human heart: affection for the beautiful, admiration for purity, reverence for a Queen, and love of a Mother. All of these come to a focus in Mary.

The beautiful: he who has lost the love of the beautiful has already lost his soul. *Purity*: even those who fall from it always admire those who preserve the ideal, toward which, again, they feebly aspire. *Queen*: the heart wants a love so much above itself that it can feel unworthy in its presence and bow down before it in reverence. "I am not worthy" is the language of all love. *Mother*: the origin of life finds peace again only by a restoration to the embrace of a mother. Beautiful, Pure, Queen, Mother! Other women have had one or more of these instincts, but not all of them combined. When the human heart sees Mary, it sees the realization and concretion of all its desires and exclaims in the ecstasy of love: "This is the Woman!"

Mary, as the Madonna of the World, will play a special role today in relieving the combined sorrows of the East and West. In the East, there is fear; in the West, there is dread. The people of the Eastern world who are not Christian have a religion based on the fear of the devil and evil spirits. There is very little practical cognizance of the good spirit there. In Tibet, for example, the farmers plow their fields in a zigzag fashion to drive out the devil. Until recent years they immolated a child to placate the evil spirit in the mountains. When they cross a mountain pass, they must still give a gift to the devil—but since they believe the devil is blind, they only throw a stone. Every tree that sways, every flower that dies, and every disease that harms is caused by an evil spirit. China, too, has its devils that have to be assuaged. There is a statue of a goddess in Shanghai with a hundred arms. More incense burns before that statue than any other. The Buddhist priest in the temple explains that her arms represent vengeance and that she must be often propitiated lest she strike.

But in the West, in recent years, there has been less fear than dread. This inner dread is caused, in part, by modern man's loss of faith, but above all by his hidden sense of guilt. Although he denies sin, he cannot escape the effects of sin, which appear on the outside as world wars and on the inside as boredom. Western man got rid of God in order to make himself God, and then he became bored with his own divinity. The East cannot yet understand the Incarnate Love of Jesus Christ because of its overemphasis on evil spirits. The West is not prepared to accept it because of its dread of penance, the ethical condition of its return. Those who have never known Christ, fear—but those who have known Him and lost Him, dread.

Since men are unprepared for a revelation of the heavenly image of Love, which is Christ Jesus Our Lord, God, in His mercy, has prepared on earth an image of love that is not Divine but can lead to the Divine. Such is the role of His Mother. She can lift the fear, because her foot crushed the serpent of evil; she can do away with dread, because she stood at the foot of the Cross when human guilt was washed away and we were reborn in Christ.

As Christ is the Mediator between God and man, so she is the Mediatrix between Christ and us. She is the earthly principle of love that leads to the Heavenly Principle of Love. The relation between her and God is something like the relation between rain and the earth. Rain falls from the heavens, but the earth produces. Divinity comes from Heaven; the human nature of the Son of God comes from her. We speak of "mother earth", since it gives life through Heaven's gift of the sun; then why not also recognize the Madonna of the World, since she gives us the Eternal Life of God?

Those who lack the faith are to be recommended particularly to Mary as a means to finding Christ, the Son of God. Mary, the Madonna of the World, exists where Christ is not yet and where the Mystical Body is not yet visible. For the Eastern people who suffer from fear of the evil spirits and for the Western man who lives in dread, the answer must ever be *cherchez la femme*. Look to the woman who will lead you to God. The whole world may have to pass through the experience of the Bantu woman. She did not know love of God until it was translated into Mother Love.

Jesus may not yet be given an inn, in these lands, but Mary is among their people, preparing hearts for grace. She is grace where there is no grace; she is the Advent where there is no Christmas. In all lands where there is an ideal woman, or where virgins are venerated, or where one lady is set above all ladies, the ground is fertile for accepting the Woman as the prelude to embracing Christ. Where there is the presence of Jesus, there is the presence of His Mother; but where there is the absence of Jesus, through either the ignorance or the wickedness of men, there is still the presence of Mary. As she filled up the gap between the Ascension and Pentecost, so she is filling up the gap between the ethical systems of the East and their incorporation into the Mystical Body of her Divine Son. She is the fertile soil from which, in God's appointed time, the Faith will flourish and bloom in the East. Although there are few tabernacle lamps in India, Japan, and Africa compared to the total population, nevertheless I see, written over the gateways to all these nations, the words of the Gospel at the beginning of the public life of the Savior: "And Mary, the Mother of Jesus, was there."

17

Mary and the Moslems

Islam is the only great post-Christian religion of the world. Because it had its origin in the seventh century under Mohammed, it was possible to unite within it some elements of Christianity and of Judaism, along with particular customs of Arabia. Islam takes the doctrine of the unity of God, His Majesty and His Creative Power, and uses it, in part, as a basis for the repudiation of Christ, the Son of God. Misunderstanding the notion of the Trinity, Mohammed made Christ a prophet announcing *him*, just as, to Christians, Isaias and John the Baptist are prophets announcing Christ.

The Christian European West barely escaped destruction at the hands of the Moslems. At one point they were stopped near Tours, and at another point, later on in time, outside the gates of Vienna. The Church throughout northern Africa was practically destroyed by Moslem power, and at the present hour the Moslems are beginning to rise again.

If Islam is a heresy, as Hilaire Belloc believes it to be, it is the only heresy that has never declined. Others have had a moment of vigor, then gone into doctrinal decay at the death of the leader, and finally evaporated in a vague social movement. Islam, on the contrary, has only had its first phase.

There was never a time in which it declined, either in numbers or in the devotion of its followers.

The missionary effort of the Church toward this group has been, at least on the surface, a failure, for the Moslems are so far almost unconvertible. The reason is that for a follower of Mohammed to become a Christian is much like a Christian becoming a Jew. The Moslems believe that they have the final and definitive revelation of God to the world and that Christ was only a prophet announcing Mohammed, the last of God's real prophets.

At the present time, the hatred of the Moslem countries against the West is becoming a hatred against Christianity itself. Although the statesmen have not yet taken it into account, there is still grave danger that the temporal power of Islam may return and, with it, the menace that it may shake off a West that has ceased to be Christian and affirm itself as a great anti-Christian world power. Moslem writers say, "When the locust swarms darken vast countries, they bear on their wings these Arabic words: 'We are God's host, each of us has ninety-nine eggs, and if we had a hundred, we should lay waste the world with all that is in it.'"

The problem is, How shall we prevent the hatching of the hundredth egg? It is our firm belief that the fears some entertain concerning the Moslems are not to be realized, but that Islam, instead, will eventually be converted to Christianity— and in a way that even some of our missionaries never suspect. It is our belief that this will happen not through the direct teaching of Christianity but through a summoning of the Moslems to a veneration of the Mother of God. This is the line of argument:

The Koran, which is the Bible of the Moslems, has many passages concerning the Blessed Virgin. First of all, the Koran believes in her Immaculate Conception and also in her Virgin

Birth. The third chapter of the Koran places the history of Mary's family in a genealogy that goes back through Abraham, Noah, and Adam. When one compares the Koran's description of the birth of Mary with the apocryphal gospel of the birth of Mary, one is tempted to believe that Mohammed very much depended upon the latter. Both books describe the old age and the definite sterility of the mother of Mary. When, however, she conceives, the mother of Mary is made to say in the Koran: "O Lord, I vow and I consecrate to you what is already within me. Accept it from me."

When Mary is born, the mother says: "And I consecrate her with all of her posterity under thy protection, O Lord, against Satan!"

The Koran passes over Joseph in the life of Mary, but the Moslem tradition knows his name and has some familiarity with him. In this tradition, Joseph is made to speak to Mary, who is a virgin. As he inquired how she conceived Jesus without a father, Mary answered: "Do you not know that God, when He created the wheat, had no need of seed, and that God by His power made the trees grow without the help of rain? All that God had to do was to say, 'So be it', and it was done."

The Koran has also verses on the Annunciation, Visitation, and Nativity. Angels are pictured as accompanying the Blessed Mother and saying: "Oh, Mary, God has chosen you and purified you, and elected you above all the women of the earth." In the nineteenth chapter of the Koran there are forty-one verses on Jesus and Mary. There is such a strong defense of the virginity of Mary here that the Koran, in the fourth book, attributes the condemnation of the Jews to their monstrous calumny against the Virgin Mary.

Mary, then, is for the Moslems the true *Sayyida*, or Lady. The only possible serious rival to her in their creed would be

Fatima, the daughter of Mohammed himself. But after the death of Fatima, Mohammed wrote: "Thou shalt be the most blessed of all the women in Paradise, after Mary." In a variant of the text, Fatima is made to say: "I surpass all the women, except Mary."

This brings us to our second point, namely, why the Blessed Mother, in this twentieth century, should have revealed herself in the insignificant little village of Fatima, so that to all future generations she would be known as Our Lady of Fatima. Since nothing ever happens out of Heaven except with a finesse of all details, I believe that the Blessed Virgin chose to be known as "Our Lady of Fatima" as a pledge and a sign of hope to the Moslem people and as an assurance that they, who show her so much respect, will one day accept her Divine Son, too.

Evidence to support these views is found in the historical fact that the Moslems occupied Portugal for centuries. At the time when they were finally driven out, the last Moslem chief had a beautiful daughter by the name of Fatima. A Catholic boy fell in love with her, and for him she not only stayed behind when the Moslems left but even embraced the Faith. The young husband was so much in love with her that he changed the name of the town where he lived to Fatima. Thus, the very place where Our Lady appeared in 1917 bears a historical connection to Fatima the daughter of Mohammed.

The final evidence of the relationship of the village of Fatima to the Moslems is the enthusiastic reception that the Moslems in Africa and India and elsewhere gave to the pilgrim statue of Our Lady of Fatima, as mentioned earlier. Moslems attended the church services in honor of Our Lady; they allowed religious processions and even prayers before their mosques; and in Mozambique the Moslems, who were

unconverted, began to be Christian as soon as the statue of
Our Lady of Fatima was erected.

Missionaries in the future will, more and more, see that
their apostolate among the Moslems will be successful in the
measure that they preach Our Lady of Fatima. Mary is the
advent of Christ, bringing Christ to the people before Christ
Himself is born. In any apologetic endeavor, it is always best
to start with that which people already accept. Because the
Moslems have a devotion to Mary, our missionaries should be
satisfied merely to expand and to develop that devotion, with
the full realization that Our Blessed Lady will carry the Moslems the rest of the way to her Divine Son. She is forever a
"traitor" in the sense that she will not accept any devotion for
herself, but will always bring anyone who is devoted to her to
her Divine Son. As those who lose devotion to her lose belief
in the Divinity of Christ, so those who intensify devotion to
her gradually acquire that belief.

Many of our great missionaries in Africa have already
broken down the bitter hatred and prejudices of the Moslems
against the Christians through their acts of charity, their
schools and hospitals. It now remains to use another approach, namely, that of taking the forty-first chapter of the
Koran and showing them that it was taken out of the Gospel
of Luke, that Mary could not be, even in their own eyes, the
most blessed of all the women of Heaven if she had not also
borne One Who was the Savior of the world. If Judith and
Esther of the Old Testament were prefigures of Mary, then it
may very well be that Fatima herself was a postfigure of
Mary! The Moslems should be prepared to acknowledge that,
if Fatima must give way in honor to the Blessed Mother, it is
because she is different from all the other mothers of the
world and that without Christ she would be nothing.

18

Roses and Prayers

No human who has ever sent roses to a friend in token of affection or ever received them with gladness will be alien to the story of prayer. And a deep instinct in humanity makes it associate roses with joy. Pagan peoples crowned their statues with roses as symbols of their own hearts. The faithful of the early Church substituted prayers for roses. In the days of the early martyrs—"early" because the Church has more martyrs today than it had in the first four centuries—as the young virgins marched over the sands of the Colosseum into the jaws of death, they clothed themselves in festive robes and wore on their heads a crown of roses, bedecked, fittingly, to meet the King of Kings in Whose name they would die. The faithful, at night, would gather up these crowns of roses and say their prayers on them—one prayer for each rose. Far away in the desert of Egypt the anchorites and hermits were also counting their prayers, but in the form of little grains or pebbles strung together into a crown—a practice that Mohammed took for his Moslems. From this custom of offering spiritual bouquets arose a series of prayers known as the Rosary, for Rosary means "crown of roses".

Not always the same prayers were said on the Rosary. In the Eastern Church there was a Rosary called the Acathist

(*Akathistos*), which is a liturgical hymn recited in any position except sitting. It combined a long series of invocations to the Mother of Our Lord, held together by a scene from the life of Our Lord on which one meditated while saying the prayers. In the Western Church, St. Bridget of Ireland used a Rosary made up of the Hail Mary and the Our Father. Finally, the Rosary as we know it today began to take shape.

From the earliest days, the Church asked her faithful to recite the hundred and fifty Psalms of David. This custom still prevails among priests, who recite some of these Psalms every day. But it was not easy for anyone to memorize the one hundred and fifty Psalms. Then, too, before the invention of printing, it was difficult to procure a book. That is why certain important books like the Bible had to be chained like telephone books; otherwise people would have run off with them. Incidentally, this gave rise to the stupid lie that the Church would not allow anyone to read the Bible, because it was chained. The fact is, it was chained so people could read it. The telephone book is chained, too, but it is more consulted than any book in modern civilization!

The people who could not read the one hundred and fifty Psalms wanted to do something to make up for it. So they substituted one hundred and fifty Hail Marys. They broke up these one hundred and fifty, in the manner of the Acathist, into fifteen decades, or series of ten. Each part was to be said while meditating on a different aspect of the life of Our Lord. To keep the decades separate, each one of them began with the Our Father and ended with the Doxology of Praise to the Trinity. St. Dominic, who died in 1221, received from the Blessed Mother the command to preach and to popularize this devotion for the good of souls, for conquest over evil, and for the prosperity of Holy Mother Church and thus gave us the Rosary in its present classical form.

Practically all the prayers of the Rosary, as well as the details of the life of Our Savior on which one meditates while saying it, are to be found in the Scriptures. The first part of the Hail Mary is nothing but the words of the angel to Mary; the next part, the words of Elizabeth to Mary on the occasion of her visit. The only exception is the last part of the Hail Mary, namely, "Holy Mary, Mother of God, pray for us sinners, now and at the hour of our death. Amen." This was not introduced until the latter part of the Middle Ages. Since it seizes upon the two decisive moments of life: "now" and "at the hour of our death", it suggests the spontaneous outcry of people in a great calamity. The Black Death, which ravaged all Europe and wiped out one-third of its population, prompted the faithful to cry out to the Mother of Our Lord to protect them at a time when the present moment and death were almost one.

The Black Death has ended. But now the Red Death of communism is sweeping the earth. In keeping with the spirit of adding something to this prayer when evil is intensified, I find it interesting that, when the Blessed Mother appeared at Fatima in 1917 because of the great decline in morals and the advent of godlessness, she asked that, after the "Glory be to the Father, Son, and Holy Spirit", we add, "Have mercy on all souls; save them from hell and lead us to Heaven."

It is objected that there is much repetition in the Rosary inasmuch as the Lord's Prayer and the Hail Mary are said so often; therefore it is monotonous. That reminds me of a woman who came to see me one evening after instructions. She said, "I would never become a Catholic. You say the same words in the Rosary over and over again, and anyone who repeats the same words is never sincere. I would never believe anyone who repeated his words, and neither would God." I asked her who the man was with her. She said he was her fiancé. I asked: "Does he love you?" "Certainly, he does." "But how do you know?" "He told me." "What did he say?" "He said: 'I love you.'" "When did he tell you last?" "About an hour ago." "Did he tell you before?" "Yes, last night." "What did he say?" "I love you." "But never before?" "He tells me every night." I said: "Do not believe him. He is repeating; he is not sincere."

The beautiful truth is that there is no repetition in "I love you." Because there is a new moment of time, another point in space, the words do not mean the same as they did at another time or space. A mother says to her son: "You are a good boy." She may have said it ten thousand times before, but each time it means something different; the whole personality goes out to it anew, as a new historical circumstance summons forth a new outburst of affection. Love is never monotonous in the uniformity of its expression. The mind is infinitely variable in its language, but the heart is not. The heart of a man, in the face of the woman he loves, is too poor to translate the infinity of his affection into a different word. So the heart takes one expression, "I love you", and in saying it over and over again, it never repeats. It is the only real news in the universe. That is what we do when we say the Rosary—we are saying to God, the Trinity, to the Incarnate Savior, to the Blessed Mother: "I love you, I love you, I love you." Each time it means something different because, at each decade, our mind is moving to a new demonstration of the Savior's love: for example, from the mystery of His Love that willed to become one of us in His Incarnation, to the other mystery of love when He suffered for us, and on to the other mystery of His Love where He intercedes for us before the Heavenly Father. And who shall forget that Our Lord Himself in the moment of His greatest agony repeated, three times within an hour, the same prayer?

The beauty of the Rosary is that it is not merely a vocal prayer. It is also a mental prayer. One sometimes hears a dramatic presentation in which, while the human voice is speaking, there is a background of beautiful music, giving force and dignity to the words. The Rosary is like that. While the prayer is being said, the heart is not hearing music, but it is meditating on the life of Christ all over again, applied to one's own life and one's own needs. As the wire holds the beads together, so meditation holds the prayers together. We often speak to people while our minds are thinking of something else. But in the Rosary, we not only *say* prayers, we *think* them. Bethlehem, Galilee, Nazareth, Jerusalem, Golgotha, Calvary, Mount Olivet, Heaven—all these move before our mind's eye as our lips pray. The stained-glass windows in a church invite the eye to dwell on thoughts about God. The Rosary invites our fingers, our lips, and our heart in one vast symphony of prayer and for that reason is the greatest prayer ever composed by man. The Rosary has a special value to many groups: (1) the worried, (2) the intellectual and the unlearned, (3) the sick.

1. *The worried.* Worry is a want of harmony between the mind and the body. Worried people invariably keep their minds too busy and their hands too idle. God intended that the truths we have in our mind should work themselves out in action. "The Word became flesh"—such is the secret of a happy life. But in mental distress, the thousand and one thoughts find no order or solace within and no escape without. In order to overcome this mental indigestion, psychiatrists have taught soldiers suffering from war shock how to knit and do handicrafts in order that the pent-up energy of their minds might flow out through the busy extremities of their fingers.

This is, indeed, helpful, but it is only a part of the cure.

Worries and inner distress cannot be overcome by keeping the hands alone busy. There must be a contact with a new source of Divine Energy and the development of confidence and trust in a Person Whose essence is Love. Could worried souls be taught the love of the Good Shepherd Who cares for the wayward sheep, so that they would put themselves into that new area of love, all their fears and anxieties would banish. But that is difficult. Concentration is impossible when the mind is troubled; thoughts run helter-skelter; a thousand and one images flood across the mind; distracted and wayward, the spiritual seems a long way off. The Rosary is the best therapy for these distraught, unhappy, fearful, and frustrated souls, precisely because it involves the simultaneous use of three powers: the physical, the vocal, and the spiritual, and in that order. The fingers, touching the beads, are reminded that these little counters are to be used for prayer. This is the physical suggestion of prayer. The lips move in unison with the fingers. This is a second or vocal suggestion of prayer. The Church, a wise psychologist, insists that the lips move while saying the Rosary, because she knows that the external rhythm of the body can create a rhythm of the soul. If the fingers and the lips keep at it, the spiritual will soon follow, and the prayer will eventually end in the heart.

The beads help the mind to concentrate. They are almost like the self-starter of a motor; after a few spits and spurts, the soul soon gets going. Airplanes must have runways before they can fly. What the runway is to the airplane, that the Rosary beads are to prayer—the physical start to gain spiritual altitude. The very rhythm and sweet monotony induce a physical peace and quiet and create an affective fixation on God. The physical and the mental work together if we give them a chance. Stronger minds can work from the mind outward, but worried minds have to work from the outside inward. With the spiritually trained, the soul leads the body; with most people, the body has to lead the soul. Little by little the worried, as they say the Rosary, see that all their worries stemmed from their egotism. No normal mind yet has ever been overcome by worries or fears who was faithful to the Rosary. You will be surprised how you can climb out of your worries, bead by bead, up to the very throne of the Heart of Love Itself.

2. *The intellectual and the unlearned.* The spiritual advantages that one derives from the Rosary depend upon two factors: first, the understanding that one has of the joys, sorrows, and glory in the life of Christ; and second, the fervor and love with which one prays. Because the Rosary is both a mental and a vocal prayer, it is one where intellectual elephants may bathe, and the simple birds may also sip.

It happens that the simple often pray better than the learned, not because the intellect is prejudicial to prayer but because, when it begets pride, it destroys the spirit of prayer. One always ought to love according to knowledge, for Wisdom and Love of the Trinity are equal. But as husbands who know they have good wives do not always love according to that knowledge, so too the philosopher does not always pray as he should, and thus his knowledge becomes sterile.

The Rosary is a great test of faith. What the Eucharist is in the order of sacraments, that the Rosary is in order of sacramentals—the mystery and the test of faith, the touchstone by which the soul is judged in its humility. The mark of the Christian is the willingness to look for the Divine in the flesh of a babe in a crib, the continuing Christ under the appearance of bread on an altar, and a meditation and a prayer on a string of beads.

The more one descends to humility, the deeper becomes the faith. The Blessed Mother thanked her Divine Son because He had looked on her lowliness. The world starts with what is big; the spirit begins with the little, aye, with the trivial! The faith of the simple can surpass that of the learned, because the intellectual often ignores those humble means to devotion, such as medals, pilgrimages, statues, and Rosaries. As the rich, in their snobbery, sneer at the poor, so the intelligentsia, in their sophistication, jeer at the lowly. One of the last acts of Our Lord was to wash the feet of His Disciples, after which He told them that out of such humiliation true greatness is born.

When it comes to love, there is no difference between the intellectual and the simple. They resort to the same token of affection and the same delicate devices, such as the keeping of a flower, the treasuring of a handkerchief or a paper with a scribbled message. Love is the only equalizing force in the world; all differences are dissolved in the great democracy of affection. It is only when men cease to love that they begin to act differently. Then it is that they spurn the tiny little manifestations of affection that make love grow.

But if the simple and the intellectual love, in the human order, in the same way, then they should also love God in the Divine order in the same way. The educated can explain love better than the simple, but they have no richer experience of it. The theologian may know more about the Divinity of Christ, but he may not vitalize it in his life as well as the simple. As it is by the simple gesture of love that the wise man enters into the understanding of love, so it is by the simple acts of piety that the educated also enter into the knowledge of God.

The Rosary is the meeting ground of the uneducated and the learned, the place where simple love grows in knowledge and where the knowing mind grows in love. As Maeterlinck has said: "The thinker continues to think justly only if he does not lose contact with those who do not think at all!"

3. *The sick*. The third great value of the Rosary is for the sick. When fever mounts and the body aches, the mind cannot read; it hardly wants to be spoken to, but there is much in its heart it yearns to tell. Since the number of prayers one knows by heart is very limited, and their very repetition becomes wearisome in sickness, it is well for the sick to have a form of prayer in which the words focus or spearhead a meditation. As the magnifying glass catches and unites the scattered rays of the sun, so the Rosary brings together the otherwise dissipated thoughts of life in the sickroom into the white and burning heat of Divine Love.

When a person is healthy, his eyes are, for the most part, looking to the earth; when he is flat on his back, his eyes look to Heaven. Perhaps it is truer to say that Heaven looks down on him. In such moments when fever, agony, and pain make it hard to pray, the suggestion of prayer that comes from merely holding the Rosary—or better still, from caressing the Crucifix at the end of it—is tremendous. Because our prayers are known by heart, the heart can now pour them out and thus fulfill the scriptural injunction to "pray always". Prisoners of war during World War II have told me how the Rosary enabled men to pray, almost continuously, for days before their death. The favorite mysteries then were generally the sorrowful ones, for by meditating on the suffering of Our Savior on the Cross, men were inspired to unite their pains with Him, so that, sharing in His Cross, they might also share in His Resurrection.

The Rosary is the book of the blind, where souls see and there enact the greatest drama of love the world has ever known; it is the book of the simple, which initiates them into mysteries and knowledge more satisfying than the education of other men; it is the book of the aged, whose eyes close upon the shadow of this world and open on the substance of the next. The power of the Rosary is beyond description. And here I am reciting concrete instances, which I know. Young people, in danger of death through accident, have had miraculous recoveries—a mother, despaired of in childbirth, was saved with the child—alcoholics became temperate—dissolute lives became spiritualized—fallen-aways returned to the Faith—the childless were blessed with a family—soldiers were preserved during battle—mental anxieties were overcome—and pagans were converted. I know of a Jew who, in World War I, was in a shell hole on the Western Front with four Austrian soldiers. Shells had been bursting on all sides. Suddenly, one shell killed his four companions. He took the beads from the hands of one of them and began to say the Rosary. He knew it by heart, for he had heard others say it so often. At the end of the first decade, he felt an inner warning to leave that shell hole. He crawled through much mud and muck and threw himself into another. At that moment a shell hit the first hole, where he had been lying. Four more times, exactly the same experience; four more warnings, and four times his life was saved! He promised then to give his life to Our Lord and to His Blessed Mother if he should be saved. After the war more sufferings came to him; his family was burned by Hitler, but his promise lingered on. Recently, I baptized him—and the grateful soldier is now preparing to study for the priesthood.

All the idle moments of one's life can be sanctified, thanks to the Rosary. As we walk the streets, we pray with the Rosary hidden in our hand or in our pocket; as we are driving an automobile, the little knobs under most steering wheels can serve as counters for the decades. While waiting to be served at a lunchroom, or waiting for a train, or in a store, or while playing dummy at bridge, or when conversation or a lecture lags—all these moments can be sanctified and made to serve inner peace, thanks to a prayer that enables one to pray at all times and under all circumstances. If you wish to convert anyone to the fullness of the knowledge of Our Lord and of His Mystical Body, then teach him the Rosary. One of two things will happen. Either he will stop saying the Rosary—or he will get the gift of faith.

19

The Fifteen Mysteries of the Rosary

The Rosary relates the Christian life to that of Mary. The three great mysteries of the Rosary—the Joyful, the Sorrowful, and the Glorious—are the brief description of earthly life contained in the Creed: birth, struggle, and victory. Joyful: "Born of the Virgin Mary". Sorrowful: "Suffered under Pontius Pilate, was crucified, died and was buried". Glorious: "The third day He arose again from the dead, sitteth at the right hand of God, the Father Almighty." The Christian life is inseparable from the joys of birth and youth, the struggles of maturity against the passions and evil, and, finally, the hope of glory in Heaven.

The Joyful Mysteries

The Annunciation

In human love man desires, woman gives. In Divine Love, God seeks, the soul responds. God asks Mary to give Him a human nature with which He may start a new humanity. Mary agrees. A woman's role is to be the medium by which God comes to man. A woman is frustrated who does not bring forth a new man, either physically, by birth, or spiritually, by conversion. And every man is frustrated who knows not both his earthly mother and his Heavenly Mother, Mary.

The Visitation

Love that refuses to share kills its own power to love. Mary not only wants others to share her *love* but also her Beloved. She brings Christ to souls before Christ is born. The Gospel tells us that on seeing Mary, Elizabeth was "filled with the Holy Ghost". When we have Christ within, we cannot be happy until we have imparted our joy. Only the soul that does not magnify itself can truly magnify the Lord. Out of the humility of Mary sprang the song of the *Magnificat*, in which she made nothing of herself and everything of Him. By reducing ourselves to zero, we most quickly find the Infinite.

The Nativity

As the Virgin conceived Our Lord without the lusts of the flesh, so now she brings Him forth in joy without the labors of the flesh. As bees draw honey from the flower without offending it, as Eve was taken out of the side of Adam without any grief to him, so now, in remaking the human race, the new Adam is taken from the new Eve without any grief to her. It is only her other children of the spirit, which she will bring forth at Calvary, who will cause her pain. And the sign by which men would know He is God was that He would be wrapped in swaddling clothes. The sun would be in eclipse, Eternity in time, Omnipotence in bonds, God in the shrouds of human flesh. Only by becoming little likewise, do we ever become great.

The Presentation

Mary submits to the general law of Purification, from which she was really free, lest she should scandalize by the premature discovery of the secret entrusted to her keeping. Simeon tells her that her Son is to be contradicted—the sign of contradiction is the Cross—and a sword her own heart shall pierce. And yet all this is considered a Joyful Mystery: for, as the Father sent His Son to be a victim for the sins of the world, so would Mary joyfully guard Him until the hour of sacrifice. The highest use any of us can make of the gifts of God is to give them back to God again.

Finding of the Child Jesus in the Temple

It is so easy to lose Christ; He can be lost by even a little heedlessness; a little want of watchfulness, and the Divine presence slips away. But sometimes a reconciliation is sweeter than an unbroken friendship. There are two ways of knowing how good God is: one is never to lose Him; the other is to lose Him and find Him again. Sin is the loss of Jesus, and since Mary felt the sting of His absence she could understand the gnawing heart of every sinner and be to it, in the truest sense of the words, "refuge of sinners".

The Sorrowful Mysteries

The Agony in the Garden

Our fellow creatures can help us only when our needs are human. But in an hour of our greatest need, some of them betray and others sleep. In the really deep agony, we must cry to God. "Being in agony, He prayed." What up to that point seemed a tragedy, now becomes an abandonment to the Father's will.

The Scourging at the Pillar

More than seven hundred years before, Isaias prophesied the laceration of Our Lord's sacred body. "Here is one despised, left out of all human reckoning, bowed with misery, and no stranger to weakness; how should we recognize that face?" Great souls are like great mountains; they always attract the storms. Upon their bodies break the thunders and lightnings of evil men to whom purity and goodness are a reproach. In reparation for all the sins of the flesh and in anticipated encouragement to the martyrs who would be beaten by communists and their progenitors, He delivers His sacred body to the lash until "His bones could be numbered" and His flesh hung from Him like purple rags.

The Crowning with Thorns

The Savior of the world is made a puppet for those who play the fool: the King of Kings is mocked by those who will have "no King but Caesar". Thorns were part of the original curse upon the earth. Even nature, through sinful men, rebels against God. If Christ wears a crown of thorns, shall we covet a crown of laurel?

> I saw the Son of God go by
>   Crowned with a crown of thorn.
> "Was it not finished, Lord", said I
>   "And all the anguish borne?"
> He turned on me His awful eyes:
>   "Hast thou not understood?
> Lo, every soul is Calvary
>   And every sin a rood." [1]

The Carrying of the Cross

Many a cross we bear is of our own manufacture; we make it by our sins. But the Cross that the Savior carried was not His but ours. One beam in contradiction to another beam was the

---

[1] Rachel Annard Taylor, "The Question", from *Anthology of Jesus*, ed. Sir James Marchant.

symbol of our will in contradiction to His own. To the pious women who met Him on the roadway, He said: "Weep not for Me." To shed tears for the dying Savior is to lament the remedy; it were wiser to lament the sin that caused it. If Innocence itself took a Cross, then how shall we, who are guilty, complain against it?

The Crucifixion

Once nailed to the Cross and "lifted up to draw all men to Himself", He is taunted: "Others He saved, Himself He cannot save." Of course not! This is not weakness but obedience to the law of sacrifice. A mother cannot save herself if she would raise her child; the rain cannot save itself if it would bud the greenery; a soldier cannot save himself if he would save his country; and neither will Christ save Himself, since He came to save us. What heart can conceive the misery of humankind if the Son of God had saved Himself from suffering and left a fallen world to the wrath of God?

The Glorious Mysteries

The Resurrection

Easter Sunday was not within three days of the Transfiguration but within three days of Good Friday. Love is not to be measured by the joys and pleasures it gives but by the ability to draw joy out of sorrow, a resurrection out of a crucifixion, and life out of death. Unless there is a cross in our life, there will never be an empty tomb; unless there is the crown of thorns, there will never be the halo of light. "O death, where is thy victory? O grave, where is thy sting?"

The Ascension

In Heaven there is now a human nature like our own, the

promise of what ours will one day be if we follow His Way. Thanks to this human nature, He will always have a deep sympathy for us, even "making intercession for us". We can ascend to Him, now, only in our minds and hearts; our bodies will follow after the Last Judgment. Until then we approach His Throne with confidence, knowing that "pierced hands distribute the richest blessings".

The Descent of the Holy Ghost upon the Apostles

As the Son of God, in the Incarnation, took upon Himself a human body from the womb of the Blessed Mother over-shadowed by the Holy Spirit, so now on Pentecost He takes from the womb of humanity a Mystical Body, as the Holy Spirit overshadowed the twelve Apostles with "Mary in the midst of them abiding in prayer". The Mystical Body is the Church; He is the Invisible Head; Peter and his successors are the Visible Head; we, the members; and the Holy Spirit is its soul. As He once taught, governed, and sanctified through His human nature, so now He teaches, governs, and sanctifies through other human natures compacted into His Mystical Body, the Church. We can never thank God enough for making us members of His One Fold with one Shepherd.

The Assumption of the Blessed Virgin into Heaven

Mary was not a rose in which Divinity reposed for a time; she was the canal through which God came to us. Mary could no longer live without the Dream she brought forth, nor could the Dream live without her, body and soul. Her love of God bore her upward; His love of His Mother lifted her upward. Our Lord could not forget the cradle in which He lay. In the Annunciation, the angel said: "The Lord is with Thee." In the Assumption: "Mary is with the Lord." Her Assumption is the guarantee that one's prayers to her will be answered. The

Son is on the right hand of the Father; she is on the right hand of the Son.

The Coronation of the Blessed Virgin

Our Lord comes back to us again through Mary as Queen of Heaven, passing His Life and His blessing through her hands as the Mediatrix of all graces. He came through her in Bethlehem; through her, we go back to Him—and through her He comes back again to us.

> *Our Lady went into a strange country*
> *And they crowned her for a queen*
> *For she needed never to be stayed or questioned*
> *But only seen;*
> *And they were broken down under unbearable beauty*
> *As we have been.*
>
> *Our Lady wears a crown in a strange country*
> *The crown He gave,*
> *But she has not forgotten to call her old companions*
> *To call and crave;*
> *And to hear her calling a man might arise and thunder*
> *On the doors of the grave.*[2]

[2] G. K. Chesterton, "Regina Angelorum", from *Collected Poems* (1935).

20

Misery of Soul
and the Queen of Mercy

A little parable to illustrate a great truth: every mortal one of us remembers the day when our mother said she was going to bake us some cookies. Her plan was that we should enjoy them together. We saw her prepare the eggs, the soda, the flour, milk, sugar, butter, and chocolate—I hope I have left out none of the ingredients. When, finally, the batter was made and was allowed to settle, she told us not to touch it— not because she did not want us to be happy or because any of the ingredients of the cookies were bad but because, in her superior wisdom, she knew that we could not be happy in anything that was not brought to full perfection.

But some of us did taste the batter—I know I did—and that is when the trouble began. A stomachache resulted from the disobedience, and the cookies we were supposed to enjoy with mother were never eaten.

This is, in miniature, what happened at the beginning of human history, and it is being repeated with varying stress in every soul ever since. God did not say to our first parents: "Some fruit is good, and some is bad. You must not eat of the bad fruit." He did not say this, because all the fruit was good, just as all the ingredients of the cookies were good. But God did say: "You must not eat of the tree of the knowledge of good and evil." By this He meant: "Do not use things in their imperfect, isolated state, for they are as yet disjointed from their final purpose."

But man decided to use these things in their half-prepared state and contracted humanity's great stomachache, which is called Original Sin. It is probable that some children have accused their mothers of giving them a stomachache, just as men who rebelled against their final purpose have asked of God: "If He knew I would be so frustrated, why did He make me?" The manufacturers of automobiles give instructions about gas, oil, et cetera, in order to get the maximum service out of the car, but they do not thereby restrain our freedom. So God asks us not to treat the batter as a cookie, earth as Heaven, and the non-God as God. He does this not because He ever wants to put us in chains but because He wants us to be happy.

Every person has a destiny—a *final* destiny. He has lesser goals too, such as making a living, rearing a family; but over and above all, there is his supreme goal, which is to be perfectly happy. This he can be if he has a life without end or pain or death, a truth without error or doubt, and an eternal ecstasy of love without satiety or loss. Now this Eternal Life, Universal Truth, and Heavenly Love is the definition of God. To refuse this final perfect end and to substitute a passing, incomplete, unsatisfying object, such as flesh or ambitious ego, are to create an inner unhappiness that no psychiatrist can heal!

What the stomachache is to the body, that a complex is to an adult. A complex is basically a conflict between what we ought to be and what we are; between our ideals or Heavenly implanted impulses and our plain, matter-of-fact selves; a complex is an exaggerated tension between the

God-summons and the affirmation of our egos. If a razor were endowed with consciousness and were used to cut rock, it would scream with pain, because its life purpose was frustrated. Our inner consciences scream with neuroses and psychoses, too, when we do not freely tend to the supreme goal for which we are made, namely, the Life and Truth and Love that are God.

It is possible to draw a complex. Take a pencil and draw a line from the bottom of the page to the top. That vertical line, which points heavenward, is the symbol of our final destiny. Now draw another line across the page, splitting the vertical line. What do you have? A cross! What a complex is psychologically, that a cross is theologically. The vertical bar represents God's will; the horizontal bar represents our will, which negates it, contradicts it, and crosses it. Not all, but most, of the curable psychoses and neuroses of modern minds are effects of sin. Patients got themselves all "crossed up", because they negated their God-given natures. Opening tin cans with pencils breaks pencils and does not open tin cans. Trying to make a god out of the belly or a god out of the ego of our own will and low standards of life breaks the mind and does not bring happiness.

Every unhappy soul in the world has a cross embedded in it. The cross was never meant to be on the inside, but only on the outside. When the Israelites were bitten by the serpents and the poison seeped within, Moses planted a brazen serpent on a stick, and all who looked on it were healed. The brazen serpent was like the serpent that stung them, but it was without poison. So the Son of Man came in the likeness of man but was without sin, and all who look upon Him on His Cross are saved. In like manner, the inner cross or complex disappears when one catches a vision of the great outer Cross on Calvary, with the God-Man upon it, Who solves the contradiction by making good come from evil, life from death, and victory from defeat.

The child, by making himself wiser than his mother, discovered his stupidity. Man, by making himself a god, discovers the painful agony that he is not God. When the first man made this discovery, Scripture describes him as "naked". Naked, because the man who neglects or rejects God has nothing. He may cover himself for a while with the fig leaves of "success", "art", "science", "progress" or by rationalizing his conduct, saying that there is no truth. But he knows that these are but inadequate shreds and cannot cover all his wants. This is modern nudity—to be without God!

What we have successively called a stomachache, a complex, a cross, a nakedness is so general that our modern literature is rapidly becoming filled with what may be termed the *theology of absence*. A man without God is not like a cake without raisins; he is like the cake without the flour and milk; he lacks the essential ingredients of happiness. Not knowing God is not like not knowing Homer; it is more like having life and waking up in a tomb. The absence the atheist feels is the negation of a presence, a sense of the absurd, a consciousness of nothingness. White grace is the presence of God in the soul; black grace is the unhappiness of His absence.

The absence may be likened to a widowhood, in that existence seems spoiled because we live in the dark agonizing shadow of what is gone! All this inner misery comes from two kinds of sin: (1) the sin that takes the gift and forgets the Giver; (2) the sin that rejects the Giver with His gift. The first makes God useless; the second drives God from the soul. Adam sinned in the first way by choosing something else before God, as does the man who sets up his ego, or flesh, or power as the goal of life. The Crucifixion sinned the second way, being anti-God. The first consists of what might be called the "hot" sins, in the sense that they are inspired by passion; the second consists of the "cold" sins, for example, blasphemy, deliberate attempts to destroy all vestiges of God and morality. Killing a body is not so serious as killing one's soul: "Fear him more who has the power to ruin body and soul in hell" (Mt 10:28). The university professor and the newspaper editor who ridicule the Divine in order to purge it from the hearts, or the radio director who eliminates all prayers and substitutes antireligious poems: these are Satan's fifth column. Here is not just a refusal to acknowledge Goodness, but a pretense that Goodness is badness, or as Nietzsche said: "Evil, be thou my good." Such evil men said of Our Lord: "It is only through the power of Beelzebub, the prince of devils, that he casts the devils out" (Mt 12:24). It is not the existence of God they deny, but His essence, namely, that He is Goodness. The old atheism denied God's existence; the new atheism denies His essence and therefore becomes militant against His existence. It is worse to say, "God is evil", than to say, "God is not." To call Love a devil is to reject the very possibility of Love's forgiveness.

Sin, in all its forms, is the deliberate eviction of Love from the soul. Sin is the enforced absence of Divinity. Hell is that absence of God made permanent by a last act of the will. God does not do anything to the soul to punish it; the soul produces hell out of its very self. If we excluded air from the lungs as we exclude love from the soul, the lungs could not blame God because we got red in the face or fainted, or our lungs collapsed. What the absence of air is to the lungs, that the absence of love in the soul is to the soul. On this earth, want of love makes people red; in the next life, want of love makes a red hell.

The great problem is now how to save these two groups,

those who have taken the gift and forgotten the Giver, and those who have rejected both gift and Giver.

The answer is to be found in the attention that a mother would give to her little son with the stomachache. It is not in the nature of a mother to abandon those children who hurt themselves by their own folly. Immediately, she manifests what might be called "the mutual relation between contraries", for example, the rich helping the poor, the healthy nursing the sick, the learned instructing the ignorant, and the sinless helping the sinful. There is something about motherhood that is synonymous with the maximum of clemency and prevents us from being conquered in advance through despair and remorse by giving us hope in the midst of sins. It is the nature of a human mother to be the intercessor for the child before the justice of the father, pleading for her little one, asking that the child be dismissed, or saying that he is not understood, or that he should be given another chance, or that, in the future, he will improve. A mother's heart is always full of pity for the erring and the sinner and the fallen. No child ever offended a father without offending a mother, but the father concentrates more on the crime, the mother, on the person.

Now, as a physical mother watches over an ailing child, so does Mary watch over her erring children. The one word never associated with her is *justice*. She is only its mirror. As the Mother of the Judge, she can influence His justice; as Mother of Mercy, she can obtain mercy. Twice in history, kings of power promised half their kingdom to a woman: once when a woman solicited a king by her vice; once when a woman inspired a king by her virtue. King Herod, seeing his stepdaughter Salome dance, and being less intoxicated by the wine than by the lasciviousness of her as a whirling dervish, said: "Ask me whatever you will and I will give it to you, even though it be half of my kingdom." Salome consulted with her mother, Herodias, who, recalling that John the Baptist had condemned her divorce and remarriage, said to her daughter: "Ask for the head of John the Baptist—on a dish." Thus John lost his head. But it is always better to lose one's head in John's way than in Herod's!

The other king was Assuerus, who had made the dust of the land run red with the blood of the Jews. Esther, the beautiful Jewish maid, fasted before petitioning him to have mercy on her people; the fasting made her more lovely than before. The cruel tyrant, as cruel as Herod, seeing the loveliness of the woman, said: "Ask me whatever you desire and I will give it to you though it be half my kingdom." Unlike Salome, she asked not for death but for life, and her people were spared. Woman is by nature the temptress. But she can tempt not only toward evil as Salome did but also to goodness as Esther did.

Through the centuries the Church Fathers have said that Our Lord keeps for Himself half His regency, which is the Kingdom of Justice, but the other half He gives away to His Mother, and this is the Kingdom of Mercy. At the Marriage Feast of Cana, Our Lord said that the hour of His Passion was not yet at hand—the hour when Justice would be fulfilled. But His Blessed Mother begged Him not to wait but to be merciful to those who were in need and to supply their wants by changing water into wine. Three years later, when not the water was changed into wine, but the wine into blood, He fulfilled all Justice, but surrendered half His Kingdom by giving to us that which no one else could give, namely, His Mother: "Behold thy Mother." Whatever mothers do for sons, that His Mother would do, and more.

Throughout all history the Blessed Mother has been the link between two contraries: the eternal punishment of hell for sinners and the universal, unlimited Redemption of her Divine Son. These extremes cannot be reconciled except by mercy. Not that Mary pardons—for she cannot—but she intercedes as a mother does in the face of the justice of the father. Without justice, mercy would be indifference to wrong: without mercy, justice would be vindictive. Mothers obtain pardon and forgiveness for their sons without ever giving them the feeling of "being let off". Justice makes the wrongdoer see the injustice in the violation of a law; mercy makes him see it in the sufferings and misery he caused those who love him deeply.

An evil man who is let off will probably commit the same sin again, but there is no son saved from punishment by his mother's tears who did not resolve never to sin again. Thus, mercy in a mother is never separated from a sense of justice. The blow may not fall, but the effect is the same as if it had.

What mysterious power is it that a mother has over a son that, when he confesses his guilt, she strives to minimize it, even when it shocks her heart at the perversity of the revelation? The impure are rarely tolerant of the pure, but only the pure can understand the impure. The more saintly the soul of a confessor, the less he dwells on the gravity of the offense and the more on the love of the offender. Goodness always lifts the burden of conscience, and it never throws a stone to add to its weight. There are many sheaves in the field that the priests and sisters and the faithful are unable to gather in. It is Mary's role to follow these reapers to gather the sinners in. As Nathaniel Hawthorne said: "I have always envied the Catholics that sweet, sacred, Virgin Mother who stands between them and the Deity, intercepting somewhat His awful splendor, but permitting His love to stream on the worshipper more intelligibly to human comprehension through the medium of a woman's tenderness."

Mary will assist us if we but call upon her. There is not a single unhappy soul or sinner in the world who calls upon Mary who is left without mercy. Anyone who invokes her will have the wounds of his soul healed. Sin is a crime of *lèse-majesté*; but the Blessed Mother is the refuge. St. Anselm said that she "was made the Mother of God more for sinners than for the just"—which could hardly be doubted, since Our Lord Himself said that He came not to save the just but to call sinners to repent.

St. Ephrem calls the Blessed Mother the "charter of freedom from sin" and even dubs her the protectress of those who are on their way to damnation: *Patrocinatrix damnatorum*. St. Augustine said of her: "What all the other saints can do with your help, you alone can do without them."

There are some sorrows in life that are peculiar to a woman and that a man cannot understand. That is why, as there was an Adam and an Eve in the Fall, there had to be a new Adam and a new Eve in redemption. Fittingly, therefore, is a Woman summoned to stand at the foot of the Cross where Our Lord redeemed us from our sins. He also redeemed her. Our Lord could feel all agonies mentally; but the agonies and griefs that only woman can feel, Mary could suffer in union with Him. One of these is the shame of the unmarried mother. Not of course that Mary was that, for she was espoused to Joseph; but until the angel told Joseph that she conceived by the Holy Spirit, Mary had to share the bleeding heart of all her sisters who bear within themselves a child born out of wedlock. Mothers whose sons are called to war call on Mary, who also had a Son summoned to the war against the principalities and powers of evil. She even went onto the battlefield with her Son and received a soul-wound.

Mothers who have children born with an affliction, crippled in body, broken in mind, mute in speech, or who have lengthening shadows of impending death or disaster hanging over them and their children, can take their worries to Mary, who lived under an incoming tide of sorrow. She knows what it is to have a child who will be a daily cross. At His Birth, Magi brought myrrh for His burial, signifying that He was destined for death. When He was forty days old, the aged Simeon told her that her Son would be a sign to be contradicted, which meant crucifixion, and that the lance that pierced His heart would pierce her own soul! There is now no excuse. There are some who say they would be "hypocrites" if they came to God. They would be hypocrites if they said they were prepared to be clean when they intended to go on being dirty. But they would not be hypocrites if they admitted they were sinful and really wanted to be children of God.

Those whose spirituality is harsh, whose Christianity is cold, who know Christ but who are severe in judgment, with a touch of bigotry and hatred of fellowman, should realize that their condition comes from a lack of Mary's Motherhood. As, in the physical order, a man who grows up without the loving attention of a mother misses something that makes for gentleness and sweetness of character, so, in the spiritual order, those who grow up in Christianity without Mary lack a joy and happiness that come to those only who know her as mother. Orphans of the Spirit! Your Mother lives!

Throughout the Christian centuries those who were burdened with guilt and afraid to approach God, or who had not come to the Divinity of Christ, or who, having come, were so stricken with shame that they fell back into sadness, have had recourse to the Blessed Mother to lift them out of the abyss. Typical of this spirit are two modern writers. W. T. Titterton, the poet and essayist, on the occasion of Shaw's death, wrote: "Shaw was great friends with a Reverend Mother who prayed daily for his conversion. Once he confessed to her his difficulty: he could not believe in the Divinity of Christ. 'But', he said, patting her shoulder, 'I think His Mother will see me through.' " Shaw put his finger on the sublime truth that those who are not yet ready to accept Christ as the mediator between God and man will come to that truth through Mary, who will act as the mediatrix between widowed souls and Christ, until they finally come to His embrace.

Marcel Proust says that when he was a young man he went to his mother and recollected many of the evil things he had done in his ignorance and passion, things his own mother could not understand, but to which she listened without understanding. He said that somehow or other she lessened their importance with a gentleness and compassion and lifted the weight of his conscience. But how can Mary know what the un-Christed suffer or sympathize with the bleeding soul-wounds of the sinners? As the pure lily rests immaculate on a foul pond, so Mary came to know what sin is in a moment that matched, in her love's capacity as a creature, what Our Lord felt on the Cross.

What is sin? Sin is separation from God and an alienation from love. But Mary lost God, too! She lost Him not morally but physically, during those seemingly endless three days when her Divine Son was only twelve years of age. Searching, questioning, knocking from door to door, pleading and begging, Mary came to know something of the despairing emptiness of those who have not yet found Christ. This was the moment of her widowhood of the soul, when Mary came to know how every sinner feels—not because she sinned, but because she felt the effect of sin, namely, the loss of God and the loneliness of the soul. To every soul who is lost, she can still truly address the same words: "Son, we have sought Thee sorrowing."

We have no record of it in the Gospels, but I have always believed that Judas, both on the way to betray Our Lord and after the betrayal, going with a halter over his arm to hang himself on an aspen tree, deliberately went out of his way to avoid contact with the Mother of Jesus. Probably no one in the history of the world would Our Blessed Mother more willingly have pardoned than Judas, though he did send her Son to the Cross. When Our Lord gave us half His Kingdom in His Mother, He made it almost impossible for any soul to go to hell who ever pleads to her to intercede to her Divine Son. If Judas is in hell, it is because he deliberately turned his back on Mary when he went out to hang himself. If he is not in hell, it is because in that split second, as he looked from his hill to the Hill of Calvary, he saw there the Mother with her Divine Son and died with this prayer on his lips: "Mother of sinners, pray for me!"

Our Blessed Mother shows mercy to all souls because she has a right to do so. She accepted Motherhood not as a personal title but as the representative of all humanity. Her consent is, to the new order of grace, what the consent of Eve was to the fallen humanity. Therefore, she had some claim on the redemptive merits of her Son. What is more, her Divine Son affirmed it, for the last act of Our Lord on earth to which He visibly demanded our adherence was his plea to take His Mother as our Mother: "Behold thy Mother." A child may forget a mother, but a mother never forgets a child. She is not only the Mother of Jesus; she is also the Mother of all whom He redeemed. "Shall a woman forget the child of her womb?" But beyond all sweet remembrance is the consoling human fact that a mother embraces and fondles that child who falls and hurts himself most often.

With St. Bernard, the Church has repeated the prayer to Mary as the Queen of Mercy: "Remember, O Most Gracious

Virgin Mary, that never anyone who had recourse to thy protection, implored thy help or sought thy intercession, was left unaided." As Christ intercedes for us at the throne of His Father, so Mary intercedes for us to her Divine Son. But this role of mercy she cannot fulfill unless there are those who are miserable.

In her *Revelations*, St. Bridget of Sweden quotes the Blessed Mother as saying: "The people of earth have need of a triple mercy: sorrow for their sins, penance to atone for them, and strength to do good." And Mary promised these mercies to all who would call upon her. As the Son shows the Father the wounds He received in saving man in the Battle of Calvary, so Mary shows the body pierced with seven swords in the same Siege against Sin. No sinner in the world is beyond the hope of redemption; no one is so cursed that he cannot obtain pardon if he but calls on Mary. It is necessary to be in the state of sanctifying grace to be saved, but it is not necessary to be in the state of grace to call on Mary. As she was the representative of sinful humanity who gave consent to the Redemption, so she is still the representative of those who are not yet in the state of friendship with God. It is easy for the brothers of Christ to call on the Father, but it is not easy for the strangers and the enemies. This role Mary plays. She is not only the Mother of those who are in the state of grace but also the Queen of those who are not. The true name of Satan is "Without Mercy" (Hos 1:6, 8), one whose nature cannot ask for pardon. He first tries to convince a soul that evil is not evil; then, when evil is done, he tries to convince it that there is no hope. Thus does presumption beget despair. Satan refuses the humiliation of pardon both for himself and for others, but Mary asks pardon even for those who, as agents of Satan, would recrucify her Son. Her name is the antithesis of

Satan: "One who has received Mercy" (Hos 2:1), and there-fore one who dispenses it.

St. Gemma Galgani, of modern times, one day was inter-ceding with Our Lord for the soul of a certain sinner. As Gemma pleaded for mercy, the Savior recounted one by one the person's frightful and abnormal sins. After the Savior had refused three times, St. Gemma Galgani said: "Then I shall ask Your Mother." Our Lord answered: "In that case, I can-not refuse." An hour later the sinner in question came to the confessor of the saint and made his full confession.

> *Sweet girlhood without guile,*
> *The extreme of God's creative energy;*
> *Sunshiny Peak of human personality;*
> *The world's sad aspirations' one Success;*
> *Bright Blush, that sav'st our shame from shamelessness;*
> *Chief Stone of stumbling; Sign built in the way*
> *To set the foolish everywhere a-bray;*
> *Hem of God's robe, which all who touch are heal'd;*
> *To which the outside Many honour yield*
> *With a reward and grace*
> *Unguess'd by the unwash'd boor that hails Him to His face,*
> *Spurning the safe, ingratiant courtesy*
> *Of suing Him by thee:*
> *Ora pro me!* [1]

---

[1] Coventry Patmore, "The Child's Purchase", from *I Sing of a Maiden*.

21

Mary and the Sword

One of the penalties of Original Sin was that a woman should bring forth her children in sorrow:

> *Nothing begins and nothing ends*
> *That is not paid with moan—*
> *For we are born in others' pain*
> *And perish in our own.*

But the heart, too, has its agony, for although the new life is lived apart from the mother, the heart always keeps that new life as its own. What is disowned in the independence of a child is owned in the love of a mother-heart. Her body for a time follows her heart, as to each child at her breast she speaks the language of a natural eucharist: "Take ye and eat. This is my body; this is my blood." The time finally comes for the soul of the child to be nourished in the Divine Eucharist by the Lord, Who said: "Take ye and eat. This is My Body. This is My Blood." Even then the mother heart pursues, never ceasing to love the life that changed her from a woman to a mother.

The other side of the picture is: as every woman begets a child, so every child begets a mother. The helplessness of the infant, in language stronger than words, solicits the mother, saying: "Be sweet, be self-sacrificing, be merciful." A thousand temptations of a mother are crushed in that one radiating thought: "What of my child?" The child summons to duty before he can speak duty. He bids the mother think twice before leaving a father to start a new pseudo-home. The child makes the fatigue and weariness of the mother, as he makes her joy in his success and her agonies in his falls from grace. The child brings the impact of another life, and no mother escapes his vital rays.

Applying this to Our Blessed Mother: not only did she beget a Son, but the Son also begot her. This is the connection between Bethlehem and Calvary. She gave Him Sonship, but He also gave her Motherhood. At the crib she became His Mother; at the Cross she was called the "Woman". No Son in the world but Christ could ever make His Mother the mother of all men, because the flesh is possessive and exclusive. Making her the Woman or the Universal Mother was like a new creative word. He made her twice: once for Himself, and once for us in His Mystical Body. She made Him as the new Adam; He now installs her as the new Eve, the Mother of mankind.

This transfer of His Mother to men was, appropriately, at the moment He redeemed them. That word "Woman" from the Cross was the second Annunciation, and John was the second Nativity. What joy went with her mothering Him! What anguish went with His Mothering her! Mary's mind was filled with the thought of Divinity in the stable; but at Golgotha it is sinners that are uppermost in her mind, and she now begins their mothering. The curse of Eve hangs heavily on Mary: "Thou shalt bring forth children in sorrow." When we contrast the great difference between her Divine Son and us, her sorrow, from our point of view, must have been not only "How can I live without Him?" but also "How can I live with them?" This was the miracle of substitution, for how can one be satisfied with straggling rays when one has been with the sun? The humility of which she sang at the *Magnificat* was not only a confession of unworthiness to be the Mother of God, but also the admission now of her readiness to be the Mother of man. It was a grief not to die with Him; it was a greater grief to live on with us.

Tradition indicates that Mary was pierced seven times with swords of sorrow and that these constitute her Seven Dolors. The position we will take is not that there were *seven swords, but seven thrusts of the one sword, and the sword that pierced her soul was Christ Himself. This Sword has a double edge: one edge ran into His Own Sacred Heart, the other into her Immaculate Heart.* How is Christ a sword? First of all, the Epistle to the Hebrews tells us the word of God is a two-edged sword. "God's word to us is something alive, full of energy; it can penetrate deeper than any two-edged sword, reaching the very division between soul and spirit, between joints and marrow, quick to distinguish every thought and design in our hearts. From him, no creature can be hidden; everything lies bare, everything is brought face to face with him, this God to whom we must give our account" (Heb 4:12, 13). The "word" here is undoubtedly Scripture and the living voice of the Church. But the root, the source is the Divine Word, Who is Christ Himself. St. Thomas in his *Commentary* on this passage makes that identification. Furthermore, St. Thomas quotes St. Ambrose as giving the same interpretation: "For the Word of God is living and effectual and more piercing than any two-edged sword."

One edge of this sword—to speak metaphorically—Christ ran into His Own Sacred Heart, in the sense that He willed all the sufferings from Bethlehem to Calvary. He was the cause of His own death, St. Thomas tells us, and in two ways: *di-*

rectly, by being in such antagonism to the world that the world could not endure His Presence. Simeon foretold this by saying He was "a sign to be contradicted". The essence of evil is not robbing, stealing, murdering; it is the crucifixion of Goodness, the elimination of the Moral Principle of life, so that one may sin without remorse and with impunity. *Indirectly*, Christ was the cause of His own death, as St. Thomas tells us, "by not preventing it when He could do so; just as one person is said to drench another by not closing the window through which it is raining; and in this way Christ was the cause of His own Passion and Death." He could have used His Power and hurled thunderbolts against Pilate and Herod; He could have appealed to the masses with the magnetism of His Word; He could have changed nails into rosebuds and a crown of thorns into a golden diadem; He could have come down from the Cross when He was challenged to do so. But "since Christ's soul did not repel the injury inflicted on His body, but willed His corporeal nature to succumb to such an injury, He is said to have laid down His life or died voluntarily", St. Thomas tells us.

The Sword, therefore, was His Own will to die, that we might be saved from the double death. But He also willed that His Mother should be as closely associated with Him as any human person could be associated with a Divine Person. Pius X declared that the bond between them was so intimate that the words of the Prophet could be applied to both: *Defecit in dolore vita mea, et anni mei in gemitibus* (Ps 30:11). If it be granted with Leo XIII that "God willed that the grace and truth which Christ won for us should be bestowed on us in no other way than through Mary", then she, too, had to will cooperation in redemption, as Christ willed it as the Redeemer Himself. Christ willed that she should suffer with Him, some theologians say, *per modum unius*. If He willed His death, He willed her Dolors. And if He willed to be a "Man of Sorrows", He willed that she be the "Mother of Sorrows". But it was no imposed will; she accepted it all in her original *Fiat* in the Annunciation. The Sword He plunged into His Heart, He, with her cooperation, plunged into her own. He could hardly have done this if she were not His Mother and if they were not in a spiritual sense "two in one flesh", "two in one mind". The sorrows of His Passion were His, but His Mother considered them her own, too, for this is the meaning of compassion.

There were not seven swords but only one, and it plunged into two hearts. The Seven Dolors are as seven thrusts of the Sword Christ, one edge for Him as Redeemer, the other edge for her as the Mother of the Redeemer. Christ is the Sword of His own Passion; He is the Sword of her compassion. Pius XII says that she, as the true Queen of Martyrs, more than any of the faithful, filled up for His Body the Church the sufferings that were wanting to the Passion of Christ!

This was the first reason why God permitted her Dolors, that she might be the first after the Redeemer Himself to continue His Passion and death in His Mystical Body. Our Lord warned: "As they hated me, so will they hate you." If the law that Good Friday is the condition of an Easter Sunday binds all the faithful, then it must with greater rigor bind her who is the Mother of the Savior. An unsuffering Christ who ignored sin would be reduced to the level of an ethical reformer, like Buddha or Confucius. An unsuffering Madonna to the suffering Christ would be a loveless Madonna. Who is there who loves, who does not want to share the sorrows of the beloved? Since Christ loved mankind so much as to want to die to expiate their guilt, then He should also will that His Mother, who lived only to do His will, should also be wrapped in the swaddling bands of His griefs.

But she also had to suffer for our sakes as well as for His. As Our Lord learned obedience by which He suffered, so Mary had to learn motherhood, not by appointment but by experience with the burdens of the human heart. The rich cannot console the poor unless they become less rich for the sake of the poor; Mary cannot wipe away human tears unless she herself has been their fountain. The title "Mother of the Afflicted" had to be earned in the school of affliction. She does not expiate for sins; she does not redeem; she is not a savior—but by His will and by her own, she is so much bound up with Him that His Passion would have been entirely different had there not been her compassion.

He also plunged the sword into her own soul in the sense that He called her to be a cooperator with Him, as the new Eve, in the regeneration of humanity. When the mother of James and John asked political preferment for her sons, they were asked if they could drink of His chalice. That was the condition of being in His Kingdom. What draining of the chalice, then, shall be the condition of being the Mother of the Crucified! St. Paul tells us that we cannot be partakers of His glory unless we partake also of His crucifixion. If, then, the sons of Mary are not exempt from the law of sacrifice, certainly Mary herself, who is the Mother of God, shall be less exempt. Hence *Stabat Mater* pleads that Mary's compassion with Christ be shared with us:

> *These five wounds of Jesus smitten,*
> *Mother in my heart be written*
> *Deeply as in thine they be;*
>
> *Thou my Saviour's Cross who bearest*
> *Thou thy Son's rebuke who sharest,*
> *Let me share them both with thee.*

The seven thrusts of the Sword are Simeon's prophecy, the flight into Egypt, the three days' loss, meeting Jesus with His Cross, the Crucifixion, the taking down from the Cross, the burial of Jesus.

First Thrust of the Sword

The initial thrust was the prophecy of Simeon. The Divine Child, only forty days old, is brought to the Temple; no sooner is the Light of the World laid in Simeon's arms than he breaks out into his swan song: he is ready to die because he has seen the Savior. After foretelling that the Child is a sign to be contradicted, he tells Mary: "Thine own soul a sword shall pierce." Note that Simeon did not say that the sword would pierce her body. The lance of the centurion might do that to the Heart of Christ, and His body might be so bruised that "even the bones of His body could be numbered", but the Virginal body would be spared an outer assault. As in the Annunciation when she conceived—unlike human love—the ecstasy was first in her soul and then in her body; so now in her compassion, the pains of martyrdom are first in her soul and only then in her sympathetic flesh, which echoed to every scourge that fell on her Son's back or pierced His hands and feet.

The Sword is only forty days old, and yet He knows how to unsheath it. From that moment on, every time she would lift infant hands, she would see fall across them the shadow of nails. If her heart was to be one with His, then like Him she must see every sunset as a blood-red image of the Passion. In one sense, her dead would not be buried, as the Sword in her own soul would not be plucked out. Simeon threw away the sheath as her own Child flashed the blade. Every pulse in His tiny wrist would sound like the echo of an oncoming hammer. But her sorrow was not what she suffered but what He had to suffer. That was the tragedy. Love never thinks of itself. If He belonged to sinners, so would she.

The Savior's edge of the sword was telling His Mother, through Simeon, that He was to be a victim for sin; her edge was knowing that she would be a Trustee of His life until the hour of sacrifice. With one word Simeon foretells His Crucifixion and her sorrow. No sooner is this young life launched than an old man foretells the shipwreck. A Mother has only forty days of embracing her Infant Child when she sees the shadow of a contradiction thrown across His life. She had no chalice of sin to drink, no cup of the Father's bitterness such as her Son would drink in the Garden, and yet He holds the cup to her lips.

The enmity of the world is the lot of everyone closely associated with Jesus. How few are the converts to the Faith who have not felt the scorn and bigotry of the world that protests their leaving the mediocrity of humanism for the high level of the supernatural. Our Lord, speaking of the opposition they would evoke, said: "I came to bring the sword, to set father against son, and mother against daughter." If a convert feels that contradiction, then how much worse shall Mary, who mothered the Cross-bearer! Truly, He came to bring the Sword, and His Mother is the first to feel it, not in the sense of an unwilling victim but rather one whose free *Fiat* made her united with Him in the act of redemption. If you were the only person who had eyes in a world full of the blind, would you not be their staff? If kindness before the wounded binds up the sores, then shall virtue in the face of sin seek to be dispensed from cooperation with Him who wipes out the guilt? If Mary, who was sinless, would with joy accept a Sword from Divine sinlessness, then who of us, who

are guilty of sin, shall ever complain if the same Jesus permits
us a sorrow for the remission of our sins?

> *O Mary pierced with sorrow*
> *Remember, reach and save*
> *The soul that goes tomorrow*
> *Before the God that gave;*
> *As each was born of woman*
> *For each, in utter need,*
> *True comrade and brave foeman*
> *Madonna, intercede.*[1]

Second Thrust of the Sword

The second piercing by the Sword was the summoning of His
Mother to share sorrow with all the exiles and the displaced
persons of the world, of whom He Himself was the first
born. The dictator Herod, fearful lest He Who came to bring
a golden crown would steal a tinsel one, sought to kill the
Infant Jesus not yet two years old. Two swords are now swing-
ing: one wielded by Herod, who would kill the Prince of
Peace to have the false peace of the reign of power; the other
by the Sword Himself, Who would have His Own Mother
see the Exodus reversed, as He now goes back to the land
from whence He once led His own people. And Joseph is still
charged with guarding the Living Bread! Hearts could bear
sorrows more readily if they could be assured that they came
directly from God. That her Divine Son should have used
Simeon as the instrument of the first thrust was understand-
able, for "the Holy Ghost was in him". But this second thrust
used the instrumentality of wicked men. How often we feel

---

[1] Rudyard Kipling, "Song before Action", from *I Sing of a Maiden*.

that God has abandoned us when He allows the perversity of men to grieve us, and yet Divine Omnipotence is in Mary's arms and still allows it! The Cross seems to be double-crossed when it does not come from Him, but in such cases it is not our patience that is tried but our humility and our faith. And yet if the Son of God in His human nature and His Blessed Mother did not both feel the tragedy of millions in our civilization pursued by other Herods; if they did not share the experience of violent uprootings from homeland and that forced grafting into the wild olives of Siberia; if both the new Adam and the new Eve were not the first displaced persons of Christian history, then refugees would raise their fists to Heaven and say, "God does not know what I suffer" or "No woman ever bore such grief."

It was for the sake of womanhood that Mary had to suffer, with Jesus, the heart-rendings of an unhospitable earth. That primal gift of the Immaculate Conception and her Virginity were walls of partition between herself and the evil world. But now the Sword was cleaving the wall, breaking it down, allowing her to feel what He Himself would feel in the prime of His life. She, too, must have her Pilates and her Herods! As a priest carrying the Blessed Sacrament to the sick would defend it unto the shedding of his blood, so Mary carrying Emmanuel was learning that to be His Mother meant to suffer with Him, that she may reign with Him. Simeon's word touched her only internally; Herod's wrath, the Egyptian flight shifted the battle against evil to the outside, as Her Son would later move from the Agony of a Garden to the Crucifixion on a Hill. One word from that Babe at her breast could have silenced all Herods from that day until Stalin or Mao Tse-tung, but that word He would not speak. The Word was now a Sword. And yet, how inexpressibly more poignant must have been the grief of her Infant Son, Who, with His

Infinite Mind, knew and willed all that was transpiring! A mother watching surgery on her infant suffers for the child and yet endures it for a greater future good; here the Son is the surgeon who, with a two-edged sword, pierces first His Own Heart before He pierces that of His Mother, as if to blunt the piercing when it touches her. The Word is a two-edged sword! Were it but single-edged, then He would hold the handle and only she would feel the blade, which would be cruel. But here nothing enters into her soul that has not first entered into His. He willed the tragedy He would suffer from the hands of evil men. She willed it, too, but first because it was His will that, as He would undo Adam, so should she undo Eve.

Mary knew that the Infant in her arms had not yet raised His voice against evil, but she nevertheless sees all the bigots and tyrants, dictators and communists, the intolerant and libertines rage and storm against Him. He was as light as a feather in her arms, but He was heavier than a planet on their hearts—"set for the fall and the resurrection of many." A Babe was hated! That was the point of the second thrust of the Sword. "As they have hated Me, so will they hate you." The hatred of men against Him she would feel as her very own! But, as He bore love to those who hated, so did she. She would go down to Egypt a thousand times and amidst a thousand fears, could she but save one single man from committing a single sin, for His sake as well as God's.

Now that Mary is crowned in Heaven, as she looks down on the earth, she sees millions of men still banishing the Creator out of their lands and driving Him out of their hearts. Many men do not spend most of their time making a living; they spend most of it flying from God! He, on His side, will not destroy their freedom, and they, on their side, will not choose Him. But as Mary in this second dolor was not angry with the wicked but unhappy for their sakes, so now in Heaven her compassion and love of sinners almost seem to rise with the measure of their sin. The more closely a soul is united with Jesus, the more it loves sinners. A patient can be so sick with fever that in his delirium he believes himself to be well; a sinner can be so engrossed in sin as to believe himself to be good. Only the healthy really know the sickness of the patient, and only those without sin know the gravity of sin and seek to cure it. Both Jesus and Mary in the flight to Egypt experienced in their goodness (infinite in the one, finite in the other) the two psychic effects of sins: fear and flight. Unless fear is overcome in forgiveness, it ends in the persecution of others; unless escapism is conquered by a return to God, it drowns itself in alcoholism, opiates, the boredom of excitement! Would that all the psychiatrists of the world knew that both these effects of sin are conquered not by self-indulgence in the flesh but by love, which masters fear, and by penance, which arrests flight. Our Lord and His Blessed Mother willingly suffered both these psychological effects so that sinning souls might be freed from them. The real "shock treatment" the guilty have not yet experienced is the shock of invoking a Woman with a Babe who will take them down to Egypt to eat the corn of tribulation and the wheat of penance! When the heart of man is not at home in Nazareth but in escape from reality, it may still have hope; for the Madonna and the Child will meet it, even in its wild flight to the desert Egypts of this world.

Third Thrust of the Sword

The three days' loss of the Divine Child was the third thrust of the Sword. One edge went into His Own soul as He hid from His Mother and His foster father, to remind them, as He said, that He must be about "His Father's business". But since Heaven, too, plays hide and seek, the other edge of the Sword was the grief of Mary's loss and seeking. He was hers: that is why she sought Him. He was on the business of redemption; that was why He left her and went to the Temple. Not only was there a physical loss, but there was also a spiritual trial. "But the boy Jesus, unknown to His parents, continued His stay in Jerusalem" (Lk 2:43). Our Lord said: "What reason had you to search for me? Could you not tell that I must needs be in the place which belongs to my Father?" (Lk 2:49). "These words which he spoke to them were beyond their understanding" (Lk 2:50). Later on there would be another three days' loss when the body of Jesus would be laid in a tomb. This loss was a foretaste and prelude to that loss, as well as a shadow of the three years' loss during His public ministry.

Something now was hidden from Mary, in the sense that she did not understand. This was not a mere negative ignorance but a privation, a deliberate hiding by her Son of the fullness of His purpose. She had her Dark Night of the Body in Egypt; she would now have her Dark Night of the Soul in Jerusalem. Spiritual darkness and desolation have always been one of the trials of God's mystics. First it is His Body and Blood that are hid from her; now it is the brilliance of His Truth. If the second thrust companioned her with the displaced persons of the world, this third thrust would lift her into fellowship with the saints. The Cross was now casting its shadow on her soul! Not only her virginal body must pay dearly for the privilege of her Immaculate Conception, but also her soul must pay the cost of being the Seat of Wisdom.

The two-edged sword affects both souls in the sweet beat of a rhythm. One day on Golgotha He will feel the pessimism of atheists, the despair of sinners, the loneliness of the selfish as He takes their own sins upon Himself and wraps up all their isolation in the one great cry: "My God, My God, why hast Thou abandoned Me?" She, too, must experience that loneliness and abandonment, not only in the physical loss of Christ, but also in the beclouding of all consolations. As, on the Cross, He would deny His human nature all the joys of His Divinity, so He would deny now to His Mother all the joys of His Father's business. If His edge of the Sword was abandonment, her edge would be darkness. The Gospel says there was darkness over the earth when He uttered that cry from the Cross; so now night creeps into Mary's mind because the Son Himself willed the eclipse of the sun. He almost seemed to question her right to seek Him as He asks: "What reason had you to search for Me?" (Lk 2:49). As He on the Cross, suspended between earth and Heaven, would feel abandoned by God and rejected by men, so now she with but one word from the Sword is as utterly "abandoned" by One Who is both God and man.

Darkness in the saints is not the same as darkness in the sinners. In the former, there is no light but love; in the latter, there is night without love. It is very likely that this mystical darkness, which the Sword drove into Mary's soul, gave rise to such heroic acts of love as to raise her to new Mount Tabors she never experienced before. Light can sometimes be so bright as to blind! Mary's failure to understand the word that was spoken to her was caused less by the defect of light than by its excess. Human reason reaches a point where it cannot describe or explain what happens to the heart. Even human love in its most ecstatic moments is speechless. Reason can understand words, but it cannot understand the Word. The Gospel here tells us that what Mary did not understand was the Word that was spoken. How hard to understand the Word when it is broken into words! She did not understand, because the Word lifted her out of the one abyss of reason to the other unimaginable abyss of the Divine Mind. At such points, Divine Wisdom in its human expressions compels a confession of ignorance. It cannot tell its secret, as St. Paul would not tell his vision of the third heaven. Words themselves were inadequate to express fully the meaning of the Word.

To prove that this darkness was unlike ignorance, the Gospel adds: "His Mother kept in her heart the memory of all this" (Lk 2:51). Her soul would keep the Word, her heart the words. He Who by His words seemed to disown her, now owns her, not only by keeping the honey of the message in the hive of her heart but also by going down to Nazareth to be subject to her.

The Divine Sword is no longer using human instruments like Simeon and Herod to brandish it. Twelve years of age, He is old enough to use it Himself. In this dolor both His natures were fastening upon her to make her a co-Redemptrix under His causality: His human nature in the physical loss, His Divine nature in the Dark Night of her soul. In the Annunciation she asks a question of an angel: "How shall this be, seeing I know not man?" Now she addresses the God-Man Himself, calling Him "Son" and asking Him to explain and to justify Himself for what He has done. Here was a supreme consciousness that she was the Mother of God. There is always a great familiarity with God whenever there is great sanctity, and that familiarity is greater in sorrow than in joy. Saints favored by revelation from Our Lord picture Him as saying that this dolor cost Him as much suffering as any other sorrow of His life: in this, as in all other cases, He ran the Sword into His Sacred Heart before thrusting it into her Immaculate Heart, that He Himself might know the sorrow first. The grief that Our Lord would feel on leaving His Mother after the three hours on the Cross was here felt in anticipation during the three days' loss. Those who sin without having the faith never feel the anxiety of those who sin with the faith. To have God, then lose Him, was Mary's edge of the sword; to be God, and hide from those who would never leave Him, was Our Lord's edge of the sword. Both felt the effects of sin in different ways: she felt the darkness of losing God; He felt the darkness of being lost. If her sorrow was a hell, His was the agony of making it. The bitterness of death is in her soul; the sadness of inflicting it is in His!

As she became the Refuge of Sinners by knowing what it is to lose God and then find Him, so He became the Redeemer of sinners by knowing the deliberateness, the willfulness, the resoluteness of those who wound the ones they love! She felt the creature losing the Creator; He felt the Creator losing the creature. Mary lost Jesus only in mystical darkness of the soul, not in the moral blackness of an evil heart. Her loss was a veiling of His face, not a flight. But she does teach us that, when we lose God, we must not wait for Him to come back. We must go out in search of Him; and, to the joy of every sinner, *she* knows where He can be found!

Fourth Thrust of the Sword

Eighteen more years with God in human form had now been enjoyed by the Blessed Mother. If He could make such a transformation in three years in a publican named Matthew, what must have been the wisdom garnered in thirty years by her who was already the Immaculate Conception? The three years of teaching have passed, during which time we hear of her only once. Now the Sword is drawing closer to the hilt, as we pass from the four trials to Mary seeing Jesus carrying the Cross. He drove the Sword into His own soul, and it appeared as a Cross on His shoulders; He drove the Sword into her soul, and it became a Cross on her heart.

As the fourth Station of the Cross has it: "Jesus, carrying the Cross, meets His Blessed Mother." Simeon had foretold that He would be a sign to be contradicted; now she sees that the sign of contradiction is the Cross. It was the advent of a long-dreaded evil. Every tree with its branches at right angles to the trunk had reminded her of the day when a tree would turn against its Creator and become His deathbed. Nails on the floor of a carpenter shop, crossbeams against a wall, arms of a youth stretched out against the background of the setting sun after a day's labor, throwing the shadow of a cross on the opposite wall—all these were advance tokens of this dread hour. But no matter how much one prepares for the misfortune of the innocent suffering for the guilty, the reality is always sadder than one had imagined. Mary had practiced for this blow, but it seemed to strike in an undefended spot. No two sorrows are alike; each has a character of its own. Although it is the same sword, the difference is in the depth of its plunging; some new area of the soul is touched that before was virginal to grief.

In each dolor it is the Son Who is the executioner, but He always makes His edge the sharper. His edge was not only to bear the sins of man on that Cross but also to permit her, who was innocent of it all, to share it as her own. But the Cross must have seemed heavier, not lighter, after His Mother saw it on His shoulders. How often Our Lord had said: "If any man has a mind to come my way, let him renounce self, and take up his cross, and follow me" (Mt 16:24). If carrying one's own Cross is the condition of being Christ's follower, then the condition of being the Savior's Mother is to carry the Savior's Cross. The curious on the roadway to Calvary could see what He was carrying, but only He knew the load she bore.

This world of ours has not only the dread of impending evil, as in Simeon's prophecy; the forced flight from a tyrant's wrath, as in the flight into Egypt; the loneliness and anxiety of the sinners, as in the three days' loss—but it has also the modern nightmare of terror. The just Abels slain by the Soviet Cains in Eastern Europe, the Chinese faithful living in mortal dread of execution, the countless multitudes panic-stricken by the injustices of communists, all these could have raised their eyes to Heaven as so much brass, did not one Man and one Woman feel the bitterness of that terror. And if only a Man Who is Innocent had felt the brunt of that terror, then what would the woman say? Must there not be among their sex, too, one whose soul was so flooded with it that she also could bring consolation and hope? If God in the flesh had not been patient at mock trials, the Chinese priests would not now have the courage to walk in His footsteps. If a creature, in the face of a maddened mob yelling for blood, had not shared that terror as her own, mankind would have said that a God-Man could bear it because He is God, but a human could not. That is why our Divine Lord had to be her Sword, with its fourth and agonizing thrust.

With this fourth dolor no word is spoken; one sees only the shimmering steel of the Sword, for terror is speechless. The Sword He drove into His Own heart made Him shed drops of blood, like beads in the Rosary of redemption over every inch of that Jerusalem roadway; but the Sword He drove into her soul made her identify herself with His redemptive sufferings, forced her to tread the streets over her own Son's blood. His wounds bled; hers did not. Mothers, seeing their sons suffer, wish it could be their own blood instead of their sons' that is shed. In her case, it was her blood that He shed. Every crimson drop of that blood, every cell of that flesh, she had given to Him. Jesus had no human father. It was always her blood that He was shedding; it was only her blood that she was treading.

Through such a dolor as this, Mary won compassion for the terrified. The saints are most indulgent to others who have been the least indulgent to themselves. Those who lead easy, unmortified lives cannot speak the language of the affrighted. So elevated above terror, they cannot bend to console; if they do, it is with condescension and not compassion. But here Mary is already in the dust of human lives; she lives amidst terror, brain-washings, false accusations, libels, and all the other instruments of terror. The Immaculate is with the maculate, the sinless with the sinner, and she bears no rancor or bitterness toward them—only pity that they do not see or know how loving that Love is that they are sending to His death. In her purity, Mary is on the mountaintop; in her compassion she is amidst curses, death cells, hangmen, executioners, and blood. A man may despair in his consciousness of sin from crying to God for forgiveness, but he cannot shrink from invoking the intercession of God's Mother, who saw sinners do these things and yet prayed for their forgiveness. If the good Holy Mother, Mary, who deserved to be spared evil, could nevertheless, in the special providence of her Son, have a Cross, then how shall we, who deserve not to be ranked with her, expect to escape our meeting with a cross? "What have I done to deserve this?" is a cry of pride. What did Jesus do? What did Mary do? Let there be no complaint against God for sending a cross; let there only be wisdom enough to see that Mary is there making it lighter, making it sweeter, making it hers!

Fifth Thrust of the Sword

The Cross unites not only the friends of Our Lord but also His enemies. Only the mediocre survive. Our Lord was too good; He disturbed consciences; therefore, He must die. The

thieves were too wicked; they disturbed false security of possessions; therefore, they must die. Our Lord Himself had said
that as Moses lifted up the brazen serpent in the desert, so He
would be lifted up. The meaning was this: when the Israelites
were bitten by serpents, God ordered that they make a brazen
serpent and hang it on a cross. All who looked at it were cured
of the serpent's poison. The brazen serpent had the appearance of the serpent that stung and yet was without venom.
Christ is the brazen serpent inasmuch as He is in the likeness
and the form of man and yet without the venom of sin. All
who look upon Him will be healed of sin that came from the
serpent, who is the Devil.

No one looked more closely at the Cross than the Blessed
Mother. Our Lord drove one edge of the sword into His Own
heart, for no one took away His life—"I lay it down of Myself." He was upright as a Priest, prostrate as a Victim. He
delivered Himself up to the iniquitous will of man so that man
might do his worst. The worst thing man can do is kill God.
By permitting man to summon forth his strongest armaments
and then defeating him by resurrection from the dead, Our
Lord showed that evil would never be victorious again.

The other edge of the Sword went into Mary's soul, inasmuch as she had been preparing the Priest to be a Victim. Her
cooperation was so real and active that she *stood* at the foot of
the Cross. In every representation of the Crucifixion, Magdalen is prostrate; she is almost always at the feet of Our Lord.
But Mary is standing; John was there, and it amazed him so
much that she was erect during these three hours that he
wrote the fact down in his Gospel.

Eden was now being reversed. Three things cooperated in
our fall: a disobedient man, Adam; a proud woman, Eve; and
a tree. God takes the three elements that led to the defeat of
man and uses them as the instruments of victory: the obedi-

ent new Adam, Christ; the humble new Eve, Mary; and the tree of the Cross.

The peculiarity of this dolor is that the seven words Our Lord spoke from the Cross were like seven notes in the funeral dirge. Our Blessed Mother is recorded as speaking only seven times in Sacred Scripture. This does not mean that she spoke only that number of times, but that only seven of her utterances are recorded. Our Lord also spoke seven times from the Cross. As He spoke each word, her heart goes back to each of the words she herself had spoken, making the sorrow more intense as she saw the mystery of the "sign being contradicted".

The first word of Our Lord from the Cross was "Father, forgive them, for they know not what they do." It is not worldly wisdom that saves; it is ignorance. If the executioners had known the terrible thing they were doing when they rejected the Son of Man; if they had known that He was the Son of God and still gone on, deliberately putting Him to death, then there would have been no hope of salvation. It was only their ignorance of the blasphemy they were doing that brought them within the hearing of the word of forgiveness and the pale of pardon.

The first word reminded Mary of her first word. It, too, was about ignorance. When the angel announced to her that she was to be the Mother of the Son of God, she asked: "How can this be, seeing I know not man?" Ignorance here meant innocence, virtue, virginity. The ignorance extolled is not ignorance of truth but ignorance of evil. Our Lord would forgive sinners because they were ignorant and not like the angels who in rebellion *knew* what they were doing and therefore went beyond redemption. Our Blessed Mother was "blessed" because she was ignorant of man through the consecration of her virginity.

Here the two words fuse into one grief: a sorrow on the part of Jesus, and a sorrow on the part of Mary, that men were not wise with that wisdom which is given only to children and the little ones, namely, knowing that Christ alone saves us from our sins.

The second word of Our Lord was to the good thief. At first he blasphemed Our Lord, but then, hearing the word of forgiveness and seeing the loveliness of His Mother, he responded to grace and envisaged his punishment as the "just reward of our crimes". The sight of the Man on the central Cross obeying the Father's will inspired him to accept his cross as God's will, and with it came a cry for pardon. Our Lord answered: "This day thou shalt be with Me in paradise."

That beautiful acceptance of his sufferings in expiation for sin reminded Mary of her word to the angel. When she was told that she was to become the Mother of Him Whom the fifty-third chapter of Isaiah described as the "one struck by God and afflicted", she pronounced her second word: *Fiat*. "Be it done unto me according to thy word." Nothing matters in all the universe except the doing of God's will, even though it brings a cross to a thief and a dolor to her at the foot of the Cross. Mary's *Fiat* was one of the great *Fiats* of the universe: one made light, another accepted the Father's will in the Garden, and hers accepted a life of selfless fellowship with the Cross.

The Heart of Jesus and the Heart of Mary were made one on Calvary in this obedience to the Father's will. Everyone in the world has a cross, but no two crosses are identical. Our Lord's was the Cross of redemption for the sins of the world; Our Lady's was lifelong union with that Cross; and the thief's was the patience on a cross as the prelude to the crown. Our will is the only thing that is absolutely our own; hence it is the perfect offering we can make to God.

Our Lord's first word was to executioners, His second to sinners, and His third to His Mother and St. John. It is a word of salutation, and yet one that completely altered all human relations. He calls His Own Mother "Woman", and John her "son": "Woman, behold thy son. Son, behold thy Mother." It was the command to all humanity who would follow Him to see His Mother as their own Mother. He had given up everything else; now He would give her up, as well, but of course He would find her again, mothering His Mystical Body.

Mary's third word, too, was a salutation. We do not know exactly what she said except that she saluted and greeted her cousin Elizabeth. In this scene too, there was another John—John the Baptist—and even he proclaimed Mary as his mother. With John leaping with joy within her body, Elizabeth spoke for him and addressed Mary as the "Mother of God". Two unborn children established a relationship before either was born. As Jesus on the Cross pronounced His Word, Mary was thinking of hers. In the Visitation she was bringing Christ's influence before He was born, because she was destined at the Cross to be the mother of all who would be born. His birth cost her no sorrow, but this birth of John and the millions of us at the foot of the Cross brought her such agony as to merit her the title "Queen of Martyrs". It cost Jesus His Mother to make her our mother; it cost Mary her Divine Son to make us her sons. It was a poor exchange, but she believes it worth it.

The fourth word of Mary was her *Magnificat*, and the fourth word of Our Lord was taken from Psalm Twenty-One, which begins with sadness—"My God, My God, why hast thou forsaken Me?"—but ends with somewhat the same note as the Song of Mary—"The poor shall eat and be filled; all the ends of the earth shall remember and adore in His sight." Both songs were spoken before there was assurance of victory.

How hopeless from a human point of view for a woman to look down the corridors of time and prophesy that "all generations would call me blessed". How hopeless, from a human point of view, was the prospect of Our Lord, now crying out to His Father in darkness, of ever exercising dominion over the earth that now rejected Him. To both Jesus and Mary, there are treasures in darkness—one in the darkness of a woman, the other in the darkness of a hill. Only those who walk in darkness ever see the stars.

The fifth word of Mary was pronounced at the end of a quest: "My Son! Why hast thou treated us so? Think what anguish of mind Thy father and I have endured searching for Thee." Mary's fifth word was that of creatures in the quest of God. Our Lord's fifth word was that of the Creator in the quest of man: "I thirst." This was not a thirst for earthly waters but a thirst for souls. Mary's word sums up the aspiration of every soul toward Christ, and His words sum up her Divine Son's affection toward every soul. There is only one thing in the world that can prevent each finding the other, and that is the human will. We must will to find God; otherwise He will always seem to be the Hidden God.

Mary's sixth word was a simple prayer: "They have no wine"—words that prompted Our Lord to work His first miracle and begin His royal road to the Cross. After Our Lord on the Cross had tasted the wine given to Him by the soldier, He said: "It is finished." That "hour" which Mary began at Cana when He changed water into wine is now finished as the wine of His life is changed into the blood of sacrifice. At Cana, Mary sent her Son to the Cross; on Calvary, her Son now declares He has finished His work of redemption. Mary's Immaculate Heart was the living altar stone on which the Sacred Heart is offered; Mary knew that the sons of men could never be saved without offering the Son of God!

Mary's last recorded word in Scripture is abandonment to the will of God: "Do whatever He tells you" (Jn 2:5). At the Transfiguration the Heavenly Father spoke, saying: "This is My beloved Son—Hear ye Him." Now Mary speaks His valedictory, "Do His will." The last word of Jesus on the Cross was the free surrender of His life to His Father's will: "Father, into Thy hands I commend My spirit." Mary surrenders to Jesus, and Jesus to His Father. To do God's will until death, that is the inner heart of all holiness. And here Jesus teaches us how to die, for if He would have His Mother with Him in the hour of His great surrender, then how shall we dare to miss saying daily: "Pray for us sinners, now, and at the hour of our death. Amen"?

Sixth Thrust of the Sword

Our Blessed Lord bows His Head and dies. Certain planets only after a long time complete their orbit and then go back again to their starting point, as if to salute Him, Who sent them on their way. He, Who came from the Father, returns again to the Father with the last words: "Father, into Thy hands I commend My spirit." A double investigation is ordered to prove that He is dead. A sergeant in the Roman army then takes a spear and runs it into the side of Our Lord. He, Who had stored up a few testimonies of His Love, now pours them out from His side as blood and water—blood, the price of our redemption, water, which is the symbol of our regeneration.

Christ, Who is the Sword of His own death, continues the thrusts even after His death, by making Longinus the instrument for opening the treasures of His Sacred Heart, which becomes the new Ark into which souls to be saved from the flood and deluge of sin might enter. But, as the one edge opened the treasures of His heart, the other edge went through Mary's soul. Simeon had foretold that a sword her own soul would pierce; this time it came through the riven side of Her Son. Literally in His case, metaphorically in hers, it was a piercing of two hearts with one sword. It is this simultaneity of thrusts, this transfixion of His heart and her own soul, which unites us in adoration of the Sacred Heart of Jesus and in veneration of the Immaculate Heart of Mary. Persons are never so much united in joy as they are in sorrow. Pleasures of the flesh unite, but always with a tinge of egotism, because the ego is put in the "thou" of the other person, to find there delight in its ravishments. But in tears and sorrow, the ego is killed before it goes into the "thou", and one wills nothing but the good of the other. In these successions of thrusts, Jesus grieves for His Mother, who must suffer so much because of Him; Mary grieves for her Son, caring not what happens to herself. The more consolation one has from creatures, the less one has from God. Few there are who can console. In fact, no one can console except the departed. No human can relieve the loneliness of Mary. Only her Divine Son can do that. In order that mothers who lose sons on battlefields and spouses who lose spouses amidst the joys of love might not be without consolation, Our Lord here becomes the bereaved, as He makes Mary their consolation and their model. No one again can ever say: "God does not know the agony of a deathbed; God does not know the bitterness of my tears." This sixth dolor teaches the lesson that, in such sadness, God alone can give consolation.

After the rebellion against God in Paradise through the abuse of human freedom, Adam one day stumbled across the body of his son, Abel. Carrying it back to Eve, he laid it on her lap. She spoke, but Abel answered not. He had never been that way before. They lifted his arms, but they fell limp at his side. Then they remembered: "The day that thou shalt eat the fruit of that tree, on that day thou shalt die the death." It was the first death in the world.

The cycle of time whirls, and the new Abel, slain by the jealous race of Cain, is taken down from the Cross and laid in the lap of the new Eve, Mary. To a mother, a son never grows up. For the moment, Mary must have thought that Bethlehem had come back again, for here was her Boy once more on her lap. There, too, was another Joseph—but this time the Joseph of Arimathea. There were also the spices and myrrh for burial, now so redolent of the gift that the Magi brought at His birth. What a portent of death was that third gift of the Wise Men! A child is no sooner born than the world suggests His death, and yet with justice, for He was the only one who ever came into this world to die. Everyone else came into it to live. Death was the goal of His life, the goal that He was always seeking.

But for Mary, this is not Bethlehem; this is Calvary. Her Son is not white as He came from the Father, but red as He came from us. In the crib He was as a chalice of the offertory, full of the red wine of life. Now, at the foot of the Cross, His body is as a chalice drained of the drops of blood for the redemption of mankind. There was no room in the inn at His birth; there is no room in the inn for His death. "The Son of Man hath nowhere to lay His Head"—except in the arms of His Mother.

When Our Lord told His parables of Mercy, in particular the parable about the Prodigal Son, we hear only about the kind father of the prodigal son. Why is the Gospel so silent about the mother of the prodigal son? I believe the answer is in this sorrow of Our Mother. Our Lord is the true prodigal son; she is the mother of the Divine Prodigal, Who left His Father's house to go into a foreign land—this earth of ours.

He "wasted His substance", spent His body and blood, that we might recover our heirship with Heaven. And now He has fallen among citizens of a country foreign to His Father's will and been herded with the swine of sinners. He prepares to return to the Father's house. On the roadway of Calvary, the Mother of the Prodigal Son meets Him. In that hour she became the mother of all the prodigal sons of the world, anointing them with the spices of intercession, and preparing them for that day, not far off, when life and resurrection will flow through their veins as they walk on the wings of the morning.

Seventh Thrust of the Sword

There can be no more sorrows after the Resurrection when death will be swallowed up in victory. But until the bursting of the bonds of dust, there was still one great sorrow that Jesus had to will and Mary accept, in order that those who bury their loved ones would never be without hope and consolation. Our Lord ran the sword of burial into His own heart, inasmuch as He willed that man should never have a penalty for sin that He Himself did not bear. As Jonas was in the belly of the whale for three days, so would He be in the belly of the earth for three days. The Apostles' Creed puts so much store upon the bereavement that it mentions the fact that Our Lord was "buried".

But Our Lord did not pierce His own soul with the penalty of burial without at the same time thrusting that grief into Mary's soul. When it happens, the earth is dark, for the sun was ashamed to shed its light on the crime of Deicide. The earth also shook, and the graves gave up their dead. In that cataclysm of nature, Mary prepares the body of her Divine Son for burial. Eden has come back again as Mary plants in the earth the Tree of Life—which will bloom within three days.

All the fatherless, motherless, sonless, husbandless, and wifeless griefs that ever tore at the hearts of human beings were now bearing down on the soul of Mary. The most any human being ever lost in a bereavement was a creature, but Mary was burying the Son of God. It is hard to lose a son or a daughter, but it is harder to bury Christ. To be motherless is a tragedy, but to be Christless is hell. In real love, two hearts do not meet in sweet slavery to one another; rather there is the melting of two hearts into one. When death comes, there is not just a separation of two hearts but rather the rending of the one heart. This was particularly true of Jesus and Mary. As Adam and Eve fell through the pleasure of eating one apple, so Jesus and Mary were united in the pleasure of eating the fruit of the Father's will. At such moments, there is not loneliness but desolation—not the outward desolation such as came through the three days' loss but an inner desolation that is probably so deep as to be beyond the expression of tears. Some joys are so intense that they provoke not even a smile; so there are some griefs that never create a tear. Mary's dolor at the burial of Our Lord was probably of that kind. If she could have wept, it would have been a release from the tension; but here the only tears were red, in the hidden garden of her heart! One cannot think of any dolor after this; it was the last of the sacraments of grief. The Divine Sword could will no other thrusts beyond this, either for Himself or for her. It had run into two hearts up to the very hilt; and when that happens, one is beyond all human consolations. In the former dolor, at least there was the consolation of the body; now even that is gone. Calvary was like the bleak silence of a church on Good Friday when the Blessed Sacrament has been removed. One can merely stand guard at a tomb.

In a short time the Sword will be pulled out, for the Resurrection is the healing of the wounds. On Easter Day the Savior will bear the scars of His Passion to prove that love is stronger than death. But will not Mary bear also the hidden scar of the seven thrusts of the Sword in her own soul? The Resurrection will be the sheathing of the sword for both, as the debt of sin is paid and man is redeemed. No one can tell the griefs that either bore, and no one can tell the holiness that she achieved through sharing, as much as she could as a creature, in His act of redemption. From that day on, God will permit sorrows, griefs, and dolors to His Christians, but they will only be pinpricks of the Sword compared to what He suffered and Mary endured. The Sword that Christ ran into His Own heart and Mary's soul has become so blunted by the pressings that it can never wound so fiercely again. When the Sword does come, we must, like Mary, see "the shade of His hand outstretched caressingly".

22

The Woman and the Atom

There is an excuse for some anxiety today, but no one has a right to be without hope. Yet the prophets of gloom abound, and the disciples of hope are few. But before giving reasons for hope, it is well to inquire why there is so much apprehension today. Man is living in fear, but it is different from any fear in the past—first, because man used to fear God with a filial fear, which made him shrink from hurting One Whom he loved. Later on, man feared not God but his *fellowman*, as the world shuddered under two world wars in twenty-one years. Now we have come to the last and most awful of all the fears, in which man trembles before the littlest thing in the universe—the atom!

The atomic bomb has suddenly made *all humanity* fear that which the individual alone previously feared, namely, death. Death has unexpectedly become a phenomenon that not only the person must face, but also society or civilization itself. Those who denied personal immortality used to take refuge in collective immortality, saying that, although the individual perished, society would be preserved. The atomic bomb has made collective immortality a myth and restored personal immortality as the great problem of our age.

The second reason for fear is that religion has again become the primary factor of human life, and not for religious but for political reasons. All through pre-Christian and Christian history, wars were religious. The Babylonians, Persians, Greeks, and Romans all fought religious wars. They fought them in the names of their gods and against peoples who believed in other kinds of gods. In Christian times, wars were still religious. Islam is a religion and, as such, crushed Christianity, reducing the number of bishops in Africa from seven hundred and fifty in the seventh century to only five in the eleventh century, so that Africa now has to be re-evangelized. Islam is a religion believing in God but fighting against those who believe that God revealed Himself in His Divine Son, Our Lord and Savior Jesus Christ. There was no quarrel among the combatants in the older wars about the end of man, namely, his union with God. There was only a quarrel about the *means* to that end.

But today all this has changed. There are no more struggles of the gods against gods, or of inferior religions against Christianity, but rather the absolutely new phenomenon of an anti-religious force opposing all religion. Communism is not an atheism that intellectually denies God in the manner of the sophomore who has just read the first fifteen pages of a textbook in biology. Rather, communism is the *will* to destroy God. It does not so much negate the existence of God as it challenges Him, changes His essence into evil, and makes man in the form of a dictator, the Lord and Master of the world.

Whether we will it or not, we are being confronted not with a choice between religions but with the supreme alternative of God (or anti-God). Never before were democracy and belief in God so nearly identified; never before were atheism and tyranny so much a twin. The preservation of civilization and culture is now one with the preservation of religion. If the anti-God forces of the world conquer, culture and civilization will disappear, and we will have to start all over again.

This brings us to the third characteristic of our modern fear, namely, the dissolving of man into nature. Man to be happy must maintain two relationships: one vertical with God, the other horizontal with fellow men. In modern times, man first severs his vertical relations with God by indifference and irreligion, then his horizontal relations with neighbor by war and civil strife. Man tried to compensate for the loss of both by the new dimension of depth, in which he sought to lose himself in nature. He, who once was rightly proud of being made to the image and likeness of God, began to boast that he was his own creator and that he made God to his image and likeness. From this false humanism came the descent from the human to the animal, when man admitted he came from the beast and immediately proceeded to prove it by acting like a beast in war. More recently he has made himself one with nature, saying that he is nothing more than a complex arrangement of chemical elements. He now calls himself "the atomic man", as theology becomes psychology, psychology becomes biology, biology becomes physics.

We can understand what Cournot meant when he said that God in the twentieth century would leave men to the fate of mechanical laws of which He Himself is the author. The atomic bomb acts on humanity as excessive alcohol acts on a human. If a man abuses the nature of alcohol and drinks to excess, alcohol renders its own judgment. It says to the alcoholic: "God made me. He intended that I be used rationally, that is, for healing and for conviviality. But you have abused me. I shall therefore turn against you, because you have turned against me. From now on you will have headaches, dizziness, an upset stomach; you will lose your reason;

you will become a slave to me, and this although I want you not."

So with the atom. It says to man: "God made me. He put atomic fission in the universe. That is how the sun lights the world. The great power that the Omnipotence has locked within my heart was made to serve you for peaceful purposes: to light your cities, to drive your motors, to ease the burdens of men. But instead, like Prometheus, you have stolen this fire from heaven and used it for the first time to destroy noncombatants. You did not first use electricity to kill a man, but you first used atomic fission to annihilate cities. For that reason, I shall turn against you, make you fear what you should love, make millions of hearts shrink in terror from your enemies, doing to you what you have done to them, and turn humanity into a victim of Frankenstein, cowering in bomb shelters from the very monsters you have created."

It is not that God has abandoned the world but that the world has abandoned God and cast its lot with nature divorced from nature's God. Man throughout history has always become wicked when, turning his back on God, he identified himself with nature. The new name for nature is science. Science rightly understood means reading the wisdom of God in nature, which God made. Science wrongly understood means reading the proofs of the book of nature while denying that the book ever had an Author. Nature or science is a servant of man under God; but divorced from God, nature or science is a tyrant, and the atomic bomb is the symbol of that tyranny.

Since man trembles before nature without God, the only hope for mankind must be found in nature itself. It is as if God in His mercy, when man turned his head away from the Heavens, still left hope for him in the very nature toward which he now lowers his eyes. There is hope, and a great hope, too. The hope is ultimately in God, but people are so far away from God they cannot immediately make the leap. We have to start with the world as it is. The Divine seems far away. The start back to God must begin with nature. But is there anything unspoiled and unshattered in all nature with which we can start the way back? There is one thing, which Wordsworth called our "tainted nature's solitary boast". That hope is in *the Woman*. She is not a goddess; she is not divine; she is entitled to no adoration. But she came out of our physical and cosmic nature so holy and good that when God came to this earth He chose her to be His Mother and the Woman of the world.

It is particularly interesting that the theology of the Russians, before they were overwhelmed by the cold heart of the anti-God, taught that, when the world rejected the Heavenly Father, He sent His Divine Son, Jesus Christ, to illumine the world. Then they went on to predict that, when the world would reject Our Lord as it has done today, on that Dark Night the light of His Mother would arise to illumine the darkness and lead the world to peace. The beautiful revelation of Our Blessed Mother at Fatima in Portugal from April to October 1917 was another proof of the Russian thesis that, when the world would fight against the Savior, He would send His Mother to save us. And her great revelation took place in the very month the Bolshevik Revolution began.

What was said on those occasions is too well known to be repeated. Our present concern is with the Dance of the Sun, which took place on October 13, 1917. Those who love the Mother of Our Lord need no further evidence of this event. Since those who unfortunately do not know either would take proof only from those who reject both Our Lord and His Mother, I offer this description of the phenomenon by the atheist editor of the anarchist Portuguese newspaper *O Seculo*, who was one among the seventy thousand who witnessed the incident that day. It was

> a spectacle unique and incredible. . . . One can see the immense crowd turn toward the sun which reveals itself free of the clouds in full noon. The great star of day makes one think of a silver plaque, and it is possible to look straight at it without the least discomfort. . . . The astonished eyes of the people, full of terror, with their heads uncovered, gaze into the blue of the sky. The sun has trembled, and has made some brusque movements, unprecedented, and outside of all cosmic laws. According to the typical expressions of the peasants "the sun danced". The sun turned around on itself like a wheel of fireworks, and it fell almost to the point of burning the earth with its rays. . . . It remains for those competent to pronounce on the *danse macabre* of the sun, which today at Fatima has made Hosannas burst from the breasts of the faithful and has naturally impressed even freethinkers and other persons not at all interested in religious matters.

Another atheistic and antireligious sheet, *O Ordem*, reported: "The sun is sometimes surrounded with crimson flames, at other times aureoled with yellow and at still others, red; it seemed to revolve with a very rapid movement of rotation, apparently detaching itself from the sky, and approached the earth while radiating strong heat."

Why should Almighty God have chosen to verify the 1917 message of Our Lady about the end of World War I, about the beginning of World War II in 1939 if men did not repent, through nature's one indispensable light and heat? We may only conjecture.

There are three possible ways of interpreting the Miracle of the Sun. The first is to regard it as a warning of the atomic bomb, which, like a falling sun, would darken the world. It conceivably might be a portent of the day when man,

Prometheus-like, would snatch fire from the heavens and then rain it down as death on Nagasaki and Hiroshima.

It could also be seen as a sign of hope, namely, that the Woman who came out of nature is mightier than the forces of nature. The atomic bomb explodes through fission, or one atom rending and tearing another atom. But atomic fission is the way the sun lights the world. God put atomic fission in the universe; otherwise we would not have discovered it. At Fatima, the fact that Mary could take this great center and seat of atomic power and make it her plaything, the fact that she could swing the sun "like a trinket at her wrist", is a proof that God has given her power over it, not for death, but for light and life and hope. As Scripture foretold: "And now, in heaven, a great portent appeared; a woman that wore the sun for her mantle" (Rev 12:1).

There is a third way of viewing the Miracle of the Sun, and that is to regard it as a miniature and a cameo of what may yet happen to the world, namely, some sudden cataclysm or catastrophe that would make the world shake in horror as the seventy thousand shook at Fatima that day. This catastrophe would be a precocious or uncontrolled explosion of an atomic bomb, which would literally shake the earth. This is not beyond the realm of possibility. Einstein and Lindbergh in their scientific writings have mentioned it as a danger, But better than either testimony is the address the Holy Father gave at the opening session of the Pontifical Academy of Science on February 21, 1943—two years before the first atomic bomb was dropped.

Since atoms are extremely small it was not thought seriously that they might also acquire practical importance. Today, instead, such a question has taken an unexpected form following the results of artificial radioactivity. It was, in fact, established that in the disintegration, which the atom of uranium undergoes when bombarded by neutrons, two or three neutrons are freed, each launching itself—one being able to meet and smash another uranium atom.

From special calculation it has been ascertained that in such a way (neutron bombardment causing a breakdown in the uranium atom) in one cubic meter of oxide power of uranium, in less than one one-hundredth of a second, there develops enough energy to elevate more than sixteen miles a weight of a billion tons: a sum of energy which could substitute for many years the action of all the great power plants of the world.

Above all, therefore, it should be of utmost importance that the energy originated by such a machine should not be let loose to explode—but a way found to control such power with suitable chemical means. Otherwise there could result, not only in a single place but also for our entire planet, a dangerous catastrophe.

On October 13, 1917, believers and unbelievers prostrated themselves upon the ground during the Miracle of the Sun, most of them pleading to God for mercy and forgiveness. That whirling sun, which spun like a giant wheel and thrust itself to the earth as if it would burn it with its rays, may have been the harbinger of a world spectacle that will draw millions to their knees in a rebirth of faith. And as Mary revealed herself in that first Miracle of the Sun, so may we look forward to another revelation of her power when the world has its next rehearsal for the *Dies Irae*.

Devotion to Our Lady of Fatima is actually a petition to a Woman to save man from nature made destructive through the rebellious intellect of man. At other moments in history, she was a Mediatrix of her Divine Son for man; but here she is a Mediatrix for nature. She seizes the original atomic power, which is the sun, and proves it is hers to use for peace. And yet it is not apart from man that she would save him from nature, as it was not apart from her free consent that God would save humanity from sin. Man must cooperate through penance. At Salette, Our Lady asked for penance. At Lourdes, three times the Blessed Mother said: "Penance, penance, penance." At Fatima, the same penitential antiphon is struck time and time again. The atom will not destroy man if man will not destroy himself. An atom in revolt is only a symbol of man in revolt. But humanity in repentance will purchase a nature in complete control. Like the threatened destruction of Nineveh, the threat of another world war is conditional. The Blessed Mother revealed at Fatima in 1917 that World War I would end in another year. If men repented, she said, a great era of peace and prosperity would come to the world. But *if not*, another world war, worse than the first, would begin in the reign of the next Pontiff (Pius XI). The Civil War in Spain in 1936 was thus looked upon by Heaven as the curtain-raiser and the prologue of World War II. This war would be the means by which

> God will punish the world for its crimes by means of war, of hunger, and of persecution of the Church and the Holy Father.
>
> To prevent this I come to ask the consecration of Russia to my Immaculate Heart and the Communion of Reparation on the first Saturdays. Russia will be converted, and there will be peace. If not, Russia will scatter her errors throughout the world, provoking wars and persecutions of the Church. The good will be martyred, the Holy Father will have to suffer much, and various nations will be annihilated.

There then comes a missing paragraph, which the Church has not yet given to the world. It probably refers to these times. Then, as if to indicate that it will be a time of trouble, comes the concluding paragraph: "In the end my Immaculate Heart will triumph. The Holy Father will consecrate Russia to me, and it will be converted and a certain period of peace will be granted to the world."

Repentance, prayer, sacrifice—these are conditions of peace, for they are the means by which man is remade. Fatima throws a new light on Russia, for it makes a distinction between Russia and the Soviets. It is not the Russian people that must be conquered in war; they have already suffered enough since 1917. It is communism that must be crushed. This can be done by a revolution from within. It is well to remember that Russia has not one but two atomic bombs. Her second bomb is the pent-up sufferings of her people under the yoke of slavery, and when *that* explodes it will be with a force a thousand times greater than that which comes from the fission of an atom! We need a revolution, too, as well as Russia. Or revolution must be from within our hearts, that is, by the remaking of our lives. As we proceed with our revolution, the revolution in Russia will grow apace.

O Mary, we have exiled thy Divine Son from our lives, our councils, our education, and our families! Come with the light of the sun as the symbol of His Power! Heal our wars, our dark unrest; cool the cannon's lips so hot with war! Take our minds off the atom and our souls out of the muck of nature! Give us rebirth in thy Divine Son, us, the poor children of the earth grown old with age! "Advance, Woman, in thine assault upon Omnipotence!" Shame us all into enlisting as thy warriors of peace and love!